# English for Meaning

*David Holbrook*

*NFER Publishing Company*

Published by the NFER Publishing Company Ltd.,
Darville House, 2 Oxford Road East,
Windsor, Berks. SL4 1DF.
Registered Office: The Mere, Upton Park, Slough, Berks. SL1 2DQ.
First published 1979
© David Holbrook
ISBN 0 85633 184 8

Typeset by King, Thorne and Stace Ltd.,
Kingthorne House, School Road, Hove, Sussex BN3 5JE in 10 on 12 Plantin
Printed in Great Britain by
Page Bros. (Norwich) Ltd., 10 Roseberry Avenue, London EC1R 4PE.
Distributed in the USA by Humanities Press Inc.,
Atlantic Highlands, New Jersey 07716 USA.

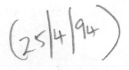
(25/4/94)

For my daughter, Suki
whom I admire for her success
as a primary school
teacher
and for her devotion as
a mother.

*The author acknowledges assistance from
the Arts Council of Great Britain*

*Other studies by the same author*
*on Education and the Teaching of English:*

| English for Maturity | Cambridge | 1964 |
| English for the Rejected | Cambridge | 1964 |
| The Secret Places | Menthuen | 1964 |
| The Exploring Word | Cambridge | 1967 |
| Children's Writing | Cambridge | 1967 |
| English in Australia Now | Cambridge | 1972 |
| Education, Nihilism and Survival | Darton, Longman & Todd | 1977 |

# Contents

# *English has lost its way*

Despite all the publications about the teaching of English issued in the last 15 years or so, and despite the ever-changing (it is symptomatic that it is ever-changing) flood of new books for use in the classroom, teachers can still write to say, 'We have lost our way'.

There is a failure of confidence in English. It can be felt from the university to the primary school – for even in the latter there is a retreat to what my small son used to call 'grey English', because the cover of his Ridout book was that colour. It is felt at NATE conferences, at which, according to an intelligent visitor from Australia, people sit round 'pooling their lack of convictions'. It lies behind the retreat to utilitarianism which I shall examine – the feeling that at a time of economic trouble we must turn to the 'more practical subjects' and make English more 'basic' and 'realistic'. It is apparent in the lengthy booklists on linguistics given to primary teachers on in-service courses, bafflingly abstract and totally irrelevant to their work.[1] What seems to be forgotten in these developments is the recognition, which one would suppose I have made incontrovertibly clear, that since English has to do with the development of powers of symbolizing in the human consciousness, the most effective way of training children to use English is through imaginative disciplines. Teaching English is an art, to do with the pursuit of meaning, and, in this, abstract rules and theories are of minimal use, as I hope to show.

The failure of confidence in English is part of a widespread demoralization in our society. This goes with a pervasive loss of a sense of meaning and values, and the collapse of our symbolic systems, from nihilism in art to the decline of the value of the pound. As I hope to

---

[1] I went to one such course to talk about the writing of less able children and found the teachers had all been given a list of 120 books. I reckoned it would have taken me five years to read all those books, as a full-time reader and writer.

indicate, the failure in English is part of the bankruptcy of a philosophical tradition, and the dismal reduction of life to its functions which goes with it.[1]

In this situation, much that has happened in English shows a shrinking from problems of meaning and values: even those who pride themselves on being 'radical' have sunk into aridity, while the 'official' approach takes on a new 'practical' air at the expense of vision and imagination.

In 1975 was published a government report on English in schools, the Bullock Report, *A Language for Life*. Just after it appeared I was asked to lecture on this report by a college of education in the autumn of that year. The thick Stationery Office volume with its eggy yellow cover dogged my summer holiday in France, as I sat reading it by the Source du Lison and other delectable places. Alas, despite, the title, I did not find it full of life. It seemed to me badly dead. It was dull to read. It lacked touch with the child and the child's lively language. It seemed dominated by theory, and bad theory at that – of intrusions into arts subjects from linguistics, disciplines based on a physicalist psychology, even with neuro-physiology and behaviourism in the background – at a time when the essential failure of such disciplines to explain consciousness and experience was being widely recognized and discussed.[2] At a time when teaching was being criticized for poor standards, when it was being said that children could not use their own language, the Bullock Report must have appeared to some as an 'authentic' assault on the problems of language teaching and use. It is really a confused and heavy compromise which marks a retreat to utilitarian approaches to language use and teaching and to a methodology and epistemology with which many are now becoming disenchanted, quite properly, as they are fallacious.

What is happening in English parallels those developments in the universities in which the humanities are in retreat, while technology and other 'practical' subjects are gaining predominance. Yet the real crisis in our world is not really a practical crisis: it is fundamentally a spiritual crisis, or a crisis of meaning.[3] The problem as it affects

---

[1] For a lively and provocative statement of this theme see Roger Poole, *Empiricism in Crisis, Tract* No. 21, Gryphon Press: 'We are called upon, not to pull back into the analytic habit, but to advance into human responsibility.'

[2] See, for example, a review of work on 'Memory and verbal learning', in the *Annual Review of Psychology*, 1970, Tulving and Madigan. Also Liam Hudson, *The Cult of the Fact;* Jan Foudraine, *Not Made of Wood;* and the work of John Shotter.

[3] See my essay, 'Politics and the need for meaning' in *Human Needs and Politics*, ed. Ross Fitzgerald, Pergamon, Australia, 1977, obtainable here from Pergamon, Oxford.

culture in society is discussed in an illuminating way by a Swedish publisher, Per Gedin in his book *Literature in the Market Place*. In Sweden literary studies and the humanities are losing ground, and this is part of the process of making people more passive and subservient to new commercial developments, in a mass or 'service' society, with palpable effects even in education. Gedin quotes one observer as saying that 'A whole world of education lies in ruins . . . the literary educated public, which was a product of our former school education, is melting away . . .' (p.132). This is happening here, too, under the influence of the new utilitarians, Left or Right, and of confused and inadequate intellectualizations such as those evident behind the Bullock Report, from 'the language men' and educational theorists.[1]

In some areas, as in the polytechnics, 'English' is absorbed into 'communications',[2] moving away from the imaginative disciplines, the literary culture and poetry. It seems that those who will have it that way must at the same time give up concern for meanings and values such as one might expect an attention to creative art to develop. So, the Bullock Report, as the best government can do to find a valid basis for English, must *studiously* ignore the kind of emphasis I placed in *English for Maturity* and subsequent works, on English as an imaginative discipline concerned with whole being and the growth of effective personal capacities.

Why did this government report so deliberately reject the principle stated by one of the greatest poets and psychologists, that 'The primary *imagination* I hold to be the living power and prime agent of all human Perception' – an emphasis by Samuel Taylor Coleridge which modern philosophy and psychology confirm?

When I wrote *English for Maturity* towards the end of the 'fifties I remember saying to myself that unless I put my chapter on poetry first, and made it plain in that definitive chapter why I felt the poetic discipline to be the key discipline, I should not be able to do my job properly, of providing an adequate basis for English teaching for the secondary teacher. Yet Bullock, after all those years of effort by so many from George Sampson to Peter Abbs, can give us only a few feeble pages on literature, pathetically inadequate: and even fewer

---

[1] See Frank Whitehead in *The Present State of English Teaching, The Use of English*, Autumn 1976, Vol. 28, No.1, p.11.

[2] And I am told one polytechnic offers with nice distinction 'Elitist literature' (e.g. Shakespeare) and 'Socialist literature' (e.g. Sillitoe).

pages, limp and apologetic, on poetry. In a sense it abandons the recognition that teaching is an art, that teaching English especially is an art, rooted in intuitive powers.

It needs to be said, and I shall try to argue it here again, that anyone who has experienced the work of a good college of education or teacher's in-service training centre *knows* what disciplines and forms of understanding are valuable in practice. They are developed from experience of the tacit, intuitive and imaginative processes of 'encounter' in the classroom. If one knows what goes on in a good classroom, and in a good college preparing teachers for such work, it is possible to see that *the courses on language for students based on explicit approaches to language proposed in the Bullock Report are wasteful and futile.* It is not only that they are based on dry bad theory, but that they substitute such theory for the living practice of teaching and learning: an intellectual 'explicit' approach pervades Bullock. The very fact that such theories and 'abstract rules' approaches are proposed as the real clue to effective English teaching is a measure of the Bullock Report's ignorance of the true disciplines in English. This in turn marks a failure of thought about the nature of the teaching experience, and of 'English'.

A useful corrective here is the late F.R. Leavis's *The Living Principle.* I have many reservations nowadays about Leavis, and many disagreements with his views. But he stuck tenaciously to the central principle: the literary work exists only in 'the criss-cross of utterance between us': in the mysterious encounter between the 'words on the page' and our inward life, between ourselves and others in the possession of language, and between teacher and taught.

'English' only exists *there,* in that mysterious flux, between word, consciousness and reality. Literature is nowhere else, and cannot be tripped over, measured or brought into a laboratory. It lives only in the *geist* and is known only in the dimension of the *Geisteswissenschaften,* the attempt to understand consciousness. Moreover, imagination can never be adequately dealt with, except in recognition that it is bound up with problems of meaning, and so with 'life'.

This essential recognition of the existence of 'English' in the region between perception, imagination, 'encounter' and moral being has been established – by many besides Leavis who have pursued his kind of serious responsible concern with education. For the Bullock Report to ignore all this authentic work is a serious offence to education, learning and research. The act of deliberate exclusion is meant, evidently, to distract attention from one of the most important streams of educational thought in Britain in the last few decades.[1]

When it comes to literature, the Bullock Report is illiterate. Where is the indication in it that 'English' deals must deal, gratefully and seminally, with some of the greatest works of art in the world, in man's whole history, from *King Lear* to *Great Expectations,* from Chaucer's Marriage Debate to *Four Quartets?* Bullock, like the *New English Bible,* is a catastrophic bureaucratic act of hacking away our best connections with the past – towards a new obsession with 'morphemes' and mechanistic concepts of 'processing' and 'structures', rather than living mysteries, speakers and writers as human beings, children or men.[2]

Those movements which have achieved 'leadership' in English over the last decade, supplanting the 'Use of English' movement and the inspiration of individuals like Denys Thompson, have, in fact, delivered the subject over to a new narrow 'practical' approach. At the moment of writing, utilitarianism seems rampant in political attitudes to the schools. Even with a Labour government (from 1977 to 1979) we were back with Mr Gradgrind, with the concept of education as the servant of a materialistic, industrial, Benthamite civilization. It is against this impulse that such great writers as Dickens and Lawrence have protested, resisting the attempt to subdue 'being' and to substitute for it a dehumanized functionalism. When Mr Callaghan made his speech about education, and the debate about returning to the 'Three R's' began, I was teaching Dickens's marvellous novel, *Hard Times,* to students. Was the Prime Minister echoing Thomas Gradgrind?

> 'Now, what I want is, Facts. Teach these boys and girls nothing but Facts. Facts alone are wanted in life. Plant nothing else, and root out everything else. You can only form the minds of reasoning animals upon facts . . .'

---

[1] A Schools Council Research English Project on 'the middle years' says it is 'placed in a theoretical framework drawing on the work of Vigotsky and Britton'. The predominance of the influence of Professor J.N. Britton has been examined by Frank Whitehead (See *'What's the use indeed?'* in *The Use of English,* Spring 1978, Vol. 29, No.2, p.15). The effect has not been the predominance of imaginative disciplines, but of these theoretical approaches to language indicated by the name coupled here with him, and disciplines of abstract classification established on a doubtful schematic basis, derived from a partial and awkward use of D.W. Harding, linguistics and positivist psychology: essentially a pretentious and damaging intellectualism.

[2] As Professor C.B. Cox pointed out in *The Times* (3 April, 1978) there was not one Professor of English on the Bullock Committee.

Thomas Gradgrind, sir. A man of realities. A man of facts and calculations. In his school, children were thought of as little pitchers, to be filled with facts.

We find something of Mr Gradgrind today in those who seek to restore the old utilitarian belief that at the centre of education is a body of information, to be conveyed to the little pitchers. Drills and rotes must return, to supplant imaginative approaches. Of Gradgrind Dickens says:

He seemed a kind of cannon loaded to the muzzle with facts, and prepared to blow them clean out of the regions of childhood at one discharge. He seemed a galvanizing apparatus, too, charged with a grim mechanical substitute for the tender young imaginations that were to be stormed away.

The opening scenes of *Hard Times* are great comedy. But they have a serious purpose, which becomes more apparent every time one reads the book. Dickens was aware of a kind of knowledge, and a kind of human creativity, which meant nothing to the utilitarian calculus of his time, and still means little to ours. There was an unholy partnership in Victorian England, between the pragmatic philosophy of a Gradgrind, and the blustering inhumanity of the mill-owner, Bounderby. Both display nothing but contempt for the personal life, for the inward life – and the *moral* life – of human beings. When a workman comes to Bounderby with a personal problem, of social ostracism or a broken marriage, he is given a punitive moral lecture, ordered out, or dismissed. When faced with the deep intuitive knowledge of the circus, from one of his pupils, Thomas Gradgrind, seeks to crush it.

'Girl Number Twenty,' said Mr Gradgrind, squarely pointing with his square fore-finger. 'I don't know that girl . . . What is your father?'

'He belongs to the horse-riding, if you please, sir.'

Mr Gradgrind frowned, and waved off the objectionable calling with his hand.

'We don't want to know anything about that, here. You mustn't tell us anything about that, here. Your father breaks horse, don't he?'

The circus, horse-riding community is not to be mentioned in Mr Gradgrind's sphere, because it stands for all those dynamics of warm community life, of 'play', of accomplishment – *'useless'* accomplishment – that go with art, with 'life', with the skills of the body, with all these meanings and dynamics explored, as a central aspect of human existence, by such modern philosophers as Maurice Merleau-Ponty, in *The Phenomenology of Perception*. They stand for the mysteries of being-in-the-world, love, and creativity, which resist quantification, yet are the grounds of learning and prowess. Dickens's genius was to put the best expression of what this means, in the end, in the mouth of Sissy's manager, the boozy Mr Sleary:

> 'It theemth to prethent two thingth to a perthon, don't it, Thquire,' said Mr Sleary, musing as he looked down into the depths of his brandy and water: 'One, that there ith a love in the world, not all Thelf-interetht after all, but thomething very different; t'other, that it hath a way of ith own of calculating or not calculating, whith thomehow or another ith at leatht ath hard to give a name to, ath the wayth of the dogth ith!'

At this Mr Gradgrind looks out of the window and makes no reply, because his world has come to ruin, despite the integrity with which he holds his utilitarian philosophy. The ruin overtakes him because he puts 'fact' before love and imagination: before being. The same fate is gradually overcoming our politicians and administrators, of whatever colour: it overcame the Bullock Committee on English in Schools.

At the beginning of the novel, Sissy cannot define a horse. Bitzer, who is a perfect product of the system, can: 'Quadruped. Graminivorous. Forty teeth, namely twenty-four grinders, etc.' 'Now,' says Mr Gradgrind 'girl number twenty . . . you know what a horse is.' But evidently, Sissy knows perfectly well what a horse is, since she was brought up with those who rode horses, and balanced one another on horses's backs, in the circus.

The kind of 'factual' education to which Mr Gradgrind adheres belongs to a world which, since the Industrial Revolution, has increasingly seen human life in terms of 'functional man'. Indeed, the world itself, in this modern view, consists not of our experience of it, from the unique perceiving 'I', but of entities apprehended by the abstractions of mathematics. When Gradgrind's daughter is to be married to Bounderby, there is a certain discrepancy in age. But, in the light of the calculations of the actuaries, this disappears. 'I find,' says

Gradgrind, 'on reference to the figures, that a large proportion of those marriages (i.e. in the statistics) are contracted between parties of very unequal ages . . . among the Calmucks of Tartary, the best means of computation yet furnished us by travellers, yield similar results . . .' But what are the Calmucks of Tartary to the heart of a girl? Yet our world, with its concrete dehumanizations, has been constructed on such statistics. Such social ideas, since they threaten unique being, menace the meaning of our existence.

Sissy June does very badly in the Gradgrind school. When she is presented with statistics, showing that only a small proportion of those travelling by sea actually get drowned, she cannot help thinking about the misery of their relatives. She is a bad pupil, who doggedly and wickedly thinks about the individual human experience of the world, and the quality of individual life: about 'life'. She attends to the I-Thou, and existentialist uniqueness, and is not to be put down by the I-It, or the 'world of outcomes'. In this, Dickens anticipates the existentialist protest against nineteenth-century natural scientism and its economic theories.

Mr Gradgrind's smallest children are named Adam Smith and Malthus, and his chief mentor is Jeremy Bentham. The philosophical point Dickens is making is clear from John Stuart Mill's account of Bentham:

> In many of the most natural and strongest feelings of human nature he has no sympathy; from many of its gravest experiences, he was altogether cut off; and the faculty by which one mind understands a mind different from itself, and throws itself into the feelings of the other mind, was denied him by his deficiency of Imagination.[1]

If, as Coleridge believed, the primary imagination is the living power and prime agent of all human perception, then an education which does not make the training of the imagination control in its curriculum will fail, and prove ineffective. If the utilitarian calculus of our industrial society is extended to an attempt to train the human soul, then this society itself will break down. This is Dickens's important message, for us in English – and the point is as fresh now as it was last century.

---

[1] One of F.R. Leavis's most useful works is *Mill on Bentham and Coleridge*, Chatto and Windus, 1950.

In Mr Gradgrind's classroom, imagination is actually denounced and driven out. That's a horse:

> 'Now, let me ask you girls and boys, would you paper a room with representations of horses?'
> After a pause, one half of the children cried in chorus, 'Yes, sir!' Upon which the other half, seeing in the gentleman's face that Yes was wrong, cried out in chorus, 'No, sir!' – as the custom is, in these examinations.
> 'Of course, No. Do you ever see horses walking up and down the sides of a room in reality – in fact? You are not to see anywhere, what you don't see in fact. This is the new discovery.'

But there *is* something else. It has to do with *'those subtle essences of humanity which will elude the utmost cunning of algebra until the last trumpet ever to be sounded shall blow even algebra to wrack.'* And Dickens works out in the drama of his moral fable what the consequences are of an education which neglects those subtle essences. Louise Gradgrind married Bounderby, for whom she had only loathing and contempt: it doesn't matter, to her deadened view of life, for her authenticity is stifled by her father's wilful moulding. And so, when she is exposed to the blandishments of an egoist who seeks to seduce her and destroy her marriage and her life, she does not *know* how to make choices. She does not *know*, she tells her father, whether she should be ashamed; she does not *know* how to save herself. She has no moral sense because his universe contains no such thing. In the end she never has a good love relationship, no children – and her future is relieved only by the radiance of Sissy, whose world is that of vision, play and imagination: and love. But at the end Dickens makes this profound comment:

> Louise was never to see herself a wife – a mother – lovingly watchful of her children, even careful that they should have *a childhood of the mind* no less than a childhood of the body, as knowing it to be an even more beautiful thing, and a possession, any hoarded scrap of which is a blessing and happiness to the wisest . . . (my italics)

The great achievement of our educational system, in the last century, has been to recognize the primary need for children to have 'a

childhood of the mind' – and that this is a question for fostering play
and symbolism, *exercising the imagination,* so that children can become
aware of what is going on in other minds and can 'find' the world. In
*Hard Times* the lives of the protagonists are seriously damaged by the
exclusion of imagination from their life and training as children.
Because of this, when faced with moral issues, they do not know how
to act. For one thing this makes them impotent in personal relationships, so that Tom, Gradgrind's son, simply betrays Louise to the man
who toys with the idea of seducing her; while he cannot, on his part,
having been brought up on the principle of intelligent self-interest, see
why he should not rob Bounderby's bank. In this development, we
have a glimpse of the deep and radical inadequacy of the predominant
philosophy of British society, which is still essentially Benthamite.
Inspired by the belief that all that matters is a calculating utilitarian,
acquisitive approach to life ('You've never had it so good'), people at
large today seem to be becoming less and less able to contribute to
good community life. One aspect of this is growing dishonesty, and a
tendency increasingly to live at the expense of others. Under the
impact of a new kind of egoism those values and meanings which
belong to good community seem threatened with collapse, while
commercial persuasions seem likely to deepen the impulses in people
to withdraw consideration from others, a trend which could make
social life impossible.

Sometimes, to my dismay, the rise in violence among youth and
such aberrations are blamed on 'progressive method' in schools! And
now, in the wake of political campaigns, we seem to be faced with a
'retrenchment' away from informal and creative methods. This could
be disastrous. The school, in fact, is today often the one centre of
humanness in many children's lives, perhaps their one experience of
care and gentleness, of human values in action. By comparison with
the grim streets around, the best schools display a delight in the 'subtle
essences', as by the imaginative paintings and poetry pinned up all
round the building. If we wish to see the real threat to the 'childhood
of the mind', we may reflect on the hysterical response of 11-year-old
girls to forms of 'pop' hysteria,[1] or watch some of the trivial rubbish

---

[1] See Charles Parker *'Pop' – the Manipulated Ritual in The Black Rainbow,* ed. Peter
Abbs, Heinemann, 1975. Parker's important point is that commerce has been allowed to
pervert the complex natural engagement between adolescent and adult, by selling a life-
style instead of mere goods, and generating division for marketing purposes, doing
serious social harm.

many children watch on television for many hours a day. We may consider what Dickens would have said about the sadistic and obscene films which many children, at the age of 11, see, as a 'dare', in the natural course of events, or watch even in their own homes late at night, through television. Here is a corruption the Black Paper people never mention, and which Bullock dismisses (as the Annan Report on Broadcasting did not).

If we look at these new influences on children's imaginations, we could conclude that they ought by now to be utter barbarians, utterly reduced to the mean level of the dehumanized society which exploits them. Anyone who is moved by *Hard Times* can only be sickened by the immense education in evil and hate, to which children are exposed today.[1] By contrast, their schools, especially where imaginative disciplines are properly organized, are often little Athenses, when the solemn emphasis Dickens makes on the need for a deep and rich imaginative life in childhood is fully understood.

If a child's imagination is inspired, he will produce remarkable writing, paintings and poetry, dances, mimes, and music. Once this flow is established, the teacher has, of course, to improve it, edit it, make the punctuation good, and train articulateness of a 'practical' kind. But Dickens is right: if the imagination is stifled or neglected, children will grow up to be ineffective in whole human terms, unable to realize their potentialities, or to understand others as a basis for their ethical living. So, we must try to give every child some touch with the finest in the cultural inheritance, to enrich the dynamics of his imagination, however much the Left, in their philistine way (which often merely matches Bounderby's philistinism) declares this is 'élitist'.[2] The Secretary of State for Education at the time of writing, Mrs Shirley Williams, says we must not give up the advance of the last twenty years. Let us hope that governments will accept this. It would be a sad waste of our cultural resource if political pressures from present-day Gradgrinds of the Right or Left led to any retreat from the valuable attention paid today in our schools to the imagination, creativity, and 'the childhood of the mind.'

---

[1] See Professor Sir Martin Roth's Goodman lecture of 1978.

[2] Geoffrey Summerfield, reviewing *English for the Rejected* in *Harvard Educational Review*, called it an 'élitist' book: Vol. 40, No.2, May 1970. 'His notion of the English curriculum . . . is over-literary and unduly preoccupied with the written word . . . For a fuller sense of what English is about we must look to James Britton . . . Unfortunately, Holbrook's view of the pupil's predicament is characterized by the weaknesses that we can now see as having marked – and marred – much of the *Scrutiny* tradition: it pays insufficient attention to the politics of education, and it allows its own élitist assumption to undercut and in effect, deny its more humane tendencies.'

# I

*Towards English for Meaning*

I say, moreover, that you make a great, a very great mistake, if you think that psychology, being the science of the mind's laws, is something from which you can deduce definite programmes and schemes and methods of instruction for immediate schoolroom use. Psychology is a science, and teaching is an art; and sciences never generate arts directly of themselves.

William James, *Talks to Teachers*, 1899.

*Chapter One*

# The Dead End of Bullock

By the time this book is published the influence of the government report on the teaching of English, *A Language for Life,* may have faded away naturally. I hope so. It cost £95,000, and was prepared under the chairmanship of Sir Alan Bullock, FBA. It has a foreword by Mr Reg Prentice, who declares it an 'authoritative statement' which 'will be of value for many years to come'. God forbid!

The Bullock Report has some good things in it, but on the whole is bad and boring. Indeed, it was a disaster, and it would be more of a disaster if it were taken, by teachers who ought to know better, as authoritative – by contrast with the voice of all that rich experience that has come, for decades, for example, from the Inspectorate.

This book is not about the Bullock Report, and should not be taken as offering a fair critical account of that volume. The Report went out of the way to snub me, as some have pointed out. [1] I use it here as a foil, towards offering a more adequate account of the nature and purpose of English in education. Then, having burned up its huge dull hulk, as it were, in the first few chapters, we can soar into a better orbit.

*The Bullock Report* arose from good intentions: it was part of an ambition on the part of the authorities to do something about the anxiety believed to be at large that not enough attention has been paid to 'English'. Some said there had been complaints that pupils had not been taught well enough to use language. Others declared that standards had not fallen – not as they might have been expected to fall, in an age of increasing distraction, triviality, debasement and illiteracy. Certainly, concern about literacy is fundamental in a civilized society, and everyone should welcome such government concern. The sheer size of *A Language for Life* marks a commendable attention to an important question, at least.

---

[1] 'Holbrook, one of the founding collaborators of *The Use of English,* was consciously excluded from the enquiries of the Bullock Committee . . .' Arthur Capey in *The Use of English,* Vol. 29, No. 3, Summer, 1977.

There are sound things in the Report. Fortunately Bullock rejects
the old-fashioned kind of 'grammar' instruction, and the fill-in-the-
blanks kind of exercise. To my delight it also rejects the 'sociological'
approach to English.[1] But our doubts centre on what Bullock means
by 'language'. When it talks about the need for teachers and parents to
'acquire a deeper understanding of language in education' or 'helping
parents to understand the process of language development in the
children and to take their part in it', it does not mean what I mean by
attention to language, a full responsiveness to the meaning of words,
and this is the real problem with which I want to deal. Bullock means
an attention like that of the 'language men': it does not mean a concern
for the whole rich poetic subtlety of words. But it also fails to
emphasise that language is bound up with feeling and thought. As
Leavis said,

> Intelligent thought about the nature of thought and the
> criteria of good thinking is impossible apart from intelligence
> about the nature of language, and the necessary intelligence
> about language involves an intimate acquaintance with a subtle
> language; its literature is very rich; and its continuity stretches
> over centuries . . .
>
> *The Living Principle,* p.13

It is not, unfortunately, this kind of emphasis which is predominant
in the Bullock Report.[2] There are in it no demonstrations of what
might be meant by attention to a 'subtle language in its fullest sense'.
On the contrary, as we shall see in a moment, in some of its more
detailed and powerful proposals it demonstrates a serious misunderstanding of what is needed in English, in terms of response to language.
    Let me be quite clear about my position. I am very much in favour
of disciplined attention to language. But the question is – what kind of
attention? Leavis says, 'To be intelligent about *meaning* is central to
"English" as a discipline of thought' (p.57, my italics), and at this
point he mentioned Michael Polanyi. He also says, 'It seems to me that
some presence of the force of "intent" is necessary to the meaning of

---

[1] 1.9, page 7: 'We are not questioning the place of social concern in the curriculum of the
secondary school. But we are questioning the philosophy of those teachers for whom it
had become the core and essence of the English programme.'

[2] As Arthur Capey points out in the article mentioned above, Bullock 'managed also to
restrict mention of Leavis's name . . . to a subordinate clause'.

"means"' (p.58). That is to say, to quote a phrase from Edmund Husserl, 'meaning is an intention of the mind': it has to do with 'protensions', with moving forward in time into new perceptions and significances. I have mentioned two philosophers, in a very different sphere from that inhabited by the Bullock Report, insofar as it can be said to have a philosophy behind it. More of all this later. For my purposes here the word *meaning* is central: what English is concerned with is not only 'language' but meaning, that which is *beyond the words*, in 'life'.

The crux of my argument will be that Bullock attends too narrowly to the 'words'. Polanyi gives an example: I point, in a lecture. *The audience does not look at my pointing finger.* The finger points beyond itself – and so does language. The audience attends to what might lie beyond the pointing finger, the 'shaft of attention' of each individual being ready to perceive what lies there, signed towards, out there in the living world.

That is not to say that we shouldn't look 'at language', its form and structure, or the structure of creative works. But it is to say that it is what lies before and after the words that is important, in the complex interaction between the individual and his world, with all those complicated processes of the identity and inner life to which we give the term 'life'. The title *A Language for Life* seems to suggest that those who wrote the Bullock Report were aware of this: but their reference to 'life' is not substantiated in the event. They do not really grasp the intentional relationship between mind, symbol, language and reality which Leavis calls 'the living principle'.

It is not only that the Report gives so little space to poetry and literature. It is rather that it managed to be so craven and ignorant about the necessity to find the poetic dynamics at the centre of all English studies. It simply fails to find what George Sampson so long ago (1934) called the 'living creation' which an English lesson at best can be: 'If literature in schools is not a delight, if it is not, in all senses, a 're-creation', an experience in creative reception, it is a failure' (p.78). It dismisses, in a philistine way, a whole honourable tradition in the theory and practice of English teaching, associated with the names of many from Sampson, through Leavis and Denys Thompson, to more recent books like *The Education of the Poetic Spirit, Coming into their Own, An Experiment in Education, English for Diversity*, a tradition to which I aspire to belong. Bullock absurdly gives a mere caricature of this thoroughly argued tradition: 'Some teachers see English as an instrument of personal growth, going so far as to declare that "English is about growing up".' Bullock simply does not give a fair and considered account of this position, and this is a disgraceful example in itself. The ostracism is breathtaking in its chosen offence to proper standards of fair discourse, of adequate procedures in 'education, learning and research'.

'English' and 'language' cannot be discussed to any satisfactory purpose without discussing the word in complex relationship with the whole growth of human capacities of the child, the interaction between his personal dynamics of mind and body, and the inherited culture to which Leavis refers, with its 'continuity'. In becoming able to take on, and use, that culture, the child enters the 'human world', the 'mansions of consciousness', the 'life world' that *is* civilization. *L'enfant sauvage,* not belonging to that world, did not have the powers of human being. He never took on that culture which is neither merely personal nor 'out there in the public world', which language creates between us, in the context of a creative relationship. For these human powers which we have, whose consideration must never be absent from the consideration of English, are developed by natural processes which are inaccessible, in the sense that we can neither fully understand nor control them. *L'enfant sauvage* was not human, because he had not experienced the long processes of intersubjectivity without which there is no human consciousness and culture. These imaginative powers are a product of the evolutionary growth of higher intelligence in the higher animals, and supremely in man, of *encounter,* as a primary biological reality.[1]

Of course, in the course of its long and tedious progress, *The Bullock Report* does recognize the way in which English relies on the 'tacit' processes and that teaching depends upon the interpersonal dynamics behind culture. It speaks of 'the many intuitions of teachers', for example, and implicitly admits from time to time that the whole professional edifice relies on what Polanyi calls 'tacit inference' and 'personal knowledge'. But primarily it tends to imply that progress lies with the explicit, with 'focal awareness', abstract concepts of 'rules' such as emerge from the treatises of linguistics, to the structure of language, as analysed in theory by experts who deal with 'language acquisition'. Leavis, however, was right when he declared that when we are faced with the question 'What is the English language?' 'a linguistician's treatise will do nothing to help you towards an answer'

---

[1] Truffaud's film *L'Enfant Sauvage* is deeply moving, around these themes.

(*The Living Principle*, p.37). The Bullock Report tends to suggest that many of the answers *are* to be found in the treatises of the linguisticians, while the rest are to be found in functionalistic accounts developed by 'objective' psychology: this is the nonsense it substitutes for approaches based on vision and imagination.

Let us look at the moment where such a report is most likely to influence practice: teacher training. When it comes to preparing teachers for the classroom, Bullock proposes 'basic language courses': 'All teachers should acquire a more complete understanding of language in education than has been required of them in the past' (23-24, p.343). The kind of understanding it means is evident from the courses proposed in detail in the Report:

TWO EXAMPLES OF A BASIC LANGUAGE COURSE
(see 23.12)

23.25 *Example 1*
(1) THE NATURE AND FUNCTION OF LANGUAGE
(based on (a) the students' own language and (b) the language of school children).
Language as rule-governed behaviour: reference to phonology, grammar, lexis. Accents, dialect, standards. Spoken and written media. The functions of language – some theoretical models.

(2) LANGUAGE ACQUISITION
Pre-speech behaviour in the family.
'Speech for oneself' and the regulative role of language.
Speech and the development of higher mental processes (Piaget, Vygotsky).
Creativity and language (Chomsky).
The development of syntax; transitional grammars.

(3) SPEAKING AND WRITING AS SOCIAL PROCESSES
The context of situation.
Language and role relations.
Language and social control.
Language and the presentation of self.
Conversation and the validation of social reality.

(4) THE PROCESSING OF CODED INFORMATION
Stages in data-processing (a) perceptual, (b) encoded in speech, (c) encoded in writing.

'Ear language' and 'Eye language'.
'Linguistic awareness' and reading.
Storage and retrieval of information.

## (5) LEARNING TO READ

The initial stages: sight vocabulary, phonics, reading for meaning, context cues, the role of expectations.
Reading and the internalization of written language forms.
Reading and the purposes of the curriculum.
Development reading: suiting the skill to the purpose.
Diagnosis, testing, observational techniques.
The rôle of fiction in developing reading.
Children's literature and patterns of individual reading.

## (6) LANGUAGE IN SCHOOL

The language behaviour of the teacher (the language of instruction of questioning, of control; the teacher as listener).
The language of text books.
The heuristic function of language – talking and writing as ways of learning.
The development of expressive, transactional, and poetic writing.
Literature as language.
Language across the curriculum – a language policy for a school.
Organization: class organization for talk, for writing, for reading
          organization of resources.
          diagnosis and recording.
Evaluation: educational aims and the uses of language in school.

23.26 *Example 2*

## (1) INTRODUCTION

(a) An historical introduction to language change and stability.
(b) A sketch of linguistic theory, with psychological and sociological links.[1]

---

[1] Fundamental criticisms have been made of the psychology and other positivistic approaches to human behaviour, as by Erwin Straus (*Phenomenological Psychology, The Primary World of Senses*): yet it is extremely unlikely that students of this proposed course would ever be given these.

## (2) COMMUNICATION IN THE CONTEXT OF COGNITIVE AND AFFECTIVE DEVELOPMENT

(a) Goals of communication in speech and writing: Information needs; negotiation processes; control processes; thinking; forms of self-expression.

(b) Sociological and psychological factors affecting communication

(i) Accents and dialects: styles of print and writing: conventions of presentation; linguistic constraints in a multicultural society; attitudes and preconceptions; knowledge structures; motivations.

(ii) Social context and style; comparative study of a range of texts; the kinds of writing required of children at school; the kinds of writing relevant to a teacher's professional role.

## (3) THE COMMUNICATIVE EVENT

(i) Strategies and tactics used in accomplishing communication goals.

(ii) Receptive organization-information access and selection procedure.

## (4) SKILLS AND STRUCTURES

(a) Primary skills – Language substance.

(i) The sound system of English, with an emphasis on intonation, auditory perception and discrimination.

(ii) The graphic system of English, including punctuation, visual perception of letter shapes and groupings.

(iii) Correspondences and anomalies in the sound and graphic systems. Auditory and visual association.

(b) Intermediate skills – Language form.

(i) Syntactic structures in speech and writing.

(ii) Semantic structure: words and collocations; semantic relationships.

(iii) Inter-sentential structures in speech and writing: the paragraph and beyond.

(iv) Redundancy as a feature of natural language: context cues in reading and listening, writing and speaking arising from redundancy, stochastic processes.

(c) Comprehension skills – Language function.

(i) Kinds of comprehension – literal, interpretative, reorganization, inferential, evaluative, appreciative, applicative.

(ii) Factors affecting comprehension.

(a) Reader/listener preconceptions; reader/listener goals.

(b) Behaviour of speaker/writer; language variation (e.g. restricted codes); sensitivity to situations (e.g. registers, language for special purposes); awareness of audience – aiming at target groups of listeners/readers.

(iii) Aids to comprehension; questions; note-taking techniques, models and diagrams.

## (5) SELF-DEVELOPMENT: SKILLS AND STRATEGIES

(a) Developmental analysis and evaluation.

(b) Learning to use verbal skills in communication; self-evaluation, recording techniques and personal resource management.

(c) Interdependence of resources and skills; the limiting effect of deficiencies in either; techniques for overcoming transitory and developmental deficiencies.

## (6) ORGANIZATION OF LANGUAGE AND READING IN THE CURRICULUM

(a) Varieties of media for learning.

A. Reading: reading schemes and workshops, subjective-area textbooks and materials, other types of printed media.

B. Speech: the language of the teacher; verbal styles and strategies; recorded and broadcast speech.

Other varieties of spoken language – language interaction in group learning situations.

(b) Evaluation of media for learning.

A. Intelligibility, legibility, readability of media.

B. Analysis of content, logical and ideological.

(c) Language across the curriculum.

(i) activities for developing the full range of language/reading behaviour in each curriculum area.

(ii) Organization of learning situations within the normal curriculum.

## (7) TEACHING THE INDIVIDUAL CHILD
(i) Assessment of individual language and reading performance-record keeping.

Creative analysis of the child's idolect[1] using the skills acquired earlier in the course.

(ii) Devising of individual learning activities based on the assessment of analysis.

Assessment and selection of appropriate materials to match individual needs.

(iii) Special individual problems in language and reading: an awareness of the various influencing factors.

## (8) DEVELOPMENT OF THE LANGUAGE CURRICULUM
(a) Evaluation of teaching materials and procedures in use.

(b) Resource development.
  (i) storage and retrieval systems for the teacher.
  (ii) management for audio-visual resources.

## REFERENCES
1. *Teacher education and Training.* HMSO, 1972.
2. *Education: A framework for Expansion.* HMSO, 1972.
3. Ministry of Education pamphlet No.324, *The Training of Teachers.* HMSO, 1957.

The primary emphasis here is on *learning the rules:* learning about language theoretically, 'from the outside', in an abstract, explicit way. The emphasis is not on *training response to meaning,* such as we experience in a good poetry seminar.[2] The student is to study 'language' as 'rule-governed behaviour'. There is a reference to 'creativity and language' – but this is followed sharply by '(Chomsky)' in brackets, so this, too, is to be an intellectualization, an attention to theories *about* the structure and functioning of language, *'about'*

---

[1] Were *English for the Rejected, Children's Writing* and Marjorie Hourd's *Coming Into Their Own* meant here? Clearly, in the light of the rest of the Report, they were not. Can one imagine the work of Susan Isaacs, Mrs. Len Chaloner (*Feeling and Perception in Young Children*), D.W. Winnicott's *The Piggle,* or Sybil Marshall's *An Experiment in Education* being involved here? Yet if our goal is the phenomenological understanding of the child's *meanings* they should surely be?

[2] May I refer the reader to my verbatim report of a seminar with student teachers in *The Exploring Word?*

creativity. The emphasis is not on developing the natural processes of language, neither its exercise nor its practice as a way of gaining experience of a rich and subtle enjoyment of words such as must be central to English. 'In the beginning was the Word' is to be reduced to 'the communicative event', together with Babel and Whitsun.

That is, the Bullock Report puts forward a positivistic, functional approach, choosing this *deliberately,* while consigning the imaginative approach to oblivion. A false analogy is even set up (as, indeed, it is often throughout *The Bullock Report*) between computers and the human mind:

(4) THE PROCESSING OF CODED INFORMATION
stages in data-processing (a) perceptual, (b) encoded in speech, (c) encoded in writing, 'Ear Language' and 'Eye Language' . . . *Storage and retrieval of information* . . .

Such computer analogies often seem convincing.[1] But how do they help? Does it help us to understand meaning in English to use the new technological terms: 'cybernetical', 'codes', 'retrieval systems', and 'information-retrieval'?

Here we are in a serious dilemma, because the mechanistic cybernetic model is so deeply entrenched that people tend to become bemused when the question of doubts about it is even raised. On the book-jacket of Dr Colin Blakemore's 1978 Reith Lectures on *The Mechanism of Mind* there is a picture of a cut-away human head with wires inside – surely the brain must work something like that, and we can understand it by analysis of the operations of circuits and bits? But the implied analogy is false.

The cybernetic model is absurd because it regards 'the brain' as an instrument which the human being 'uses', just as he uses the computer. Any computer, in fact, is an instrument, just like my small son's electronic calculator, which I borrow to do my income tax. The computer has to be programmed, and it cannot by itself *learn* or *initiate,* a fact which the cybernetics enthusiast will often simply not admit. Confidence here is so high that Dr Blakemore can declare that a conscious and choice-making machine is perfectly conceivable. This is surely to fail to see the mystery of human consciousness and

---

[1] And in psychology are used to study 'cognitive development': I have just heard an Open University programme in which cognitive development was studied entirely in relation to models derived from computer science. The mysteries of learning and thinking escaped notice.

autonomy: and, in its tendency to over-simplify, such a view reveals inability to grasp the vast complexity of the subject. This in turn indicates the futility of the task which science takes on in this area, of explaining in particulate terms, and in cause and effect terms, processes which can only be understood in terms of a whole complex higher being, and his subjectivity which cannot be found by a physico-chemical positivist approach.

As E.W.F. Tomlin points out, it will not do to attribute to 'the brain' alone all rational, intelligent, purposive thought and activity, together with the faculties of memory and invention, for some of these are needed in some form in the development of the brain. For one thing, this would imply a leap from the non-conscious to the conscious which is inexplicable. Life and consciousness must be seen as the same, and the brain is an instrument which enables the organism to live increasingly outside itself. We must see those capacities which are attributed so often to the brain as aspects of the whole creature:

> . . . far from being the whole of consciousness, cerebral consciousness, as we may call it, is a *specialization* whereby the organism is enabled, through its sense-organs, to register stimuli and compose an internal 'pattern' of external objects, and, in the light of this information, to 'act on' its environment.

The consciousness of which cerebral consciousness is a specialization is the 'immediate unity of the organism itself', its form. To this Professor Tomlin gives the name 'subjectivity' in its original sense of 'existing in itself'. In the light of such an extended view of consciousness, 'the brain is an organ for mediating or "transacting business" between the organism and its environment. To identify it with the mind is like identifying a transformer with the electric current which it regulates.'

The relationship between the apparent 'parts' of the human being, and consciousness, are not the same as or fundamentally parallel to the relationship between the parts of a computer and its various functions. Moreover, in any account of consciousness and learning a cultural dimension is evident, and this the positivist must fail to find since he seeks to reduce the operations of the computer mind to what can be reduced to his kind of logic. Something more adequate is needed in the account, and Tomlin uses such phrases as 'cerebral consciousness surveys the whole complex of the structures of our social life' and 'the

B

brain carries into the environment the formative instinct of the organism, and by endowing its inventive faculties with sensory equipment, it "forms" or "informs" the environment in such a way as to prolong organic evolution in the form of cultural evolution'.

As Professor Tomlin discusses the nature of consciousness and the mind, it becomes clear that we are moving into dimensions which cannot be dealt with in the terms of concepts of physics: 'psychological phenomena occupy a dimension distinct from the spatio-temporal world of physics.' Nor will it do, to rest on mechanical models. The attempt to explain the 'brain' in machine terms develops from the desperate attempt of science, driven by its anti-teleological metaphysic, to reduce mental processes to the merely mechanical. In truth, the brain (and indeed the whole body)

> is the appearance of which the *reality* is consciousness, and in this way it is possible to accept the view that the mind is 'outside time' without resorting to the occult. Indeed, there is nothing abstruse or 'mystical' in this view, for the truth is a commonplace experience. If two persons hold a conversation, they must reach outside the spatio-temporal framework in order to communicate their thoughts.

We are in the dimension of subjectivity and inter-subjectivity, which we shall discuss here later in such terms as 'mansions of consciousness', 'encounter', and the 'space between' mother and child, in the early stages of the origins of culture and language. In this area, of the study of consciousness, machine-thinking simply misleads:

> the machines of the extra-organic world imitate the brain and the bodily organs only in respect of their delegated *function*. Such machines cannot replace the vital activity of primary consciousness, so that a computer can never be a living brain. Conversely, a fully-functioning brain can never be a dead machine. And since a machine is dead in the sense that all machines are dead unless 'surveyed' by consciousness, and since the disparate parts of a machine enjoy their connection and integration only in the unity of the organism, a machine-brain cannot, as Dr Blakemore and his fellow-mechanists would have us believe generate the consciousness which it presupposes.
> 'The Mechanics of Dr Blakemore's mind', in *New Universities Quarterly*, Vol. 32, No.1, Winter, 1977/78, p.67.

The cybernetical analogy will always be inadequate to explain behaviour. The plausibility of mechanistic models arises from the fact that both human actions and machines are directed to achievements. But as Marjorie Grene points out, cybernetics theory, like behaviourism, reduces actions to mechanistically conceived causal chains in a monolithic time sequence. Organic time is structured in reference to natural goals; 'life manifests itself as configured time' (Adolf Portmann). Then, the learning of machines is only pseudo-learning, as for instance when learning machines are programmed to avoid wrong moves in a game. Human beings by contrast are capable of holding their responses to a situation in ambiguity, in a yes-no response, and are also capable of real learning – of suddenly coming to recognize something new in a situation, when they had no previous knowledge of what it was they were hoping to find out. Moreover, living organisms have a special relationship to their environment which involves 'so long as they are alive, openness and restriction at one and the same time'. (*Approaches to a Philosophical Biology,* pp.137-8) Yet a good deal in the first of these two Bullock Courses is based on cybernetics analogies which are open to such criticisms, implying mechanical models where these are simply erroneous, at the deepest level of understanding human nature.

Example 2 is no better, in its underlying assumptions. Its intention is not that 'the student should learn to read closely' or that 'the student should become more subtly responsive to language', but he is to get

(b) a sketch of linguistic theory, with psychological and sociological links.

We know what kind of psychology they mean. It will not, for example, help us to understand the child's talk or painting or play, as does the psychology of Len Chaloner, Susan Isaacs, D.W. Winnicott and others we shall discuss. It doesn't mean Marjorie Hourd or the reports on classroom experience of Sybil Marshall. Bullock means the abstractions of sociolinguistics and psycholinguistics, neither of which can find the subjective realities of creative being.

Creative expression itself becomes submerged in a theoretical communications scheme:

B. Communication in the context of Cognitive and Affective Development.

(a) Goals of communication in speech and writing: Information needs; negotiation processes: thinking; forms of self-expression . . .

Behind the syllabus is a certain model whose origins are in a specific philosophical tradition (e.g. of Hobbes and Hume)[1] – a machine-man, whose primary *functions* are communication, information, and *'control processes'*. His 'goals' are not those of being-in-the-world, as a creative and autonomous *being*: they are of a homunculus operating like a robot, according to certain physical rules. His role is to fit into a utilitarian society and serve it, not *to be*. The complexities of language in existence, of communing with oneself, of sustaining a human identity in touch with a real world, of intentionality in creative living are here eliminated. Again, beyond the words and 'functions' is the *problem of life*, here conveniently ignored. And in any case when it comes to our area of concern, creative writing, to speak of 'self-expression' is not enough: as a concept of creativity this was always woefully inadequate, as we have made plain enough.

The reference to creativity is tagged on the end: the dominant assumption is that literacy is to be inculcated by a set of rules and procedures derived from linguistics and psychology:

Intermediate skills . . .

(iii) inter-sentential structures in speech and writing; the paragraph and beyond . . . stochastic processes . . . Learning to use verbal skills in communication . . . recording technique . . .

It all sounds so 'authentic', 'scientific', and effective in that way. But look at it closely: 'learning to use verbal skills in communication . . .' – is that quite what happens? It is, we know, much more mysterious than that. And then perhaps we come up with a jolt at 'the paragraph and beyond . . .': so that is all linguistic science comes to! Have we not heard this, years and years ago, from our worst English teachers, who bored us, and did all those futile 'drill' exercises in 'writing a sentence' and 'building a paragraph'? Perhaps all we have here is a retreat to the old dullness, masked by a language which suggests we have in all this a 'properly authentic' discipline which should satisfy the university and its demands for 'rigour'? The two

---

[1] See 'Hobbes and the modern mind', in *Philosophy in and out of Europe*, Marjorie Grene, 1976 and on Hume in her *The Knower and the Known*, 1966.

proposed courses are boring enough simply in outline: and they miss 'English' altogether.

But, as we shall see, while the basis for this kind of approach might seem to have authenticity, there has been a philosophical revolution which exposes them as ill-based. This has found the empirical, objective model to be bankrupt, while developing a richer under-standing of humanness of its own. Since the work of people like Susan Isaacs, the child had been seen as a complex and mysterious, autono-mous, creature, whose culture develops between the responding adult and his own inner spirit. Anyone entering a good primary school can see this new understanding of the child in action. This recognition of creative autonomy in the human child is perhaps one of the greatest achievements in British life in the last quarter-century, and has been a powerful contribution to the civilized quality of our society at best. In a good primary school one experiences a meeting between the imagination of child and teacher which establishes a certain kind of essentially humanistic atmosphere – of friendly co-operation, of care, of attention to human problems of development of dealings through symbolism with joy, sorrow, love, conflict and resolution. In this atmosphere children learn with evident depth and quickness, even though many have serious difficulties (of broken homes, of belonging to a remote ethnic culture, of being unable to speak much English at all, and so on). Many a primary school seems a little Athens, because there is no conflict in it about the main purposes; everyone there enjoys learning in the fullest and truest sense, in kindness and order-liness. Something happens which is far more complex and rich than 'learning to use verbal skills in communication' – not least when teacher is reading her class *Never Go Down to the End of Town without Consulting Me, Tom's Midnight Garden,* or *Charlotte's Web.*

I have visited schools where there is a rich atmosphere of creative living, even in grim areas; where young teachers work happily and enthusiastically, with negro, Japanese, Greek, and Italian children, as well as children of working-class parents on the one hand and TV producers on the other (in NW1). These teachers would, I believe, obtain no benefit from the kind of linguistics courses recommended as above in Bullock. Indeed these would inhibit them. As George Sampson said, English is 'a condition of existence rather than a subject of instruction' (p.25). The best training for such work is good reading and good writing: the enjoyable study of literature, and the experience of creative writing. Student teachers should have hours specifically set aside for reading the vast literature of childhood, from *The Tinder Box*, to de la Mare, Chinese poetry and *Huckleberry Finn;* and, for their own satisfaction, William Blake, Dickens and Edward Thomas. Student teachers need to spend hours and hours discussing the symbolism of children's writing, their stories and their meaning; fairy tales, and child speech; game-rhymes and babies' patter. They need to read *poetry* and talk about poetry, at the level of their own interest.[1] *These are the real disciplines of English.* Yet at the moment, apart from some notable exceptions, not enough of this responsive activity with words goes on. No wonder the *choice* of works for study and for presentation is often so poor! So few teachers have a rich range of literature and child literature in their acquaintance, from which to draw. Yet if colleges of education were to follow the *Bullock Report*, students would instead be subjected to even more tedious and irrelevant abstract courses, like those quoted above – taking up valuable time, and even blunting responsiveness by dry theorizing. The Bullock kind of training in explicit analytical attention to words would inhibit them further, because the assumption that such attention improves 'language use' is based on theories which are seriously wrong, in their account of how language use develops, as Polanyi shows.

---

[1] And to practice other arts, dancing, painting and music. At Homerton College of Education, Cambridge, the students once could choose to do sculpture with the late Betty Rea, a superb artist. At one time a committee argued that it would be better if they did *The History of Art* – a characteristic university response. Fortunately the move was restricted, though I gather the conflict continues.

*Chapter Two*

# Some Philosophical Problems Behind 'A Language for Life'

There is an urgent need, then, to prevent prescriptions like Bullock wasting our time. The Bullock Report is too massive a compromise however to reply to in detail as a whole. All I can do is to pursue some of the philosophical issues posed by it, to try to justify my remarks at the end of the last chapter.

The fundamental error in this element of the Bullock Report may be made clear by looking at one paragraph (1.11): 'If a teacher is to *control* the growth of *competence* he must be able to examine the *verbal inter-action* of a class or group in terms of an *explicit* understanding of the *operation of the language.*'

This is the typical language now of any 'education' course on language. It turns a natural process into a mechanical theory, with implications which are seriously misleading. To show what kind of confusion lies behind it, let me quote an earlier sentence (p.xxxii) already referred to, for contrast: 'The quality of learning is fashioned in the day-to-day atmosphere of the classroom through the knowledge, intuitions and skill of individual teachers.' This is the language of a different world, and it is to be preferred: 'fashioned' is a better word than 'control', 'quality' a better word than 'competence', and the word 'intuition' points to the mystery of the whole powers of the teacher, to draw out capacities in pupils. The word 'intuitions' invokes a recognition of 'nous', of the reliance on tacit powers which are beyond our explicit awareness and control. For when we stand in front of a class of children – *we do not know what is going to happen.* We sink or swim. Will it be any good? Will the end-product make sense when we read them through next morning? Will there be anything there at the end of the hour that wasn't there at the beginning? Will there be something with order and meaning in the pupils' souls at the end rather than mere blots and scrawled paper? Will they beat us? Or refresh us?

These are moments of 'life'. They have to be lived through, and God alone knows what the outcome will be. Every creative act, and every lesson, is a 'surrender to creative fate'.

The other terminology – 'control' and 'competence' – avoids the complexities by implying that we can deal explicitly with entities. This is to falsify. We can only make these capacities *seem* more accessible and controllable if we implicitly reduce them thus to mechanistic and functional dimensions by our terminology. We can make 'the criss-cross of utterance between us' seem more susceptible to our will, if we speak of 'verbal interaction', or 'competence'. We can seem to make everything seem more malleable, and deprive events of their disturbing mystery, if we speak of 'explicit understanding of the operation of the language'. But these analytical and abstract terms may well delude us into thinking we can will what cannot be willed, and triumph where we can only live through an experience.

I am not urging irrationality. There are, of course, many benefits to be obtained from a rational and even analytical approach to problems of knowledge as in medicine. But even there diagnosis will always remain an art, employing tacit processes, and so even will (say) the recognition of germs.[1] Many important activities in our lives depend upon such powers. In truth, in our sphere, the 'explicit' is often an enemy to all those processes upon which creativity depends: and there are good epistemological grounds for this view.

An *'explicit'* understanding of the 'operations of the language' is a highly specialized achievement, only possible for a small number of experts. While it has its own authenticity as a study, it contributes little or nothing to the capacity of a teacher to respond to, and to judge, the achievement of a child, as he is learning to speak or write. Will linguistics help the teacher to 'examine the verbal interaction' of a class better? Anyone who has taught poetry will surely doubt that, as will anyone who has discussed children's writing with teachers: listening, even, is an imaginative activity, since we are always wondering what the speaker's 'real' meaning is. Will 'explicit' under-standing really help to 'control' the growth of *competence*'? Before we answer that, let us first examine the implications. In what sense 'control'? Is the growth of the capacity for language use really controllable? I doubt it. We put all kinds of cultural material before a

---

[1] A leading biologist, Dr C.A. Pantin, told his students to 'bring in any worms that sneer at you': that is, he was instructing them in the intuitive processes of recognizing the features of a species, and he recognized this as a tacit process on which his branch of science depends.

child, and we respond to him in a loving way – but what happens belongs to the 'going concern' inside him. His 'living principle' in dealing with his world, including language use, is an unfathomable mystery, taking its own pace and developing at its own rate. We must simply live with these truths: it is self-deceiving to believe we can control, rather than foster, competence, while it will not do to see competence as a mere function apart from his whole emotional life.

Within the child is a whole complexity, involving his 'formative principle' – so that he can become the kind of person he has within himself to become; an existential process. Of this overall growth his powers to listen, speak, hear, write and read in words and other signs and noises is part. Rather than a mere 'competence', his capacity to use words is an aspect of the development of the whole 'life-world' of a complex being trying to make sense of his life. All knowing is that kind of quest for meaning.

The words in the paragraph above about 'intuition' are words that allow nature to take its course, aided (albeit) by some knowledge on the teachers' part. The words in the paragraph about 'control' and 'explicit understanding' belong to the philosophical tradition against which many are now arguing, because it falsifies both the knower and the known. For one thing it implies that we must 'divide and rule', break everything down into fragments. Examine processes in terms of items occurring in a commonsense world of a one-after-the-other sequence of strict cause and effect, and you will gradually, step by step, arrive at the whole. This whole will be no more than an assemblage of these parts and these processes, which in 'the last analysis' can be accounted for by the laws of physics and chemistry. Activities and forms will eventually be reducible to substance and processes governed by physical laws: so we may rule over Nature, by dividing and fragmenting. Reverse the process, and we can control mental processes by technical approaches, or devise machines that will be conscious.

So deeply entrenched are these assumptions that we are easily persuaded that this is the proper way to set about problems, such as that of the improvement of English. This is where Bullock goes wrong: and it is over such issues we must find an alternative philosophical base.

The word 'competence' as used in The Bullock Report probably derives from Chomsky. As Ian Robinson shows, this use of the word virtually implies that there is a kind of apparatus of linguistic ability in the child's head, which belongs to his organic make-up. It is assumed, virtually, that this competence can be 'tuned up' by a teacher-technician who understands its structure. Of course, if we accept this model, the teacher must know how the thingy 'works', and so should study linguistics. But in this there is a confusion of the physical (apparatus) and the psychic (consciousness). In the phrase 'operation of the language' there is a lurking confusion as we shall see between linguistic system or grammar and the human-being-using-words. In the word 'control' lurks a falsification in the implied analogy between using an apparatus (like a computer coding it and so forth) and what a teacher does in the art of teaching. 'Control' implies 'outcomes' where there are no clear outcomes since we are dealing with developing complex unique beings who are living. How can we ever be sure that any aspect of their living is attributable to anything we have done? And in the word 'explicit' there is an implication that there can be 'clear and distinct ideas' (Descartes) in a region where nothing of the kind is possible, not even in verbal statements, as Polanyi and Marjorie Grene have made clear.

Thus the whole terminology invokes a model which determines discourse. As Erwin Straus says, 'any description is already theory':

> The very language we learn dictates a definite interpretation of the world. We *see* the world through the medium of language, and this language is that of our parents. It is also the language of our generation; it binds us to tradition.
>
> *The Primary World of Senses*, p.36

Erwin Straus is discussing Pavlov, whom he accuses of accepting with astonishing naïvety certain concepts from physics as the universal categories of his exploration of the world, and as a *meta-physic*. In our commonplace thinking about the world and ourselves, our view, whether we are aware of it or not, embodies a metaphysic, and very often today it is a thoroughly mechanistic one. Pavlov was able to assume that his physicalistic theory was self-evident. His theory was not the beginning but the end of a long development of Western thinking which is now coming into question.

In this situation it is perhaps inevitable that we should have a Bullock Report. In adopting a physicalist model where it embraces linguistics the Report menaces the whole 'humanities' tradition which regards English as a creative subject, whose roots are in the imaginative disciplines. But on what grounds? In what sense is it 'scientific' when a great scientist like Polanyi speaks of the child and words in *our* kind of way? The child's discovery of semantic sense-giving and sense-reading arises, says Polanyi, within a multitude of parallel achievements. His heuristic powers are set at work by the puzzlements he encounters, and his acquisition of language is explained by the dynamics of tacit knowing – that is, coming to know which, by such processes as 'subception' and 'indwelling' – *imaginative* acts – involving the whole person and his intentional capacities.

This is perhaps the place to establish Michael Polanyi as an important figure in the debate on the mind, language and culture. His work has the more force because was an outstanding scientist. Polanyi was a chemist and a Fellow of the Royal Society. He trained as a doctor of medicine at Budapest University in 1913. In 1917 he published the outlines of his theory of absorption which was much later recognized as a major contribution to this phenomenon. In the period 1940 to 1949 he worked on the fundamental mechanics of molecular dissociation at surfaces and other problems in chemistry and physics. In 1946, after the publication of *Science, Faith and Society,* he embarked on a philosophical study of knowledge, *Personal Knowledge.* His change of field of interest from physical chemistry to philosophy was an intellectual journey of profundity which has yet to be fully understood. As Robin Hodgkin has said, his central insight was a discovery about discovery: that all human creativity prior to the verbalization of it is rooted in what Polanyi called 'tacit knowledge'.

> We know more than we can tell. In the actual performance of a work of art or in the execution of a skill we integrate both our conscious understanding of the art and many less accessible physiological processes, in a "focused passionate endeavour". Important acts are the acts of a whole persons acting freely, not of detached intelligence or of automata.

In these few sentences alone (from Dr Hodgkin's obituary in *The Times*) we have enough of a clue to those investigations of Polanyi's which make it evident that the Bullock Report is often seriously wrong in its concepts of how the mind works. This most relevant statement here has force because it is from a scientific essay: 'The child's discovery of semantic sense-giving and sense-reading arises within a multitude of parallel achievements. *His imagination is at work from the start in exploring the nature of the things he is encountering . . .'* (p.206, my italics).

This emphasis on the creative powers of the imagination, together with intuition, as the basis of all language and thought, arises from Polanyi's experience of scientific endeavour itself.

Throughout Polanyi's work we encounter the concept of imagination. The Bullock Report displays something of a tendency to shrink from such terms: much talk about 'creativity', it declares, is 'hazy', and it seems to the Report doubtful that English is a 'vehicle for the child's emotional development'. In this we have a strange paradox. A distinguished scientist-philosopher finds no difficulty in recognizing and discussing tacit modes of being – because he has the strength to encounter the complexities. 'English' experts find it difficult.

Those who follow the narrow empirical-objectivist paradigm in Britain often refuse to encounter consciousness, or the inner life, or creativity. But they also tend to commit the 'blasphemy' (as Kierkegaard called it) of applying natural scientism to human existence. They seem commonsensical, yet often, when examined, their ways of approaching human experience are alchemical, as Roger Poole has declared, accusing H.J. Eysenck of quantifying the unquantifiable and then putting it through a computer. The Bullock Report often displays a mechanistic model of 'language use' in relation to experience: 'English is rooted in the processing of experience through language. The pupil uses language to represent the experience to himself, to come to terms with it, to possess it more completely' (p.7). The approach to how language relates to our lives is here a natural consequence of the modes of thought of Hobbes and Hume, and belongs to the kind of analysis made in pre-gestalt psychology. It belongs to a somewhat over-simplified and crude application of scientific analysis to processes of perception, thinking, and the nature of behaviour.

It is because he is the greater scientist that Michael Polanyi can speak of the individual's relationship to his world in different terms – *and* recognize at the same time the existence of the body in complex with the mind, and the primacy of imagination:

> . . . we integrate the muscles moving our limbs, without any focal[1] knowledge of this muscular performance. This was first described by William James as the structure of all voluntary motion, and he observed that it was set in motion *by the imagination striving to anticipate* the result of the action.
>
> *Knowing and Being*, p.200

In the Bullock Report there is an assumption that the learning of theories and rules must come first in the teaching of English. To teach well the student must study linguistics, while he must see language as a tool for 'processing experience'. This is clear from the proposed linguistic courses I have examined. Yet in any holistic study of the processes of learning or acquiring skills it seems clear that the explicit is less significant than dynamics such as 'indwelling' which involve the extension of ourselves into the world by imagination. As Polanyi makes plain, the *'aim of a skilful performance is achieved* by the observance of a set of rules *which are not known as such to the person following them,* (p.49).

Even riding a bicycle depends upon tacit processes we barely understand. The principle by which the cyclist keeps his balance is not generally known.

> The rule observed by the cyclist is this. When he starts falling to the right, he turns the handlebars to the right, so that the course of the bicycle is deflected along a curve towards the right. This results in a centrifugal force pushing the cyclist to the left and offsets the gravitational force dragging him down to the right. This manoeuvre presently throws the cyclist out of balance to the left, which he counteracts by turning the handlebars to the left: and so he continues to keep himself in balance by winding along a series of appropriate curvatures. A simple analysis shows that for a given angle of unbalance the curvature of each winding is inversely proportional to the square of the speed at which the cyclist is progressing.
>
> *Personal Knowledge*, p.49-50

---

[1] 'Focal' – explicit or 'clear and distinct'. One of the points made by Marjorie Grene following Polanyi is that modern science follows Descartes in pursuing 'clear and distinct ideas', forgetting in fact that there are no such things: even the most definite scientific truths only exist in scientists knowing. The whole 'reflective' movement in thinking about thinking is thus anti-Cartesian, and this may be found in Roger Poole, in Leavis, in Marjorie Grene and Polanyi.

Now, if we wish to teach a class of children how to ride bicycles, we shall have an adult with each child, to allow the child to 'get the feel' of riding. After a few minutes, the sense of balance will begin to come to each child, and he will want to 'try' alone, by the great mystery of body and being – as he 'dwells in' the bicycle, making it an extension of his self, the child will suddenly 'learn to ride a bicycle'. He will want to learn because he wants to *show us:* another tacit element. Of course, he will fall off, and we will say, 'You can't ride as slowly as that', or 'Don't forget to put your foot down, when you feel you are losing balance!' *But we can't tell him how to keep balance.* A child achieves the amazing feat of riding a bicycle through subception, indwelling, and other processes involving imagination, before he could possibly learn the 'rules', from his own body-in-being centre.

No 'linguistics' of bicycle-riding, velocipedistics, could enable a child, by abstract studies of the physics of balance, to ride a bike: yet even the dullest child can ride a bike like the best of them!

The calculation Polanyi refers to is quite complicated. A child would not even be able to work it out, let alone learn it: the 'rules' would be absolutely useless to him. So, they would also be useless to a bicycling instructor. One cannot learn to swim by theoretical instruction in hydro-dynamics, either. We swim, bike and talk by doing these naturally, 'picking it up', 'mastering' them.

Yet, by analogy, the main recommendations of the *Bullock Report* are that teachers should learn such rules for language on the assumption that explicit knowledge *is* an essential for the fostering of language competence. *This is a serious fallacy,* and, if followed, would land us back in something akin to the old assumption that grammar and clause analysis are the way to learn to write.

Such errors may be traced to the kind of 'objective' paradigm within which Chomsky thinks (see the analysis made by Ian Robinson in *The New Grammarian's Funeral*). In his attempt to make a scientific analysis of language, Chomsky comes to *confuse grammar with language:* that is, to confuse his analytical abstraction (made into an intellectual scheme) with the natural process of using words, as a manifestation of those tacit processes of which Polanyi writes.

Chomsky begins to talk of a grammar as 'internalized' by speakers:

> By a generative grammar I mean simply a system of rules that in some explicit and well-defined way assigns structural descriptions to sentences. Obviously, *every speaker of a language*

> *has mastered and internalized a generative grammar that expresses*
> *his knowledge of his language.*
>> *Aspects of the Theory of Syntax,* p.8 (my italics)

But the speaking child has *not* mastered a *grammar:* he speaks, without knowing the rules. The truth is, as M.O'C. Drury puts it, that the child's use of language comes by nature:

> I want to say that the existence of language, and the development of the ability to speak in a child is a miracle, something that the notion of explanation as to how it came, and comes to be, does not make sense. It is something indeed for us to wonder at and be thankful for.
>> M.O'C. Drury, *The Danger of Words,* p.76

Such a mere reliance on 'mysteries' annoys your analytical 'expert', who wants to satisfy 'university demands' for 'intellectual rigour.' But there is no other way to come at the tacit. The tacit elements manifest in everyday achievements like riding a bicycle, painting, learning to swim, speaking cannot be found by positivist analysis: they are 'subsidiary' in the sense that they are beyond access of clear and definite enquiry.

Of course, artefacts such as pictures may be discussed in analytical terms, and compared, in that intellectual, critical way, with other paintings, comparing flesh-tones, fore-shortening, perspective, 'balance' and so forth. But it is not possible to turn the process round and paint good pictures just by knowing the analytics. There is a passage in D.H. Lawrence's *Phoenix* (p.34) in which he ridicules a young man who supposes that 'now we know about how a good picture should be made . . . we should be able to paint good pictures'. Lawrence offers a hilarious list of the supposed ingredients of a good painting: but makes it clear that no such explicit knowledge of the parts could even enable a man to paint a good picture: that can only happen in the living moment of creation. Either we can paint or we can't, by some mysterious *endowment,* some capacity to indwell and symbolize. Yet there are some who cannot see the problem, because they are stuck with a machine analogy: and Bullock cannot see the problem, which is its danger.

In his *Syntactic Structures* Chomsky says, 'This conception of language is an extremely powerful and general one. If we can adopt it, we can view the speaker as being essentially a machine of the type considered' (p.20). Chomsky has just previously used the word 'machine' to mean an abstraction in grammar. From saying that a grammar is a machine it is but a short step to saying that the speaker is a machine of a kind in using that grammar. But the machine analogy is fallacious, as we have seen, at a very deep level: the higher organisms display creative powers inexplicable by any machine analogy – not least in the capacity to hold both 'yes' and 'no' responses, at the same time; to initiate; and (most significantly) to *learn*. Not to see what learning involves, which must bring a recognition that a machine *can't learn*, is a serious defeat in educational discourse. The truth is, as Polanyi emphasizes, that a child grows up to use his language in the most marvellous and complex ways, using all the rules, and creating new sentences, far beyond (as it were) the sum of all the previous sentences he has ever used – *without knowing one rule*.

Chomsky was struck by the fact that children, naturally, learn to use language with all its complex rules, without knowing the rules.

> It seems plain that language acquisition is based on the child's discovery of what from a formal point of view is deep and abstract theory – a generative grammar abstract theory – many of the concepts and principles of which are only remotely related to experience by long and intricate chains of unconscious quasi-inferential steps.
>
> *Aspects of the Theory of Syntax*

Moreover, Chomsky saw, there is another fundamental fact of language:

> namely, the speaker's ability to produce and understand instantly new sentences that are not similar to those previously heard in any physically-defined sense . . . not obtainable from them by any sort of 'generalization' known to psychology or philosophy.
>
> op.cit., pp.57-8

Without knowing the rules, a child may produce new sentences which a computer (fitted with generalizations to enable it to deduce from previous 'data' and to put known processes together) could never formulate: the child does something it would not be possible to 'programme' for. This amazing act of creative intentionality is a feat even the least able child can achieve, and any mechanistic analogy simply cannot account for this at all.

How can children 'learn to perform a vast set of complex rules, intelligible only to a handful of experts'? Chomsky has not been able to solve this problem, says Polanyi. The problem *is* solved by recognition of the existence of tacit and subsidiary elements. That is, the use of language grows from within the body-life of a being-in-the-world, through an interplay between perception, subjectivity and inter-subjectivity, to become a wholeness of capacity. Below we shall look at ways in which thinkers like Martin Buber and D.W. Winnicott have sought to understand these processes in a very different way from the approach of theoretical 'scientific' linguistics. The child's capacity for metaphor, for symbolism, for being logical, for being able to use mathematics, and for communicating to another being – all these emerge from the whole complex process of the growth of consciousness and intersubjectivity. In learning to paint, students practise painting, copy masters, learn by doing – but only long after do they come to realize what they have done, and even then cannot explain it. These all go together; and if these processes generate structures and modes which can be examined subsequently by the linguist as a generative grammar, then that is wonderful. But the human processes come first, and the linguist's analysis after: *it is not possible to perform the creative act on the basis of the theory, or explicit analysis.* In any case, any theory like linguistic theory remains only a feeble and inadequate, *partial*, account of *some* of the features of the living act itself – and the limitations of the theory will be at one with the limitations of the paradigm, in this case one which cannot find consciousness. Nor is it a question of waiting until the linguisticians are clever enough to understand complex phenomena which have so far eluded them. As we have seen, there is something fundamentally wrong with the assumption that such complex realities as the workings of the human mind can be understood by the physicalist principle of reducing everything to the one simple level by micro-reduction. New, holistic, subjective disciplines are required.

It is not that the child internalizes a systematic grammar which *'expresses his knowledge of the language'*; he does not know his language in that way. He uses it, as an artist uses a paintbrush, exercising his protensions (to use a word from Edmund Husserl). Anyone 'uttering' in that way is working with lightning speed, or in unscrutinized tacit ways, trusting upon his subsidiary capacities to sustain the miraculous process of painting a picture, or even just telling Daddy about the pub being on fire, breathlessly.

Chomsky, however, moves on as if from the belief that a child (or anyone) couldn't speak unless he had 'internalized' a 'grammar', in a belief that 'competence' must be present in the speaker's mind, something the speaker has 'acquired' and now puts to use. The long processes of development of consciousness and culture, from the first discovery of the mother as another, this mysterious 'meeting' between inner potential and intersubjective 'reflection', the built-up sense of self and world with symbol in between, as the basis of language, is not present in the field of Chomsky's view. His psychology is one based upon a mechanistic model in the background, to be understood in strict cause-and-effect terms, rather than a living subject operating by creative dynamics. Where does the working 'apparatus' come from? Since it cannot, in his model, come from the 'space between' mother and infant (neither inside nor outside, in the realm of culture) it must come from some inner physical reality, the secret thing in the 'system'. Here we find such a positivist approach inevitably comes up against unsolved problems of Cartesian Dualism, and has to rely, as Tomlin has shown, on belief in the impossible.

The presence of Chomsky's 'competence', as Ian Robinson shows, is physical. Chomsky says:

> It has, I believe, become quite clear that if we are ever to understand how language is used or acquired, then we must abstract for separate and independent study a cognitive sytem, a *system of knowledge* and belief, that develops in early childhood and that interacts with many other factors to *determine* the kinds of behaviour that we observe; to introduce a technical term, we must isolate and study *the system of linguistic competence* that underlies behaviour but that is not realized in any direct or simple way in behaviour.
>
> *Language and Mind,* p.4 (my italics)

This system must be abstracted, not as an abstraction in the grammatical sense, but as something 'there' parallel to the digestive 'system'. *Grammar* thus begins to become 'a finite object, realized physically in a finite human brain' (*The Sound Pattern of English,* p.6).

Those who follow the linguists and try to be scientific will try to find a scientific 'object'. The human mind in this approach must therefore become 'a particular, biologically-given system', 'the system represented in the brain'. Chomsky's excitement in this is castigated by Ian Robinson. Chomsky merely confuses 'the child using language' with 'what the grammarian does'. He 'attributes to the whole human race the grammatical understanding worked out laboriously by Western scholars since the days of the Greeks' (Robinson, p.60). That is, Chomsky supposes we are all able to speak because we are all linguists possessing a whole tradition of grammatical theory.

But neither we nor our children are linguists, even though we talk and write like billy-o. The basis of our competence could not possibly either be a natural physical competence, like a built-in code. Learning language is an exercise of *consciousness* in whole being. We have only to watch the way a child acquires language to see that he learns it by play and in the context of love, using tacit powers. Where can we put 'learning', 'play', 'love' or 'tacit powers' in a positivist scheme? To Chomsky, says Robinson, 'competence' becomes in his thinking a kind of physical entity: 'Thus fallaciously does "competence" force its way back into "performance", whence it should never have departed, and now with the additional fallacy that "competence" must be a physical object' (Robinson, p.60).

The final step in the development of this fallacy is to confuse language with grammar. 'For our purposes,' writes Chomsky, 'we can think of *language* as a set of *structural descriptions of sentences* . . .' (*Conditions on Transformation*, p.232, my italics). Of course, the way certain English sentences go, even in sentences used by children, can be seen to belong to, or embody a subtle work of grammar. But (says Robinson) 'the grammar is the act of structural descriptions, not the sentences and much less the language'. What we have to emphasize again is that 'the striving imagination has the power to implement its aim by the practice of ingenious rules of which the subject remains focally ignorant' (Polanyi, p.200).

If we are to try to improve language use, then our attention needs to be given to the child's consciousness and imagination, and to give him lots of opportunities for the exercise of his imagination in a loving context. The linguistic specialists behind the *Bullock Report* try to turn English in the direction of explicit attempts to tune up that 'competence' conceived as a physical system, in the child's computer-like head. For them, what is to be improved is *grammar*, confused with a cognitive system, a physical entity, in the 'brain'. The teacher's rôle, then, becomes one of understanding the structure and rules, which 'are' language, in order to become able to manipulate that 'biologically given system'. It is a great relief to turn back to Polanyi who, after dealing with Chomsky, simply speaks of the whole child, as in the above sentence. The rules of which one is focally ignorant in using language, he goes on, can be acquired tacitly and *only* tacitly, and it can also be practised *only* tacitly: it does not come into explicit focus and no focal awareness can perform it. So, the proposals based on linguistics theory in the *Bullock Report* simply fall down, because the authors never found the realities of *tacit knowing*, as a manifestation of that 'striving imagination' trying to make sense of its world.

> The dynamics of tacit knowing have made this problem more manageable. We are no longer faced with the question how people who learn to speak a language can identify, remember and apply a set of rules known only to linguists. They do not identify these rules, let alone memorise them and explicitly apply them, and *do not need to do so.*
>
> *Knowing and Being,* p.204 (my italics)

If children do not need to do so, and students do not need to do so, why waste time teaching them dense linguistic theories? Only a few linguists need study the rules, for the sake of truth, not in order to prescribe. The rest of us can simply do English, enjoying plays, poems and stories – and improve our language powers thus: *by art.*

This is not to say, of course, that there should not be linguists. Linguistics is an important subject but it is one which is highly specialized, a very minority subject. What I am rejecting as false and impractical is the implication that linguistics offers us a means to foster and control language development; that *'explicit'* analytical concern with the structure of language and its categories is the way to teach English. It is not, and linguistics has very little to offer the English teacher.

# Chapter Three

# *The Bullock Bête-Machine*

Besides the doubts I have about the linguistic model, there is a related model of how the human being 'works' to be found in the Bullock Report: one glimpses in it from time to time a functional model, again cybernetical. This kind of model lies behind such an account as is given here of memory: 'a word that names an object is for a young child a *filing-pin* upon which he *stores successive experience* of objects themselves . . .' (*Bullock Report*, 4.4., p.48, my italics). At the foot of the page, Vygotsky is quoted as saying that the language rules gradually internalized by a child 'become the basic structures of thinking' and that 'a child's intellectual growth is contingent on his mastering the social means of thought, that is, language'. This, the Report says, would be too close an identification of thought with language, for some psychologists: but it offers no fundamental rejection of this kind of model, and does not even suggest criticisms of it. But there have been criticisms, and they are fundamental, because they raise questions of human creativity and freedom.

Another phrase used is 'processing experience', and this seems related to the model that lies behind linguistics: 'Language provides us with a generalized representation of experience, and generalizing has the effect of *reducing the multiplicity of experience to a more manageable form*' (my italics). When we write or speak, according to Bullock, we 'impose orders upon the experiences we put into words': but what is meant is not a poetic order. The model is still that of a mechanism, 'handling' 'input'. The *Bullock Report* often talks as if the child has *not yet had its experience,* but is, as it were, a passive recipient of sensations who then uses language as a kind of instrument to service 'data' about the world, which must then be 'processed', and can then be (presumably) 'stored', ready for 'retrieval' at appropriate moments, like cheques in a machine at the bank. Of course, the whole tradition of scientific psychology leads to this view, in which the mind is a conditioned-reflex sort of mind, and the self is a bundle of impressions: sense-data are fed through some kind of 'communications' machine. The 'brain' as an autonomous entity in this mechanical process takes on a function of its own, as part of this machine. The origins of this model are traced by Marjorie Grene to David Hume's *Treatise of Human Nature,* and she warns, 'Associative mechanisms cannot make a person', while a chain of such mechanisms proceeding by habit cannot 'evaluate and choose' – the existential 'I' is missing (see *The Knower and The Known,* Chapter Four). So, the model is menacing – as is the concomitant reduction of 'English' to 'Communications'.

As we shall see, Continental reflective philosophy is striving to restore the central experiencing 'I', and it is this that we must strive to do, in English, as by opposing the essentially functional view that lurks behind Bullock. The functional mind there seems to operate as distinct from the person:

> The accumulated representation is on the one hand a storehouse of past experiences and on the other a body of expectations regarding what may yet happen to us . . . we interpret what we perceive at any moment by relating it to our body of past experiences, and respond to it in the light of that interpretation . . .
>
> *Bullock Report*

'processes' . . . 'storing' . . . 'store' . . . 'stored' . . . 'recall'. But where are the ferrous tapes, magnets and revolving wheels? There follows a reference to some experiments: *The Dynamics of Semantic Systems,* by A.R. Luris and G.J. Vinogradova, in the *British Journal of Psychology.* Vol. 50, 1958: 'Language is one of a number of ways in which we represent the world to ourselves.'

This is far too simple a view. As F.J.J. Buytendijk has put it, 'Speech is achievement.' 'Human language', says Marjorie Grene, 'becomes itself a growing world of meanings within meanings, which are not only used for practical ends but dwelt in as the very fabric of our being' (*The Knower,* p.174). This embodied complexity of being-in-the-world must be upheld. We need to protest, with Merleau-Ponty, about the 'enigmatic nature of our own body'. 'It is not a collection of particles, each one remaining in itself, not yet a network of processes defined once and for all – it is not where it was, not what it is – since we see it secreting in itself a significance upon its material surroundings, and communicating it to other embodied subjects' (*The Body as Expression*). In the objectifying positivist tradition to which the Bullock Report defers, this particular knowledge of our body, which we enjoy from the mere fact that we are a body, remains subordinated to our knowledge of it through the medium of ideas: and this leads to the strange impression given by the word 'representation' above, as though one part of our self needed another part to tell 'us' (who?) about our world. So elsewhere in the *Bullock Report* the child is a bête-machine who (p.8) reaches a 'narrative level of organizing experience', or becomes 'capable of sustained generalization'. These views are too much limited to theoretical abstractions and the cognitive view: they lack recognition of the dynamics in us of intentionality and spontaneity – all that Maurice Merleau-Ponty means when he declares, 'We are the upsurge of time'.

In Chapter Four a functionalistic influence seems most powerful. It opens with a quotation from Georges Gusdorf: 'Man interposes a network of words between the world and himself, and thereby becomes the master of the world.' The words 'network' and 'mastery' again indicate a mechanistic kind of thinking: language again is a 'communication tool'. 'Without the exchange of information in words we should not be able to achieve a fraction of our customary activities.' Yes, but surely this is to put the cart before the horse? The 'customary activities' developed in complex with those capacities for culture and language that made us man. The perspective on language use is too narrowly concerned with mere functioning.

So, Bullock prefers to seek a behavioural model of communications. We read of 'verbalised information', and 'inner representation':

> 4.1. It is the role language plays in generating knowledge and producing new forms of behaviour that typifies human existence and distinguishes it from that of all other creatures.

This all depends upon the fact that we symbolize, or 'represent to ourselves the objects, people and events that make up our environment, and do so cumulatively, thus creating an inner representation of the world as we have encountered it' (3.2).

Where is this 'inner representation'? And what does the Report mean by a 'representation'? Who represents what to whom? Is someone coming in with a print-out from the control room: showing what to whom? Surely, *I see?*

In fact, as Erwin Straus argues, 'Seeing transcends the here, the new, the thus seen.' We can apply this to the relationship between perception and language. The single views present themselves as segments of the *continuum* of the world encounter. We do not receive 'data' from our sensations, but *experience things which are objects for us.* While seeing, we experience ourselves together with and facing things. We experience the seen as an actualization. While seeing, we behave receptively, but not passively. Our body is not a receptor of 'stimuli' but the body of an experiencing being. The use of symbols and language emerges from this experience of being-in-the-world (see *The Primary World of Senses,* pp.179-180).

Objective psychology, Straus argues, contests this. According to that kind of psychology, the world which appears in experience is afflicted with a defeat, the defeat of those 'secondary qualities' which Galileo distrusted. We are not in the world: it is presented to us, as if by some film projectionist, somehow operating in the brain, showing us shadows of the world: 'It is unreal, deceptive, a phantasmagoria... The phenomena are but epiphenomenological shadows of the actual happening . . .' ('Man thinks, not the brain', in *The Primary World of Senses,* p.180). The phenomenal world is eliminated completely. The observation moves entirely on the physical plane. One must measure and compare the 'input' and the 'output' in order to understand how the brain works as a mediator between stimulus and reaction, 'processing' 'experience'.

So, to this view, language is an *instrument* of the *brain* which is a *tool* mediating between man and the natural occurrence, as we have seen. In such psychological theory, it is no longer an observer who, thanks to the function of his brain, makes the comparison, but it is the 'brain' in the skull of an observer which performs the feats, using language (etc.) as a tool to unite the disparate Humean fragments to 'represent' experience. In this, as Straus argues, there is a brain which is endowed with the human powers of which the experiencing being is bereft: 'The brain machine which is supposed to explain animal and human behaviour has been secretly equipped with gifts of observation and knowledge: it has become anthropomorphised' (Straus, p.186).

Here again it is necessary in our thinking to put the being back in his body in wholeness. As Erwin Straus says, on 'awakeness': 'Waking, we are "back again": we need no scientific apparatus, no footnotes, and no commentaries to realise we are awake':

We do not watch the coming and going of percepts in our minds to cry out at the end: Behold, this is real! We do not look on an 'outside world' from which we, conceived as mind, intellect, or consciousness, are in turn excluded; we do not project sensory data, which first occurred in our mind or our brain, into an 'outer world'. We do not use our eyes and other sense organs like binoculars to watch events on a distant stage. Awake, we find ourselves within the world; together with the world, in relation to the world. Self-awareness does not precede awareness of the world: the one is not before the other: the one is not without the other. We are not distant observers who, through a curious process of reality testing, scan neutral sensory data and arrange them into two groups, real and unreal. Awake, we experience the power of reality in our action and the world's counteraction – in its resistance and our suffering.

Quoted by Earling Eng, in a *Eulogy* for Erwin Straus, 22 May, 1975, after his death.

If we see ourselves not as 'processing experience' or 'representing the world to ourselves', but 'together with the world, in relation to the world', we shall have a better, and less functional, attitude to language use. Our goal will not be communication or 'the storing or retrieval of "information"', but *understanding*. As Erwin Straus puts it, 'The word is the bearer of meaning, hence the description of a thing which we have before our eyes can contribute to a better understanding' (see the note on 'language learning', *The Primary World of Senses*, pp.145-147). The goals of the linguists behind the Bullock Report seem quite different, they are of *functional efficiency* rather than understanding: it is to this utilitarian end that students, parents and teachers are to be trained in the explicit rules of language. The bête-machine is to be made more efficient: the primary reality is not the need of a *being* for *meaning*.

So when the Bullock Report speaks of

5.10 Helping parents to understand the process of language development in their children and to take part in it . . .

this hardly means understanding why their children love *Wee Willie Winkie* and *Tom Tit Tot*. Does it mean reading the Opies? Singing *Noyes Fludde* or playing Christmas charades? The Report makes the valuable point that the way to train parents is to train them as parents while they are pupils at school: but there is no mention of imagination or creative effort even in this enrichment. By 'responsiveness to language development' it means linguistic attention, not the kind of response we train in teaching poetry. The utilitarian approach is clear from the terms used. The Report recommends the use of films towards the ends of family and social organization:

> An awareness of the adults' rôle in the young child's *linguistic and cognitive development*. This would include a study of the *linguistics aspects of relationships* . . . and of the value of discussion and explanation in *controlling a child's behaviour* as against simple prohibition . . . (my italics)

It all seems very reasonable. But note that the pupils who are going to be future parents are not, by this emphasis, going to learn to live by the processes of love and 'fancy': *Hard Times* becomes relevant again. Children are not to become morally more autonomous and subtle by the processes of imaginative understanding of what goes on inside human beings. Parents are not urged to experience how the child develops in the context of family interrelations, in love, in play with the mother, through all the mysterious processes of intersubjectivity. Attention is limited to 'linguistic and cognitive development', because these (Bullock believes) provide the key to manipulating the thingummies inside their heads and so are the clue to the control of the functioning bête-machine. The emphasis is not on seeking understanding, in terms of the *Geisteswissenschaften*, of children's *meanings* and their relationship to adult problems in philosophy and art, such as become clear through the illuminations offered (say) by Marjorie Hourd, or D.W. Winnicott's *Therapeutic Consultations in Child Psychiatry*.

So convincing is the seeming commonsense in Bullock that we fail to notice how its whole view of language is arid and inadequate. If we think of all the kinds of delight we have experienced from words, from reading children's poems to *Henry V*, from murmuring 'Spare Thou them that confess their faults', to 'Dear heart how like you this?' where are these joys in the voluminous pages of *A Language for Life?* Language for Bullock is for 'constructing generalized representations': development is concerned with 'interacting language behaviour with . . . other mental and perceptual powers'. Human beings have 'developed languages as means of organizing their experience of the world' (p.49) as if they invented the tool to deal with experiences they were having before they had language to deal with them. A child 'gains mastery' of language, and then applies its 'organizing power to his own experience', 'and as a result his mental processes take on new form' (4.6). Heathery tethery mona dick! The world of Bullock is the world of an Edward Casaubon (see *Middlemarch*) without joy or passion.

Of course, the report declares that language has a 'heuristic' function. But its concept of what learning itself is, is inadequate, because it fails to find the mysteries in learning which, as I have shown, have never been solved by philosophers. It is not 'classifying experiences'. Who thinks of 'classifying' or 'processing' when they read lines like Donne's

> I wonder, by my troth, what thou and I
> Did, till we loved? Were we not weaned till then?

It is not true that by 'recognizing recurrences that we learn from our experience'[1] The mystery is indicated by the phenomenon Chomsky notices, that children and adults use sentences which are completely new and which cannot be made up from knowledge of other sentences. It is in moving forward by language as the 'fabric of our being' into new spheres. The mystery of learning is indicated by Marjorie Grene who refers us to Meno's question, about the very nature of knowledge itself:

> Why, on what lines will you lack Socrates, for a thing of whose nature you know nothing at all? Pray, what sort of thing, amongst those that you know now, will you treat us to as the object of your search? Or even supposing, at the best, that you hit upon it, how will you know it is the thing you did not know?
> *Meno* 8 OD. Quoted by Marjorie Grene, 'The legacy of the "Meno"', *The Knower and the Known,* p.23.

---

[1] Behind this 'classifying' impulse lie those misreadings and oversimplifications of some sentences of D.W. Harding of which Frank Whitehead accuses J.N. Britton. See *The Use of English,* Spring, 1978; 29/2, p.15. Professor Britton is the influence mainly responsible for diverting English from the art-literature-imagination approach towards one which is believed to be more academically respectable, capable, in its new positivism, of hob-nobbing with Piaget, Vygotsky, Chomsky etc. while losing sight of English as 'the child's initiation into the life of man' (Sampson).

According to the concept of language in the *Bullock Report* there can be no real learning, because their way of thinking about knowing is too explicit, and is to do with bits immediately present to the mind. But as Marjorie Grene declares:

> If all knowledge were explicit, if it consisted of pieces of information immediately present to the mind, and impersonally transferable from one mind to another, then there would be no learning and *a priori* no discovery, which is the learning of what no-one ever knew before.
>
> Grene, *The Knower and the Known*

That is, the Bullock Report cannot find all that various writers about English have meant by creativity, intentionality, and 'the living principle': the way we continually move forward into new areas of perception, thought and vision – indeed, all that makes life worth living. Yet a teacher of children lives with these every day, and this is *creativity*.

If we accept the Bullock Report's concept of English, then we shall feel a kind of paralysis. Rather than looking 'through the word' at the meaning, we shall be attending to the words with the consequent inhibiting effect: 'Switching the focus of our attention back on the object which is thereby rendered once more external to us. And as it acquires the status of externality, the object loses its meaning' (Polanyi, *Knowing and Being*, p.185). Reading the Bullock Report, we often feel threatened by a loss of meaning – a strange experience for the English teacher. The functional paradigm causes Bullock to exclude from its considerations of language everything that makes it a medium of the creative perception and the 'formative principle'. This is indeed to cast a grey cloud over a humanities subject!

It is totally false to believe that by attending to the words in the Bullock sense the child learns to use language. The child does *not* 'master the morphological rules'. It may indeed be that these 'come later than his command of syntax'. But both ways of putting it are misleading (p.52) because the child is never aware of the morphemes or the syntax. It is absurd to talk of how 'it is not always possible for the reader to sort out the syntactic structure of a sentence at first' (p.91). Not always! At first! Most readers *never* sort out the syntactic structure of the sentences they use, write and read: they don't need to, unless they belong to that tiny minority of linguists. 'At first reading'! . . . 'not always possible'! – the implication is that one *ought* to be able to do it, and *should* do it, as one reads. How much more of the ring of truth is there in Polanyi's comment on our capacities: 'We usually conduct these delicate and meaningful integrations without our being able to give more than the crudest account of such subsidiary performance' (Polanyi, *Knowing and Being*).

Bullock takes it seriously, that the quality of language may be measured by the syntax. It reports without criticism or irony that

> There have been several attempts to establish criteria for maturity in writing: mean length of composition index, the minimum terminable unit etc. We can take the last-named as an example. The minimum terminable unit, or T-unit is 'roughly any sentence or part of a sentence that is an independent clause, possibly containing, however, one or more dependent clauses'.
> W. Kellogg Hunt: *Grammatical Structures Written at Three Grade Levels*, NCTE Research Report. No.3, Urbana, Illinois, 1965

Of course, the Report says that a 'piece of writing might well have syntactic maturity and yet be wanting in organization and content'. But it fails to detect the underlying absurd concern to find a quantitative method of measuring that which essentially belongs to meaning and so can never be measured. It gropes towards 'impression marking' itself. Feeling that we ought to be more objective in this area, it suggests: '. . . the pupils' responses to a sentence or paragraph might be reliably scored by impression markings. These responses can provide a wealth of data to assist teachers and researchers alike in interpreting the empirical analyses . . .' (p.38). In its recommendations of a monitoring system, it suggests that 'assessment of the scripts' would involve 'impression marking' and 'coding schemes'. There are some doubts expressed: but there is certainly an aspiration towards quantifying that which cannot be quantified. I have heard Professor Britton on this subject, and it simply seemed to me to mark a failure of confidence in phenomenological disciplines. If we respond to literature there is no problem of responding to children's writing, and what is necessary here is responsiveness and understanding not marking or classifying.[1] Where the impulse to classify gains ground,

---

[1] See again Frank Whitehead's strictures in the article referred to above. Whitehead suggests that J.N. Britton's erroneous theoretical proposals have led to a situation in which teachers feel that if they have classified a child's work they have done their job.

poetry comes increasingly under suspicion, because the perspective of modern objectivity is so hostile to all that shadowy 'subsidiary' area with which it deals. To Gallileo poetry was at best mere tale-telling; at worst obscurity and untruth. Bentham found poetry all superstition. Following this tradition, the Bullock Report is suspicious of the view that English has to do with 'personal growth', and is inclined to follow the same kind of 'commonsense' exclusion from reality of the whole work of the imagination, myth and metaphor, dream and prophecy – with poetry.

If poety is to be allowed in at all, it must be 'realistic' and 'relevant'. The few pages on poetry are apologetic and pathetic: 'It has to be acknowledged that poetry starts at a disadvantage. In the public view ...' (p.135, 9.22). When was education a subject to defer to the public view?[1] Our duty is surely to win the public over to the convictions of those who have studied the purpose and nature of their subject, as imaginative teachers have done in the primary school? In Bullock we must get round the problem of poetry by diplomacy: the teacher must show that 'it speaks directly to children, as to anyone else, and has something to say which is relevant to their living here and now'. The magic word 'relevant'! The poetic processes of the imagination are the primary basis of *all human powers:* our very relationship with the world is sustained by a continual process of creative formative effort in the inner world of fantasy, dream, day-dream, play, game and cultural artefact. Poetry is 'all that we are'. Poetry is thus indeed 'relevant': but not in the sense Bullock means. What they mean is 'narrowly related to immediate explicit interests of social and other kinds'.

In poetry children often speak better than they know (as J.N. Britton once said). If poetry is central to our discipline, then we will be able to allow true learning: 'The fact that we can possess knowledge that is unspoken is of course a commonplace and so is the fact that we know something yet unspoken before we can express it in words ...' The failure of Bullock to place imagination first is a mark of its essential (positivist) attachment to the explicit and its failure to find these 'unspoken' roots of knowing, inaccessible, but the foundation of all education. This is surely a very radical failure. The failure is a philosophical one, common to all positivist approaches: as Polanyi says:

---

[1] As I point out in *English in Australia Now* parents actually go to the schools there to protest against their children being taught poetry, and all imaginative teaching takes place in the face of public hostility.

It has been taken for granted in the philosophical analysis of language in earlier centuries, but modern positivism has tried to ignore it, on the grounds that tacit knowledge was not accessible to objective observation. The present theory of meaning assigns a firm place to the inarticulate meaning of experience and shows it is the foundation of all meaning.

*Knowing and Being*, p.187

Although it allows the creative (for Chomsky has spoken of the 'innovative' (p.158)), the Bullock Report cannot really find this central dynamic of the pursuit of meaning.[1]

By failing to find these areas of development by which we take on a human world with our language, the Bullock Report fails to find those responsibilities which knowing inevitably brings, not least in the humanities. Under the impact of functional views of existence there is a new trend in our world to avoid urgent questions of values and meanings. Throughout the Report, questions of values are skilfully dodged and a moral relativism results. 'A good deal of emotion attaching to the terms' makes it difficult for the report to discuss literacy: opinions on the bad effects of television are 'essentially subjective'. By contrast with its feeble defence of poetry, the report is at one point even enthusiastic about the beneficial effects of television advertising jingles, while it equally absurdly rejects suggestions that television is doing harm, flying in the face of such publications as the *Report to the Surgeon General* in the United States (1970) which found a 'modest connection' between screen violence and delinquency among children and others.[2] Naïvely, it leaves responsibility with the media men: as if these had not conclusively shown their total irresponsibility, not least by being so unresponsive to public opinion. Some children are actually watching television 25 hours a week: what hope for English is this situation, since literacy depends on words? All Bullock can say is, 'That fact alone makes it a part of his experience so influential as to generate serious obligations on the part of those who provide it' (2.19, p.15).

But surely we must take a more critical stance? The whole trend of

---

[1] An exception is Professor Britton, who speaks in a personal note (pp.554-5) of potentials, 'deeply felt unconscious needs' and 'poetic language'.

[2] See also *The Annan Report on the Future of Broadcasting*. The government is evidently now persuaded that our powerful electronic media do have an effect, especially on the young, and the BBC issued new guidelines. See *The Plug-in Drug* by Marie Winn, Viking Press, 1977.

our culture at large in recent decades has a steady debasement of taste, trivialization and even the undermining of reason. It is surely becoming clear that it is impossible to uphold standards in school if culture at large continues to educate everyone to be a barbarian. In this again we must be 'custodians of mankind'.

Who wants 'objective discussion' from English experts in such a situation – even if we only go as far as the mild remonstrances of the Annan Report? The trouble is that an approach based on the functionalist view cannot find consciousness where the damage is done, so it is impotent in the face of corruption (*The New Scientist* could find nothing wrong with pornography). The Bullock Report, having no existentialist basis, can find nothing in the 'industrialization of the mind' by the electronics industry to be a threat to freedom and cultural self-realization. But surely, despite the disavowals of Bullock, we *know*, if we read Ian Robinson[1], or work with pupils or students, or study *The Guardian* now (compared with *The Manchester Guardian* 15 years ago) that there has been a steady, catastrophic decline in taste and language (see *The Black Rainbow*, ed. Peter Abbs). This is a fact we have experienced as English specialists, and no 'objective' exploration can shift our knowledge, our first-hand experience, of this decline. Anyone who is concerned with a humanities subject must surely resist, if the values inherent in our pursuit of truth have any validity?

The answer to Bullock here comes most forcibly from Leavis's *The Living Principle.* Leavis's concern is with values we recreate in ourselves, as we read literature, and take on our language, which is the way in which the 'Human World' is constructed. Every great writer in the language belongs to 'one collaboratively creative continuity':

> The discipline is not a matter of learning a deduced standard logic or an eclectic true philosophy, but rather of acquiring a delicate readiness of apprehension and a quasi-instinctive flexibility of response, these informed by the intuited 'living principle' – the principle implicit in the interplay between the living language and the creativity of individual genius.
>
> *The Living Principle,* p.49[2]

---

[1] *The Survival of English,* Cambridge.

[2] I should say I cannot accept Leavis's term 'quasi-instinctive' here, since cultural phenomena cannot be sensibly discussed in terms of instinct. Intuition, yes.

Of course, Leavis is concerned to define English as a discipline at the sixth form or university level: but we may apply his definition to the simpler levels – for the child, in coming across folksong, or the deepest wisdom of his family or village, or enjoying Hans Andersen, or hearing the *Authorised Version*, was experiencing *his* interplay between 'the living language' and creativity.

To Leavis, language is more than 'means of expression': 'it embodies values, constations, distinctions, promptings, recognitions of potentiality.' We possess these as we possess, say, a poem. Where *is* a poem (or, we could say, a nursery rhyme or a Shakespeare song)? 'It is neither merely private, nor public in the sense that it can be brought into a laboratory, quantified, tripped over or even pointed to' (p.36). The assemblings of black marks on the page is not the poem: 'The poem is a product, and in any experienced actual existence, a phenomenon, of human creativity, the essentially collaborative nature of which it exemplified in diverse distinguishable modes. And yet it is real' (p.36). Its reality belongs to the 'Third Realm', that which is neither public nor merely private: minds meet 'in' it. It is into the Human World that the child is born, and such an account of how a poem exists indicates the way in which the Human World is created and, 'in constant renewal, maintained'.

The child is able to grow into full humanity because it lives in a fully human world, says Leavis, a world shaped by all kinds of human value-judgements and informed by distinctively human 'values'. For Leavis, discussion of such values is a human world. So, he dismisses with a single phrase any division of 'thought' from 'language: he invites those who demand a more 'rational' account to consider the intractable truth of language: 'not only do they express their thought in it: without a language they would be incapable of thought.'

> Where *is* the English language? You can't point to it, and the perusal of a linguistician's treatise will do nothing to help you towards an answer to such questions. It is concretely 'there' only as I utter the words and phrases chosen by the meaning (*in* me, but outward bound) which they convey and you take them . . . I might, at the end of a seminar say: 'It was there, in the criss-cross of utterance between us.'
>
> *The Living Principle*

He places an emphasis on the 'context' akin to that of Polanyi, who

He places an emphasis on the 'context' akin to that of Polanyi, who says:

> Anything that functions effectively within an accredited context has a meaning in that context . . . We may describe the kind of a meaning which a context possessed in itself as *existential*, to distinguish it especially, from derivatives or, more generally, representative meaning.
>
> *Personal Knowledge,* p. 58

English is not the 'processing of experience through language' but a discipline of existential meaning. Polanyi, as Leavis says, insists that what for philosophers is 'mind' is 'there' only in individual minds, and his mind is the mind of his body. In this he includes the tacit, by which we acquire knowledge that we cannot tell. The ideal of a strictly explicit knowledge is itself contradictory: even an exact mathematical knowledge on which it bears and a person whose judgment upholds this bearing.

Leavis draws our attention in the chapter 'Thought, language and objectivity' to the origins of culture in the mother-infant relationship:

> Mother and child, as Buytendijk says, already form a society. The child's discovery, and construction, of the world already takes place with and through others, through question and answer, through social play, through the older child's or adult's interpretation of pictures, the teaching of language and writing . . . All the way we are shaping ourselves on the model of or in criticism of others . . .
>
> Quoted from Marjorie Grene, p.34.

In this process of developing his personal culture in intersubjectivity, the child inevitably creates *standards,* and the development of values is inherent in *knowing:*

> No discipline, however 'factual', however 'detached', can come into being or remain in existence except in so far as the evaluative acts of individuals belonging to a given culture have legislated into existence and maintain in existence the area of free enquiry and of mutual confirmation or falsification which such inquiry demands.
>
> *The Knower and the Known,* p.181, quoted by Leavis, p.33.

In the Bullock Report there are a few references to Bernstein's sociological theories of 'restricted' and 'elaborate' codes in the language of children from different classes. But there is virtually no attention at all to the way in which, in possessing their language, and creating the Human World, children are also renewing values created for themselves, by 'the fundamental evaluative arts of the individual belonging to a given culture'. Yet all this lies behind those powers to which we owe our capacity for recognizing in our experience a meaning that can be stated in words, as Polanyi puts it.

In his essay to which Leavis sends us, Polanyi writes of sense-giving and sense-reading. When a writer picks his words for describing his experience, this is an act of what Polanyi called conceptual *subsumption*. Reading the writer's account is one of *conceptual exemplification*. Polanyi tells us that Kant called the process of subsuming particular instances under a general term 'a skill so deeply hidden in the human soul that we shall hardly guess the secret that nature here employs'. The secret was, indeed, inaccessible, so long as one looked for its explicit procedure. But, Polanyi declares, the secret can be found in the tacit operations of the mind.

> Our conception of a tree, for example, is formed . . . by the tacit integration of countless experiences of different trees and pictures and reports of still others, deciduous and evergreen, straight and crooked, bare and leafy. All these encounters are included in forming the conception of a tree; they are all used subsidiarily with a bearing on the conception of a tree, which is what we mean by the word 'tree'.
>
> *Knowing and Being*, p.191

No explicit procedure can give an account of these subsidiary processes. 'The brilliant advances in phonology and generative grammar have cast no light on the strange fact that language means something.' Deprived of their tacit coefficient and of that context discussed above, all spoken words are strictly meaningless. Language arises from the exercise of human intelligence, rooted in imagination like all movements and activities of the being-in-the-body, prompted and guided by intuition: mysterious acts of consciousness.

As I have tried to show, the Bullock Report conception of mind and language falls far short of anything as adequate as the accounts given by Leavis and Polanyi: so it consigns English to meaninglessness. Of course the authors make it plain that they know that modern children have considerable verbal powers before they come to school (6.15, p.84); they see that literature can help 'resolve inner conflicts' (p.125); they are aware of the need for parents and nursery workers to talk to children (5.35, p.69); and they even see at times that teaching is an art:

> 9.24 . . . a particular poem may make its maximum impact by being dropped suddenly, . . . into a lull . . .

They recognize that teachers must promote books (9.7., p.128); and it is obvious that they recognize the interpersonal and even bodily elements in the development of language: 'Face to face speech is a very direct embodiment of the relationship between the speakers . . .' But the implications of these insights are not fundamental to its philosophical position, and its whole approach falls down on its confidence in an explicit approach: 'While many teachers recognize that their aim is to initiate a student in a particular mode of analysis, they rarely recognize the linguistic implication of doing so' (12.4, p.189).

The question is this: the old study of grammar was ineffective because it attended too exclusively to the *words*. So 'the teaching of traditional analytic grammar does not appear to improve performance in writing' (Bullock, p.171). *What then do we study?* Bullock goes on: 'This is not to suggest that there is no place for any kind of exercises at any time and in any form' (p.171). In discussing this problem *The Bullock Report* obviously makes good use, among other books, of *English for Maturity* and *The Secret Places* (see 11.17; 11.19; and especially 11.35, for example).

At times, reading the Report, I hoped it was moving towards an imaginative basis for the development of literacy. But always instead it moves towards a sociolinguistic approach, and a theoretical programme based on psychology. Of course, the Report makes some good remarks here and there. It rejects one-word answer exercises for instance because these 'afford no opportunity for the *generation* of language' (1.19, p.171). It even speaks of the 'total language experience' necessary, and of the dangers of separating language training from other aspects of English teaching, so that it 'does not commit itself to fundamental values' (11.28, p.175). But the best it can do in the end is to talk about how 'The study of language is inseparable from the study of human situations . . . we believe that the influence linguists can exercise upon schools lies in this concept of the inseparability of language and the human situation' (11.26, p.174).

But it is the outward *social* situation they have in mind: English in outward situations rather than as a contribution to the development of the powers of symbolizing of an existential being, or as an aspect of *intersubjectivity.* Though it speaks of how the 16-year-old (in a paragraph almost directly taken from *English for Maturity*) should 'have some understanding of the different uses of language . . . (as) the instrument of the creative imagination' (11.35), it does not place this creative imaginative discipline *first*, and does not confront the need to define that primary discipline, even though so many of us have laboured to define it.

So its compromise is between *relying* in practice on tacit and subsidiary processes, while still believing these can be brought within the scope of, if not actually controlled by, the explicit, the analytical, the attention to 'rules'. This is plain in such injunctions as this

> In nusery and infant schools there should be planned attention to the children's *language development.* It should be the school's *conscious policy* to *develop in all children* the ability to use *increasingly complex forms.* A careful record should be kept of their progress . . .
>
> Recommendation No.47, p.520 (my italics)

It declares that, 'In the secondary school, all subject teachers need to be aware of: (i) the linguistic processes by which these pupils acquire information . . .' (138, 329). But as Polanyi makes clear, we simply do not know how pupils acquire 'information' by 'linguistic processes' and, if we did, no knowledge of the explicit kind would enable us to teach fluency or help the children to learn.

Student teachers (it says) are to be instructed in 'the linguistic processes by which the pupils acquire information and understanding' (p.338), the processes in which 'language is said to structure reality . . .' 'Teachers themselves need to know more about the way language works' (p.73). 'In learning about the nature and operation of language, students should be made more *explicitly* aware of their own practices' (315, p.550, my italics). Such emphases must lead to futility, since good English teaching is not based on explicit awareness, but on the natural processes of *art.*

Because of this, it is not true that 'linguistics . . . (has) a considerable contribution to make to the teaching of English' (133, p.528). It is only fair to add that the Report does say that they believe this 'because it emphasizes the inseparability of language and the human situation', thus drawing attention to the best kind of language study – attention to how language is actually used. The Report also properly warns that, 'Linguistics should not enter the schools in the form of the teaching of descriptive grammar' (133, p.528). But Bullock *does* want it in the schools as a way of seeking explicit attention to language, which is nearly as bad because teachers and students will assume that this is the way to control language development, or even foster it, when it is not.

It is clear that the linguists, with all the confidence of positivist science, are unwilling to accept this. They want to establish an exclusive specialism, to take over. We get a hint of this in Bullock: 'A radical solution would be to regard language as one central synthesizing force which would serve to relate certain elements taught in philosophy and sociology courses, and otherwise to dispense with these as separate disciplines' (p.340). This is a disturbing claim, that *language* study, in terms of explicit abstracting analysis, could replace, not only English, but all these disciplines concerned with meaning and the nature of existence, consciousness and relationship. Here we have a menacing specialism: linguisticism. (Philosophy, for example, should be an attempt to understand great minds, a process not achieved by language study.)

Where English is concerned, we must insist on it as an imaginative discipline. We must demand *English* departments, not 'language' or 'communications' departments. We are concerned, of course, with fluency and the capacity to use language in the practical ways demanded by the subject, including response to literature, and so to 'life and thought' – to problems of civilization and its values. And in this we must recognize a philosophical position: we must have a philosophical anthropology, for which linguistics is certainly no substitute. We have scientific backing (as in the work of Polanyi) in making such a claim. For one thing, we shall, in invoking creativity, be assuming Polanyi's emphasis on the natural intuitive mysterious processes by which cultural powers develop in each of us. So we shall invoke those kinds of psychology and philosophy (and sociology even[1]) which can suggest an adequate philosophy behind English (it will be very different from that behind the *Bullock Report*). The pursuit of a philosophy of English, however, is a pursuit which is

---

ne work of John O'Neill, for example.

never likely to come to an end, in a finally acceptable policy document of even a series of such statements (though it could be less of a muddle and compromise than *Bullock*). Those who have attempted to define their view of English, like Frank Whitehead in *The Disappearing Dais,* or Fred Inglis in *The Englishness of English Teaching,* or Peter Abbs in *English for Diversity, Root and Blossom,* and other books, have never supposed that their work could be presented as a complete *vade mecum,* or English teacher's bible. Such efforts must continue. But the nature of our quest is suggested by E.A. Burtt's remarks about existentialism in his book *In Search of Philosophic Understanding.* He quotes Heidegger to suggest that the new forms of existentialist philosophy expect to go on always tackling the same problems, because the problems of finding and cherishing our own authenticity can never be finally solved. Because what we are really doing in a humanities subject is seeking to define creativity and freedom the task is open-ended: our kind of learning is at one with our growing and our 'being-unto-death', our quest for a meaning in life before we die.[1]

It would make many feel insecure, if they were to abjure the seemingly 'scientific' position behind Bullock, as in its embracing of linguistics and theories of 'processing experience' in its functional paradigm, to talk like that.

Where shall wisdom be found? But there are two characteristic features of the insecurity. First, it fails to feel confident in the teaching experience itself, which works at best often without theory! Secondly, it displays an ignorance of the whole of 'continental' or 'Reflective' philosophy as an alternative to western positivism.[2] I shall try to show that the basis of English must be in those disciplines which find man as the *animal symbolicum.* The *Bullock Report* makes a little bow to Susanne Langer (4.2, p.4): 'Man's individual, social and cultural achievements can be rightly understood only if we take into account that he is essentially a symbol-using animal'. But it does not apply Professor Langer's findings to the relationship between self and world. It does not really find symbolism of a primary human need. She says:

> I believe there is a primary need in man, which other creatures probably do not have, and which actuates all his apparently

---

[1] See also, for a wider perspective, Karl Jasper's *The Idea of The University* in which he declares that the central concern is the pursuit of truth.

[2] See E.W.F. Tomlin, Introduction to *The Western Philosophers* and *The Eastern Philosophers.*

unzoological aims, his wistful fancies, his consciousness of value, his utterly unpractical enthusiasm, his awareness of a 'Beyond' filled with holiness ... *This basic need, which certainly is obvious only in man, is the need of symbolization.* The symbol-making function is one of man' primary activities, like eating, looking, or moving about. It is the fundamental process of his mind, and goes on all the time.

*Philosophy in a New Key,* p.41 (my italics)

If we accept this insistence on symbolization as a primary factor, English cannot be discussed apart from the processes of seeking meaning and order in the inward life. This demands a holistic approach, which is existential, dealing with whole *experience.* The *Bullock Report* kind of attention to language concentrates on the hacked-off structures of the artefacts, the sentences, the functioning 'codes'. We must now place these back in our thinking in whole processes of life in the body and being, and in the context of what lies 'beyond the words'.

The limitation of the functionalistic thinking behind the *Bullock Report* is clear from much of its language: 't-units', 'minimum terminal units': 'code'; 'data-pool', 'item pool', 'light sampling', 'calibrated': 'rolling estimate of standards' and so on. We must speak of people experiencing, of human beings living their lives.

English has to do with such aspects of life as one's capacity to understand and perceive the world, to know oneself, to enlarge one's sympathy and understanding of other people and to realize potentialities in oneself: in all this, *metaphor* is a fundamental dynamic. One cannot begin to study words in English without linking this activity with such profound phrases as

the dungy earth
Feeds man and beast alike . . .
or     Therefore all seasons shall be sweet to thee . . .
or     At the then fair hour in the then fair weather . . .

in which words are engaged at the profoundest level with the dynamics of perception, of time, of intentionality, of questions of meaning, embodied in metaphor: symbolism which 'does what it says' is at one with 'life' through rhythm, image, texture and sound. These complexities of language use are not discussed in the Report; nor are such evanescent but primary qualities as rhythm, texture, movement and tone as part of the meaning of words.

Of course the Report seems, from time to time, to recognize the appropriate dimensions. It seems to be drawing attention to the wholeness of the process of English teaching, talking at times of the 'organic' unity of English: 'language across the curriculum' (George Sampson said it in 1934[1]). But its limitations even become clear when it seems to be declaring for a wider view of the subject: 'Reading must be seen as *part of a child's general language development* and not as a discrete skill which can be considered in isolated from it' (p.xxi). For even here it sees English as 'part of a child's general *language development*' rather than 'part of the whole development of a child's personality, his capacity for perception, and his understanding of the world, of which language is a part' – that is, as integral with the growth and living of a human being.

---

[1] '. . . *every teacher is a teacher of English because every teacher is a teacher in English.* That sentence should be written in gold over every school doorway.' p.25.

# II

*A New Philosophical Perspective*

# Chapter Four

# A New Philosophical Perspective

---

One of the principles of any existentialist approach to human experience is that we should not erect imposing palaces of theory, while we live in our actual lives alongside these in a hovel (as Kirkegaard said) – but rather, we should always try to look at experience in whole terms, as it really is. Thus, the best manifestations of philosophical anthropology, phenomenology and the rest are in particular applications – in the study of works of literature, or music, or case-histories, or just of 'experience'[1]

So let me begin my exploration of a better possible philosophical backing for English teaching by asking what exactly is happening when we teach a poem. If poetry must be at the centre of our work in English, what do we mean by this? Let me take a short poem and suppose I am teaching it in a poetry lesson. What am I doing?

### Tall Nettles

Tall nettles cover up, as they have done
These many springs, the rusty harrow, the plough
Long worn out, and the roller made of stone:
Only the elm butt tops the nettles now.

This corner of the farmyard I like most:
As well as any bloom upon a flower
I like the dust on the nettles, never lost
Except to prove the sweetness of a shower.

Edward Thomas

First, it is necessary to say that my prime aim is to get this *work of art* possessed by my pupils. I read it to them aloud, or I print it for them to

---

[1] Although I had read no 'reflective philosophy' at the time I wrote it, I would now call *English for the Rejected* a phenomenological work, since it is a study of the meaning of each child's symbolism and consciousness.

read: perhaps I ask them questions, to draw their attention to the meaning ('What is the point of setting the nettles, which grow up every year, alongside the elm butt which is presumably dead') But I also allow I do not know half of what its effect on them (or me) will be.

In this, because we are dealing with a verbal art, the English teacher will need to try to get his pupils to respond sensitively to the words. Such elements as sound and texture are part of the meaning. Take, for example, the strong consonants in 'Only the elm butt tops the nettles now . . .' These consonants give a texture (a biting quality in the mouth when the poem is read) which enacts the stumpiness of the elm, the bluntness of its cut-off butt, which tops the nettles. Both nettles and elm butt are common, blunt things, and the seeming competition between them is that of the coarse growth of wild plants: this the sounds of the words enhance.

In the background is the blunt labour of years of farm work, with the stone roller and the rusty harrow, even a worn-out plough. So, we have a powerful evocation of time and human effort, not least by the fall of the words, *'Long worn out'*. There is a rich ambiguity, in the juxtaposition of symbols of years of hard toil, of long growth eventually felled (as in the elm), and the wiry seasonal growth of the vigorous weeds.

This we must see now against two elements in the poet's life first of all the brevity of the time left to him before he goes to the front with the virtual certainty of being killed (See *As the Team's Headbrass*, discussed below p.138). The other element is Thomas's own liability to depression, against which he needs to grope for some meaningful hold on life, to relieve his pain and guilt, when everything seems futile.

Surprisingly, it is this gloomy corner of the farmyard that he likes most, *because* it reminds him of time and futile effort. What can be meaningful, if so much human effort is devoted to wearing out the plough, and if the growth of the tall elm merely comes to being felled, leaving a useless butt? If he can answer that here, he can answer it anywhere. These complex antitheses are held in suspension.

Knowing of Thomas's depressiveness, we could say that for him to find joy in a rich flower, or a rich hothouse grape, might fail to yield satisfaction, because it might deepen that guilt which underlies depression. It is easier for him (as it was for George Crabbe and Wordsworth) to find joy in the weeds, here in dust which settles on nettles. It is lowly, it speaks of time and death ('Brightness falls from the air/Dust hath closed Helen's eyes'), yet it is a gift because it coats the nettles like a bloom, and is sometimes *lost* to *prove* the sweetness of a shower. A rich ambivalence vibrates in the sensuousness of 'bloom' and a curious ambiguity hangs round the words 'lost' and 'prove'. Even the bloom of the dust, with its association with the theme of useless effort (since mortality swallows all) can be lost – that is, one can escape even from the morbidity dust evokes – by rain. Rain brings earnest of a different kind of continuity – a sense of life going on, renewing itself, not simply growing on meaninglessly. And the loss of dust on the nettles *proves* that even in such lowly circumstances life can be sweet. It is sweetened (as in Mahler's *Das Lied Von Der Erde*) by the image of continuity; and one virtually smells the rain that brings this relief ('I once more smell the dew and rain/And relish versing' – George Herbert, *The Flower*). The disturbance of the bloom on the nettles is richer than disturbance of the bloom-dust on a rich flower would be.

We are now, surely, 'beyond' the words? We have possessed the work of art: but we are also deeply involved in existential questions. The images of futility have raised what we may call the *'Dasein'* problem (see below p.93) of 'being there'. In the face of such stretches of useless effort in time, *what meaning does life have?* The answer is strange: if I attend to low and simple details in the fore-ground of the world of man and nature, I can find sweet moments, in which the mere relishing of being alive, of visual and tactile sensations, provides me with a sense of meaningful existence. The sibilant consonants of 'dust . . . lost . . . sweetness' enact the happy relish of this moment of attentive consciousness which enables me to experience 'being there', in a meaningful way. The remembered details enhance the feeling of being in existence, in the face of 'being-unto-death'.

What I have been talking about here, evidently, are philosophical questions. So we may call them phenomenological ones: Edward Thomas's poem is a distinguished work of art because it makes a phenomenological record of that moment of consciousness. We have also been talking about psychology, in the whole sense: problems of dread of death, the sense of futility, the *quest for meaning.* I am both 'with' or 'in' the words: but also beyond the words.

The trouble with our relationships with other subjects (as between, say, 'English' and 'psychology' in a college of education or a depart-ment of education at a university) is that very often a subject which offers us a study of man in fact betrays us and leaves us bored or frustrated – because it is based on an empirical fragmentation of the 'organism' and cannot find the experiencing 'I'. The 'data' and theory are not united by any recognition of an experiencing consciousness. Indeed, some scientists deny consciousness altogether.[1] Moreover, we often find in other subjects a failure to recognize the cultural dimension of man: even in Freudian metapsychology, for instance, culture is an epiphenomenon, a sublimation of instinctual drives (they being 'real' as culture is not).

The overall problem in its widest sense has to do with approaches to the nature of man. How do we know man? Ernst Cassirer has said:

> We cannot discover the nature of man in the same way that we can detect the nature of physical things. Physical things may be discussed in terms of their objective properties, but man may be defined only in terms of his consciousness. Empirical observations and logical analysis . . . prove inefficient and inadequate.
>
> *An Essay on Man*

Ernst Cassirer is a post-Kantian philosopher, concerned with Kant's fourth question, What is man? And Cassirer's conclusion is that the key to understanding man is to recognize him as the *animal symbolicum:* the symbolizing animal who has a special cultural dimension.

Here, then, is one component discipline of philosophical anthropology, which insists that the proper study of mankind must include *consciousness* and *culture*; and (of course), by implication, *meaning*.

When Ernst Cassirer tells us that we cannot give an adequate account of man in terms of the natural sciences he is, of course, making an existentialist emphasis – in the tradition of Søren Kierkegaard, who declared it a blasphemy, to try to reduce human existence to a natural science dimension. And this in turn takes us into the broader question of the nature of knowledge, and the nature of man in the universe. Our convictions in 'English' must depend upon the answers to questions

---

[1] Michael Polanyi quotes Hebb, Kubie and Lashley, from a symposium on brain mechanisms in 1954: 'The existence of something called consciousness is a venerable *hypothesis*, not a datum, not directly observable'; 'Although we cannot get along without the concept of consciousness, actually there is no such thing . . .'; 'The knower as an entity is an unnecessary postulate . . .', *Meaning*, p.25.

about what we can believe. Edmund Husserl, the founding father of phenomenology, declared that the philosopher must concern himself with the question, 'What should we, who *believe*, do in order to *be able* to believe?' Such questions are meaningless to our analytical philosophical tradition: they seem to belong to the language of religion, which Professor A.J. Ayer has pronounced to be meaningless, so that's that.

Can we achieve any meanings at all? In some areas of education, where it has come under the influence of 'objective' positivism, we are encouraged to believe that the meanings achieved in the humanities are supposed to have no reference to reality: 'they are simply works of the imagination, brilliant in some cases, often sparkling and interesting, intriguing and enjoyable, but nevertheless inescapably only ephemeral flashes of light, that never were – or could be – on land and sea' (Michael Polanyi, *Meaning*, p.64). 'Science has most commonly been thought to deal with facts, the humanities with values. But since, in this frame of reference, values must be totally different from fact, the humanities have been thought to deal only with fancies.' As 'education' comes closer to universities with a positivist scientific bent, it encounters this crisis, as Bullock displays.

But, as Polanyi argues, personal participation and imagination are *essentially* involved in science as well as in the humanities. Meanings created in the sciences stand in no more favoured relation to reality than do meanings created in the arts, in moral judgment, and in religion. Both are attempts by men, to make sense of their experience; in both 'man lives in the meanings he is able to discern'.

The fallacy of our inherited traditions of thought has been the exclusion of the subjective, and its failure to recognize the element of personal participation, the essential participation of the knower in the known. There is no 'objective' body of knowledge, known once and for all, existing as if written on a blackboard: science itself is nothing but men knowing, and all knowledge is contingent. Moreover, besides the abstractions of mathematics, to which the Cartesian revolution reduced the universe, there is the man holding the tape measure and looking through the telescope. Galileo and other pioneers in the scientific revolution won their achievements by splitting off the 'mathematical revolution' from the rest of reality, distrusting 'secondary qualities' and rejecting poetic knowledge, of the subjective realities.

They thus betrayed, Husserl argues, the original telos of the quest initiated by Greek civilization for the whole truth of man's existence. And as we absorb the intellectual framework of modern objective thought nature comes to *mean* to us Galilean nature, from which all that poetry deals with is excluded. Marjorie Grene puts it this way:

> The 'mathematical language', the instrument of an impersonal reason, is seen [in the perspective of modern objectivism] as the sole medium of truth and light . . . And it is not only poetry in the narrow sense, the craft of making verses, that is here exiled from reality, but the whole work of the imagination: myth and metaphor, dream and prophecy. In the bare mathematical bones of nature there is truth; all else is illusion. Yet that 'all else' includes the very roots of our being, and we forget them at our peril.
>
> *Approaches to a Philosophical Biology*, p.51

In the poem we have looked at Edward Thomas is grappling with real problems of the point of existence in time about which science has nothing to say. But how can these be solved if it is true that 'science says' all things are meaningless? Our efforts in constructing meaning can only be felt by us to be symbols of defiance against the meaninglessness of the universe, and poetry can only be 'superstition'.

Although it is the one unquestioned authority of our time, science itself has fallen into a crisis too, however. The world-view of man dominated by the positivist sciences has triumphed because these sciences have produced prosperity, by manipulations of the physical world. This makes science seem 'true'. But there has been, as Husserl argues, an indifferent turning away from those questions which are decisive for a genuine humanity (*Menschentum*) – the kind of questions to which Charles Dickens continually drew attention. There is even an echo of *Hard Times* in Husserl's declaration, 'Merely fact-minded sciences make merely fact-minded people.' Young people turn against science, says Husserl, because, as a repository of truth, it has nothing to say to us: 'It excludes in principle precisely the questions which man, given over in our time to the most portentous upheavals, finds the most burning: questions of the meaning, or the meaninglessness of human existence' (*The Crisis of European Sciences*, p.6). Can the world, and human existence in it, truthfully have a meaning if the sciences recognize as true only what is objectively established, by excluding all questions of the reason or unreason of human subject matter and its cultural configurations? If man is to become a free self-determining being, in his behaviour towards the human and extra-human surrounding world (*Umwelt*), then questions of meaning and value must be explored rationally, within science: it must not abstract from everything subjective.

The crisis of science, then, is its loss of its meaning for life. What we have to reassert is the primacy of our experience, and of our need to work on the problem of meaning through the exercise of symbolism.

People today even feel that they must distrust their own sense of meaning. Recently there was a survey made at Nottingham University, by a research division in the School of Education, in association with the Oxford Religious Experience Research Unit. One question asked was, 'Do you feel you have ever been aware of or influenced by a presence or a power, whether you call it God or not, which is different from your everyday self?' Seventy-two per cent of the men and 58 per cent of the women replied that they had. In a report in *The Times* (December 16, 1970) the Religious Affairs correspondent wrote:

> It may be, the author, Mr. Kay, suggests that because religious experience is regarded as unscientific it is therefore assumed to be something to be ashamed of. *One woman described an experience she thought was genuine, but which she later lost confidence in when she found she could not reconcile it with her scientific materialism.* (my italics)

This problem is very relevant to 'English' as a humanities subject. As Viktor Frankl has argued, science and science teaching convey, willy-nilly, a kind of nihilism.[1] Yet we must try to overcome the effect of this on us:

> We accept without question the picture of the world presented by physics. But how real, for example, is the entropy with which physics threatens us – how real is the universal doom, or this cosmic catastrophe which physics predicts, and in the light of which all the efforts of ourselves and posterity seem to dwindle to nought? Are we not rather taught by 'inner

---

[1] See his contribution to The Alpbach Seminar, edited by Arthur Koestler and Robert Smithies, Hutchinson. On these matters in general, see the present author's *Education, Nihilism and Survival*, Darton, Longman and Todd, 1977, and *Lost Bearings in English Poetry*, Vision Press, 1977.

experience', by ordinary living unbiased by theories, that our natural pleasure in a beautiful sunset is in a way 'more real' than, say, astronomical calculations of the time when the earth will crash into the sun?

*The Doctor and the Soul,* p.39

A man who is enjoying supreme artistic pleasure or the happiness of love never doubts for a moment that his life is meaningful. That we can be persuaded that existence is meaningless is the result of a long history of philosophical ideas which on the one hand have proved effective in manipulating the world 'out there', but which belong to the 'masculinization of knowledge', and have actually generated alienation. This alienation has led to grave consequences in man's effect on the world – pollution, the danger to species, erosion, waste of resources, atomic threats: these could even be called consequences of forms of 'male doing' which are not guided by imagination and concern and a sense of good relationship with Mother Earth. There are traditions of thought which have generated alienation because they are rooted in individual forms of psychopathology with their roots in the fear of woman. Karl Stern, a Catholic psychotherapist, has traced this philosophical tradition in history, taking account especially of Descartes, Schopenhauer and Jean-Paul Sartre. The rejection of 'feminine' modes, he says, goes with an increasing sense of alienation from 'the earth' as primal source, so that in the end, any effort to find a meaningful place in the universe is futile, and nothing is left but a kind of desperate nihilism. This nihilism deeply affects our humanities culture today, and the philosophy of science: at large, the vacuum left by the failure of meaning is filled by various forms of desperate irrationality – drugs, alcohol, the occult, pornokitsch entertainment, and violent fantasies, a very dangerous situation in which consciousness itself is under assault from desperate false solutions.

Yet, the truth is that we do not have to accept the 'facts' which 'objective' science seems to have impressed upon us. It has been the achievement of Polanyi's post-critical philosophy to make this clear to us. For one thing, the objectivity of science is itself a myth and a fallacy If a long film lasting several days were made of the history of the universe, man's period of existence, shown 'objectively', would pass in one frame – flick! Is this what we mean by 'objectivity'? Of course not: even science is anthropormorphic, in the sense that it attends to phenomena because they are of significance to man. Man as scientist is deeply involved in his science, and he relies in his work on tacit inference – bringing all his subjective proclivities to bear on the clues he can find in the world, on which to base his hypotheses, his knowing. And his knowing cannot be separated from his responsibility as the one creature, man, product of evolution, who knows. Scientific knowledge, far from being coldly detached, is thus an act of ultimate responsibility. Ours is the dreadful responsibility of being knowers.

Consciousness, as an evident aspect of the knower, must be restored to the centre of the picture: '. . . the naturalistic interpretation of man is itself in palpable contradiction of the 'facts' of our experience, even of living nature other than man, let alone of the massive fact of consciousness, of the inner lives we do in fact lead' (Marjorie Grene, *Approaches*, p.31). All those 'inner' realities which Galilean rationalism has relegated must be restored as realities. And here, for one thing, biology speaks some other language, other than the equiprobable language of what sequence or shape might be expected to emerge from mere 'laws'. So, the DNA molecules obey the laws, and there is nothing else there but what can be found by physics and chemistry: yet the code subserves some hierarchical principle, belonging to the long history of life in the universe, which cannot be reduced to chemistry and physics. It must be understood in other terms, as of systems organization, or terms of the operation of whole organisms (as, for example, must the nervous system, which cannot be broken down into initial conditions, for then the laws of nerve action would disappear[1]). There is an urgent need to find realities in biology which defy reduction to the laws of physics and chemistry: for a new holism.

In dealing with these philosophical problems, it should be clear, I am not merely rejecting science. I am asking for a better science. And a demand for a more adequate science of life is coming from philosophical biology and the philosophy of science. I am asking for a (biological) view of man which can include the subjective realities of his existence, and so include poetry and find and see that the kind of problems Edward Thomas wrote about are real ones. The facts are not that we are merely driven by our functions, as some scientists have argued. Attention to our biological development shows that it 'has been rewritten in our case in a new key', while our cultural yearnings for meaning are primary in our reality: 'The whole structure of the embryo, the whole rhythm of growth, is directed, from first to last, to

---

[1] See 'Are we only DNA making more DNA?' by the present author, New Universities Quarterly, Winter 1978.

the emergence of a culture-dwelling animal' (Marjorie Grene, *Approaches*, p.88).

We are not bound by our ecological niche, but are born to be 'open' to our world. Our upright stance, our large brain, our long period of gestation, all go with our nature which is to accept responsibility and to confront the future with intentionality. As Dr Leakey has argued, man is not the aggressive animal of Desmond Morris and Robert Ardrey, but 'cooperation man': he would not have survived if he had not been capable of good relationships. And good relationships are the product of the initial formative relationship with the mother in which we discover the reality of ourselves and the world: as Martin Buber puts it in his essay *Distance and Relation*, 'From man to man the heavenly bread of self-being is passed.'[1] Through mutual reflection men create in themselves the capacity to live in 'the mansion of consciousness' rather than, like animals, in immediate response to their environment, like a fruit in its skin. Consciousness and culture give man an extra dimension in which problems of freedom and responsibility become crucial, as does that of meaning. The discussion of these problems in the humanities is closely bound up with English.

For, in many ways, from philosophical anthropology, and from biology, we are beginning to develop a totally different picture of man, with consciousness and culture at the centre of the picture. Not only is man being put back into nature, but he is being restored to a universe which is full of meaning. Polanyi declares that the metaphysical belief we tend to hold, that everything is meaningless, is a fallacy:

> Our modern science cannot properly be understood to tell us that the world is meaningless and pointless, that it is absurd. The supposition that it is absurd is a modern myth, created imaginatively from the clues produced by a profound misunderstanding of what science and knowledge are and what they require, a misunderstanding spanned by positivistic left-overs in our thinking and by allegiance to the false ideal of objectivity from which we have been unable to shake ourselves quite free.
>
> Polanyi, *Meaning*, p.181

The world in fact is full of meaning. Scientific inquiry itself, far from being a 'mystic chant over unintelligible universe', is a 'thrust of our minds towards a more and more meaningful integration of clues'.

---

[1] Martin Buber's essay is discussed further below, **p.98.**

Living things, says Polanyi, are oriented towards meaning, 'while man's cultural framework, including his symbols, his language arts, his fine arts, his rites, his celebrations, and his religions, constitutes a vast complex of efforts – on the whole, successful – at achieving every kind of meaning.' 'We might justifiably claim, therefore, that everything we know is *full* of meanings, is not absurd at all, although we can sometimes fail to grasp these meanings and fall into absurdities' (*Meaning*, p.179).

What we need to resist is the ideal of objectivity (wholly explicit, wholly certified truth) since this 'falsifies the nature of the knower and the known, of mind and the world.' The new modes of knowledge to which I have given the name philosophical anthropology seek to remember this in their disciplines – even though we do not yet know quite what disciplines will need to be employed. (A useful discussion of this problem may be found in Roger Poole's *Towards Deep Subjectivity*, in which he emphasizes that the intention of the new approach is to enable us to give meanings to the world, rather than let the world shove its meanings down on us.)

Biology has been referred to, as a source of recognition of the primacy of consciousness and culture in any study of man. Post-Kantian philosophy (Cassirer, Langer) and post-critical philosophy (Polanyi, Grene) have been invoked. I have also mentioned Edmund Husserl, whose work leads on to the important French phenomenologist Maurice Merleau-Ponty. But there is one other important subjective discipline whose very existence provides considerable resistance – psychoanalysis. I have been employing ideas from psychoanalysis in books on English (such as *English for the Rejected*) and in phenomenological analysis of meaning in modern works of art (*Dylan Thomas: the Code of Night; Sylvia Plath: Poetry and Existence; Gustav Mahler and the Courage to Be; Lost Bearings in English Poetry*). But resistance has been considerable and it has often been made plain to me, from centres of supposed intellectual authority, that the authenticity of such ideas is doubted (even King's College once expressed doubt about allowing me to hold a conference on such ideas in the college: Cambridge University Press has told me 'There is no such thing as philosophical anthropology', and has refused to consider several of my books employing ideas for psychotherapy). However, it must be clear that the ideas of psychoanalysis, in its many branches, are now felt to be respectable by the highest authorities. Psychoanalytic theory is an important branch of philosophical anthropology.[1]

The relevance of psychoanalytical ideas is made clear in E.A. Burtt's *In Search of Philosophical Understanding* (1967). Professor Burtt is the author of, among other things, *The Metaphysical Foundations of Modern Science.* In the 1967 book Burtt declares: 'The most provocative note in the findings, I want to share is the conviction that philosophy must come fully to terms with the psychoanalytical concept of the human mind' (p.xiv). He goes on 'the crucial fact can no longer be ignored that behind anyone's thinking there are unconscious motives, to be taken into account beside the desire for the truth.' Burtt points out that Greek thought was basically a thoery of *being:* during modern times philosophy has been mainly a quest for *method.* In this Burtt is surely drawing on Husserl, who believed that the scientific revolution betrayed the original *telos* of Greek thought which sought truth in the wholeness, diverting thought into analysis and man- ipulation. Burtt sees that thought today is moving back to explore the nature of being, as in existentialism and phenomenology, and is seek- ing to cure the disastrous split between science and philosophy (and poetry too for that matter), as the exploration of the whole truth of man.

The masculinization of thought has also involved an avoidance of love. The remarkable thing about such a keen philosophical mind as that of Professor Burtt is that he is able to see that the key to under- standing in the realm of being is the experience of love. This (he says) is the central theme in both psychoanalysis and existentialism. Certainly the central insight in religious existentialism is the search for love: 'as a child a man's consuming need is to be loved, so that he may find his way from anxiety, frustration and anger in the presence of the harsh realities that surround him, to an acceptance of an adult role in the universe' (Burtt).

This confirms the findings in philosophical biology of the kind explored by Marjorie Grene in *Approaches to a Philosophical Biology,* where (as in the work of Ludwig Binswanger) the concept of *liebende Wirheit* becomes a primary fact of human existence: 'loving communion' as the basis of being. In Martin Buber, as we shall see, mutual encounter is the basis of human freedom and autonomy. D.W. Winnicott, the late great pediatrician, spoke of 'creative reflection'

---

[1] See the present author's survey of post-Freudian developments, short of existentialist psychotherapy, in *Human Hope and the Death Instinct*, Pergamon, 1971.

between mother and infant as the basis of human effectiveness. Love is the basis of our autonomy.

How can such entities, be found as human truths? Here we may find clues in psychoanalysis itself. Winnicott made a useful list of the sources of understanding, himself paediatrician turned psychotherapist. He gained his knowledge of human nature he tells us, through the following activities.

1. Direct observation of the infant-mother relationship.
2. Direct periodic observation of an infant starting life after birth and continuing over a period of years.
3. Pediatric history-taking.[1]
4. Pediatric practice, typically the management of infant feeding and excretion.
5. Diagnostic interview with children.
6. Psychoanalytical experience of adults and children.
7. The observation in pediatric practice of psychotic regression appearing as it commonly does in childhood or even in infancy.
8. Observation of children in homes adapted to cope with difficulties.
9. The psychoanalysis of schizophrenics.

*Collected Papers,* pp.158-9

Winnicott's interpretations of a child's drawing or story are really phenomenology in practice, a matter of concrete descriptive analysis of meanings (See *The Piggle,* and *Therapeutic Consultations in Child Psychiatry,* both deeply penetrating analyses of what, in a situation of love and trust, disturbed children are telling the psychotherapist, in symbolic language. Both are immediately relevant to English teaching).

Despite such phenomenological approaches in practice phenomenology itself makes little headway here. Even in the world of psychiatry phenomenological approaches have made little advance in Britain. As Professor Herbert Spiegelberg has said in his survey *Phenomenology in Psychiatry and Psychology:* 'The present rôle of phenomenology in the total picture of psychology and psychiatry,

---

[1] 'I have given a mother the opportunity of telling me what she knows of her infant's development in about 20,000 cases' (*Pediatrics and Psychiatry Collected Papers,* p.158).

particularly in the Anglo-American world, is a minor one and has not shown significant growth in recent years except at the "fringes"' (p.364). Gilbert Ryle, among philosophers, embraced German phenomenology in the 'twenties, but then rejected it. He did however refer to his own book *The Concept of Mind* (1941) as 'my phenomenology of mind', and has published an article on *Phenomenological Psychology* as recently as 1968 (by D.C.S. Osterhurzen, in *Mind,* **lxxix,** pp.487-501). This discussed Ryle's relationship to Husserl.

Phenomenology seeks to overcome the sensation-bound concept of experience which is characteristic of the British tradition since Hume. The traditional British approach to human existence and experience believes that it is to be understood by micro-analytical methods: measurement of atoms of sensations, in atoms of time. Every aspect of life is to be explained in terms of 'little casual thingummies'.

The paradigm of learning in the Human tradition is that of the conditioning reflex which Hume and animal psychologists since have considered to be common to man and other animals. This atomistic psychology meant that the mind was a 'bundle of sensations' (Hume) and all 'higher' categories were banished to the limbo of metaphysical nonsense. Mind was reduced to the parts, and thus *a fortiori* to a mechanical summation of such parts. All that could be studied was the association of elements of sensation (or of utterance).

Gestalt psychology challenged this associationist theory, by emphasizing the organization of achieved perception: the perceiving agent must be taken seriously as himself a whole more than the sum of his parts. But the most radical criticism of the objective paradigm has come from Edmund Husserl. A useful short introduction of his position is to be found in Roger Poole's *Towards Deep Subjectivity.*

> The world is thus *replaced.* It is not the spatial support of mathematically know extensions, but a world of interacting subjectivities which belongs to people, which they confer *meaning* upon and *control* through their conferring meaning upon it.
>
> p.88

A key concept in Husserl is that of 'intentionality', the power of conferring meaning on the world. As Poole says, 'With this attention to the "intentionality" of subjects in the world (the way they confer meaning and interpret their world) the massive task of re-integrating subjectivity into objective research has begun' (p.92). It should be clear how this kind of approach may be linked with existentialism. Poole goes on to discuss Kierkegaard, who declared 'What is abstract thought? It is thought without the thinker.' As Abraham Maslow said of the whole movement of which I am writing, 'We are groping . . . towards the phenomenological, the experiential, the existential, the ideographic, the unconscious, the private, the acutely personal . . .' (*Towards a Psychology of Being*, p.216). And we have to do this in an atmosphere which is 'forbidding', because of its addiction to the rational, the abstract, the objective, the impersonal. Even the Bullock Report brings this forbidding ethos into English, to drive out the imaginative dynamic. Here we may return to Ernst Cassirer:

> Physical things may be described in terms of their objective properties, but man may be described and defined only in terms of his consciousness. This fact poses an entirely new problem which cannot be solved by our usual modes of investigation. Empirical observation and logical analysis, in the sense in which these terms were used in pro-Socratic philosophy, here proved insufficient and inadequate. *For it is only in our immediate intercourse with human beings that we have insight into the character of man.*
>
> *An Essay on Man*, p.5 (my italics)

In his first chapter Cassirer discusses the crisis in man's knowledge of himself. His remarks may be read in conjunction with Husserl's command to us, to pick up again the *telos* of the whole Greek pursuit of truth.

Discussing Plato, Cassirer says that the Socratic dialogues show that knowledge of human nature cannot be gained except through a constant cooperation of the subjects in mutual interrogation and reply. 'Truth is not like an empirical object; it must be understood as the outgrowth of a social act.'

The goal is not 'objective truth' but the quest in each one of us to examine and determine our mode of life:

> Man is declared to be that creature who is constantly in search of himself – a creature who in every moment of his existence must examine and scrutinize the conditions of his existence. In this scrutiny, in this critical attitude to human life. 'A life which

is unexamined,' says Socrates in his *Apology*, 'is not worth living.' (Plato, Apology, 378, Jowett trans).

*An Essay on Man*, pp.5-6

It is by this fundamental faculty, of giving a response to himself and to others, that man becomes a 'responsible' subject, a moral subject. As Cassirer urges, 'we are still here at the beginning', even though we may recognize that 'the Socratic problem and the Socratic method' have left their mark 'on the whole future development of human civilization'. So, in philosophical anthropology we have a recapturing of the view of knowing as an aspect of that process delineated by Martin Buber: the origin of 'self-being' and autonomy in intersubjective processes, seeking values and meaning.

The new disciplines, especially existentialism, are concerned with meaning: and how meaning is possible. But this is less a preoccupation with intellectual abstraction, but is rather continually linked with attention to potentiality, and especially with the distinction between 'authenticity' and 'inauthenticity': with problems of how to live and fulfil oneself.

This makes the whole new approach less a body of theory or discourse than a mode of approach not only to knowing, but to *being*, and to the way in which each individual lives and explores his experience and realizes potentialities. Speaking of Jaspers, Professor Burtt says that

He explicitly conceives existentialism as universal – embracing the entire panorama of man's search for the true and the good, with special emphasis on the insights that have come from religious philosophies in the East and the cultural values they express . . .

p.91

Burtt points out that the existentialists have argued that every truth they attain is partial, and openness to fuller insight is therefore always needed. To talk in this way obviously appeals little to the analytical philosopher and positivist scientist: it is too vague and woolly to those who seek Cartesian exactitude and a new 'scientific' certainty by analysis and explicitness.

Heidegger maintained that the self-correcting process involved in the quest for philosophic understanding is more like a way of living, working and creating, rather than a search for abstract theories and certainties. Yet the subjective disciplines, all the same, demand more exacting disciplines of thought, and attention to the world and the self.

For the foundation of existentialism and phenomenology are admitted to be by no means secure and established and will need considerable on-going revision. Philosophical anthropology is not concerned to answer that question 'What is it to be human?' once and for all, but to point to a quest inspired by the question. In any case, the existentialist is not concerned (if he follows Kierkegaard) to persuade others to accept a new intellectual orientation so much as to help them on the quest for their own self-realization. The existentialist search for insight, says Burtt, calls for unending growth in an infinitely evolving universe, and this means openness to change at the deepest level of thought and insight.

But one new goal emerges from philosophical anthropology: a search for the 'true self' and its potentialities (see Peter Lomas, *True and False Experience*). Maslow believes there is a fundamental impulse towards self-realization.

> It looks as if there were a single ultimate value for all mankind, a far goal towards which all men strive. This is called variously by different authors, self-actualization, self-realization, integration, psychological health, individuation, autonomy, creativity, productivity . . . but they all agree that this amounts to realising the potentialities of the person, that is to say, becoming fully human, everything that a person could become.
>
> *Towards a Psychology of Being*, p.12

Here we may return to the poem discussed at the beginning of this chapter. As I tried to show, teaching such a poem has to do with the meaning of life in time: it raises the question for each of us (as do, say, Shakespeare's *Sonnets*). 'What have I achieved in my life before time overtakes me?' Here I believe one important concept in existentialist psychotherapy is relevant: that of *Dasein*, 'being for', from the philosophy of Martin Heidegger, a concept at which I have already looked, around the poem. *Dasein* means literally 'being there', and in psychotherapy influenced by these concepts the therapist seeks to draw out from his patient a sense of having 'been there', in a significant way, having achieved a sense of meaning which can never be taken away from him. (I discuss the poem by Isaac Rosenberg,

*Break of Day in the Trenches,* in this light, in *Lost Bearings in English Poetry).* Each of us lives in a state of 'being-unto-death', and all have to solve the problem of the point of our lives.

In the light of philosophical anthropology, one of our primary human needs is to establish meanings which can triumph over death – which have this 'Dasein' quality, of asserting a sense of 'hereness and nowness', in the creation of meaning, which can triumph over our ultimate nothingness. Love and human encounter too are important positive ways of solving the 'Dasein' problems of life, and while we are discussing forms of philosophy, it must also be pointed out that many artists can be said to be 'existentialist' in this way whether they know it or not: for instance Van Gogh, Gustav Mahler and D.H. Lawrence.[1] Of course, the art is not to be reduced to philosophy – but speaks for itself, as 'thought' of the 'art speech' kind.

To sum up, in this general area of philosophy, the central fact is consciousness, the experiencing 'I'. Moreover, to understand consciousness does not require ratiocination, analysis or logic, but the use of language and other forms of symbolism in *whole* terms. And this, of course, was F.R. Leavis's emphasis in his work, as defined in *The Living Principle.* Leavis sought to uphold the unique central creativity of the experiencing being, in the face of an era which would try to reduce human beings to units, to automatons, to 'functional man'. With Blake, Dickens and Lawrence, Leavis has sought to uphold the energy and freedom of the human soul against abstract reductions in the name of 'society' or political systems on the one hand, and the arid abstractions of the Newtonian universe on the other. With this holistic emphasis goes an indivisible emphasis on whole 'meaning', 'in the criss-cross of utterance between us'. This is, whether Leavis accepted it or not, an existentialist position, as Roger Poole has tried to show.[2]

Leavis himself declared that he was 'anti-philosopher', and seemed to suppose that there could be no reconciliation between that subject and English because philosophy was the kind of analysis of terms and trivialization of thought which menaced poetic meaning: which menaced *being.* Now, however, there are developments in philosophy which can make it a subject which offers us support and insight,

---

[1] See Rollo May in *Existence – a New Dimension in Psychiatry,* on these. Gustav Mahler I believe was aware he was composing existentialist music, as I try to show in *Gustav Mahler and the Courage to Be.*

[2] '*The affirmation is of life:* the later criticism of F.R. Leavis', Roger Poole, *Universities Quarterly,* Winter, 1974.

because it concerns itself with *being*, too. In the wake of Husserl, the aim is 'back to the things themselves' – that is, to return to the phenomena of consciousness, to the study of whole experience, in our living moment, not of essence, but of existence, of being-in-the-world. Husserl's major work is concerned with the failure of the scientific tradition to give an adequate account of man, and to provide an adequate basis for the pursuit of whole truth, and to find something to believe. Is there any meaning in existence? If this question is to be answered, we must have disciplines capable of finding man in his body and being as a conscious subject, in his proper place in nature, the knower in essential relation to the known. Michael Polanyi's work runs very close to this stream of thought in Husserl, emphasizing as he does the tacit, subsidiary and embodied. And Polanyi's thought in turn is in sympathy with much in European 'reflective' philosophy, such as that of the French phenomenologist Maurice Merleau-Ponty, who emphasizes the embodied nature of perception and thought. His concept of the 'ante-predicative', that is, the shadowy as yet unknown apprehension which we move towards, even while we cannot speak of it, is close to some of Polanyi's notions. Anyone who has grasped such themes in philosophical anthropology can glimpse new insights into the processes with which education deals: and English may be seen as a discipline which is itself part of philosophical anthropology. The essential dynamic is imagination. In becoming capable of human knowledge, a child is, from the beginning, growing through imagination, and this involves his whole body-mind existence. Coleridge was correct in seeing the imagination as primary in the growth and development of the human mind, and modern psychoanalysis sees the child's play with the mother as the origin through imagination of his sense of identity and his personal culture, as we shall see. These are the processes of *being*, and the new disciplines grope towards a new ontology which can study being as positivistic; 'objective' disciplines cannot. The quasi-scientific inclinations observable in the Bullock Report do serious harm by diverting attention from those new disciplines, such as are to be found in philosophical anthropology, which can help in a humanities subject such as English, to understand being by fresh forms of *Geisteswissenschaften*, and to become better able to foster developing powers because of deeper understanding.

# Chapter Five

# The Heavenly Bread of Self-Being

In this chapter I wish to look closely at a few important insights relevant to English, from philosophical anthropology.

There are two great mysteries with which we live, and which we take for granted – and yet we are often annoyed if anyone tries to inquire into them. One is our consciousness, asserting its intentionality and autonomy, as we have seen. The other is the origin of these powers in the baby and very small infant, with the concomitant residue, in each one of us, of aspects of this period of psychic gestation. As a number of thinkers have pointed out, there are considerable resistances to the exploration of these origins in adult human life: we will look everywhere but at our beginnings. And one reason is our fear of the infant within each of us, who is not fully grown, and whose existence threatens us because of his vulnerability and unsatisfied needs.[1]

However, if we dare to contemplate infancy and the amazing processes by which we become ourselves, we may find insights which will help us in our work of teaching – which, after all, is an encounter with childhood. Indeed, I believe, all teaching is a version of the processes which go on between mother and infant in the formative beginnings, and depends upon 'tacit' dynamics of the same kind.

Here I wish to focus more closely on a few of the thinkers in the realm of philosophical anthropology who have investigated childhood, or who have thought about the subjective interrelations which are peculiar to human beings. Their observations, I believe, help us to feel more confident in our attention to the imagination, because they

---

[1] W.R.D. Fairbairn gives this infant inside us the name 'regressed libidinal ego'. For a discussion of this dynamic as dealt with symbolically in the poetry of Sylvia Plath see my *Sylvia Plath: Poetry and Existence*. We both love this hidden dynamic and fear its vulnerability may wreck our lives: see Ted Hughes' poem *Littleblood* and Sylvia Plath's depiction of this 'littlesoul' in *Poem for a Birthday*, in *The Colossus*.

confirm that this is the primary dynamic in the development of our human powers. As Masud Khan has said of the work of D.W. Winnicott, for example, 'What is important . . . is the way Winnicott links the child's "true confidence" with his "creative gestures" and the *imaginative* as well as affective capacities in the mother to meet these.' The primary exchange, in play and intercommunication between mother and child, and her 'creative reflection' of the child's emerging self, are the roots of being: and here imagination plays a major part. The origin of the infant's human identity depends upon his looking into his mother's mind to see what kind of image of himself she has there; again, this is an imaginative act, and it illuminates the kind of mysterious process that lies behind education. Every teacher experiences, for example, the exhausting responsiveness of numerous pairs of eyes in the classroom, seeking to know what one has to offer:

> Out of each face, strange, dark beams that disquiet . . .
> – How can I answer the challenge of so many eyes?
> > D.H. Lawrence, *A Snowy Day in School*

One knows that children will, without explicit instruction, write the kind of poem they know, intuitively, you would like them to write (and indeed, perhaps, the adult poet writes the kind of poem to which he imagines an imaginary audience responding?) In writing creatively we both rely on powers within us that are not fully under our control. George Eliot, for example, expressed a feeling that her novels were written by another hand than her own, and this feeling has been recorded by others, including William Blake. So, the audience we write to is a postulated one which may or may not exist, while the 'writer' in us is a dæmon with whom we collaborate, strangely. The act is possible, however, because our very self was formed in the context of 'encounter' so we are able to imagine the other consciousness to which we write responding.

Our capacities to see and know the world, and other people, and to deal with these effectively, are bound up with our earliest relationships. One may even go back before anything that may be called 'relationship', since there does seem to be a time before we can even distinguish between the *me* and the *not-me*. According to Winnicott, as we shall see, there is at the beginning an at-oneness with the mother in whose the mother actually allows the baby to treat her as a

D

'subjective object', virtually as part of himself. Winnicott declared boldly to the British Psychoanalytical Society that 'there is no such thing as a baby'. He meant that we should think in terms of a 'nursing couple': whenever you come across a baby there is always someone's ears glued to it. The mother extends her identity to include the baby, and they live together for a time like a double-yoked psychic egg. If the baby dies, the strange distortion of the mother's personality shows up as a schizoid illness. But in health the mother gradually recovers from this extension and becomes herself again, while the baby is 'disillusioned' and comes to find (sometimes in pain and dread) that he is an independent separate being, in a world he must recognize as real. The pain and dread arise from his awareness that if he is separate and yet dependent he could be abandoned, while he also comes to realise that his acts can harm the 'other', or even damage the world.

These processes are bound up with problems of self and other, self and world, and thus with the deepest poetic and philosophical problems. They are thus bound up from the beginning with *meaning*, and they are worked on by *imagination*, play and symbolism. In a number of works I have tried to show what happens if these processes go 'wrong' as they have for the schizoid individual: his struggles to complete them often generate the most remarkable art.[1] Thus a study of these processes is essential for anyone concerned to see what English as a subject has to do with the discovery of the 'other', of the world, of the self; 'reparation' and love.

Here I want to look more closely at some observations by the Jewish philosophical anthropologist, Martin Buber; by Winnicott; and by other investigators such as F.J.J. Buytendijk the Dutch biologist, and Marion Milner, a psychotherapist.

In the important essay already referred to, Martin Buber discusses how our specifically human powers originate in being over against the other being: the title of the essay is 'Distance and Relation'. He speaks of a special kind of act of 'making present' between men, in which 'at such a moment something can come into being which cannot be built up in any other way'.

It rests on a capacity possessed to some extent by everyone, which may be described as 'imagining' the real: I mean the

---

[1] See for example *Dylan Thomas: the Code of Night*, on Thomas's attempts at self-cure. Much art is a form of self-mothering. Gustav Mahler's *Song of the Earth* is in part 'about' the processes discussed in the preceding paragraph.

capacity to hold before one's soul a reality arising at this moment
but not able to be directly experienced. Applied to intercourse
between men, 'imagining' the real means that I imagine to
myself what another man is at this very moment wishing,
feeling, perceiving, thinking, and not as a detached content but
in his very reality, that is, as a living process in this man.

*Distance and Relation,* in *The Knowledge of Man,* p.70

Buber is concerned with the special kind of quality of human
experience as it emerged from animal existence: and also the way the
individual human being evolves in his own beginnings, through
relationship. Man has 'a special way of being', and is 'a special category of being' derived from the 'the primal setting at a distance' and
'entering into relation'.

That the first movement is the presupposition of the other is
plain from the fact that one can enter into relation only with
being which has been set at a distance, more precisely, has
become an independent opposite. And it is only for man that an
independent opposite exists.

p.60

Man lives in a 'mansion' of consciousness, and this is created by
interaction with the 'other'. The 'being at a distance' is the Thou who
can 'be' for us: only thus, by *love,* is consciousness created. In man
there is a special category of being *because of love.* As Buber puts it, 'we
reach the insight that the principle of human life is not simple but two-
fold, being built up in a twofold movement which is of such kind that
the one movement is the presupposition of the other'. The 'great
phenomenon' of man is his 'connection with an otherness' which is
constituted as otherness by the event of 'distancing'.

Modern biology, says Buber, will speak of an animal's environment
(*Umwelt*), by which is understood the total world of objects accessible
to its senses, as conditioned by the circumstances of life which are
peculiar to this animal. Biology says something like this: the animal
perceives only the things that make its *Umwelt.* But is the animal's
really a 'world'? Isn't it simply rather a 'realm'? By this distinction
Buber is trying to emphasize that a human being lives in a 'world'
which 'is extended substantially beyond the realm of the observer who
is *in* the world and as such is independent'. Even a 'world of the senses'

is a world through being composed not of sense data alone, but through 'what is perceived being completed by what can be perceived', and it is the unity of these two which constitutes the proper 'world' of the senses.

An animal's organism gathers the elements which meet the necessities and wants of its life, in order to construct from them the circle of its existence.

> Wherever swallows or tunny wander, their bodily being (*Leiblichkeit*) carries out this selection from 'nature', which as such is completely unknown to them, and on which they in turn have an effect, again as something they neither know nor can know. An animal's 'image of the world', or rather, its image of a realm, is nothing more than the dynamic of the presences bound up with one another by the functions of life which are to be carried out.
>
> p.61

Man's existence is utterly different. it is only man, says Buber, who replaces this 'unsteady conglomeration' by *a unity which can be imagined or thought by him as existing for itself.* 'With soaring power he reaches out beyond what is given him, flies beyond the horizon and the familiar stars, and grasps a totality.'

With man, with his human life, a world exists. The animal lives in 'masses of usable sense data' which constitute its realm of life. But man both comprehends and transcends this realm.

> An animal in the realm of its perceptions is like a fruit in its skin; man is, or can be, in the world as a dweller in an enormous building which is always being added to, and to whose limits he can never penetrate, but which he can nevertheless know as one does know a house in which one lives – for he is capable of grasping the wholeness of the building as such. Man is like this because he is the creature (*Wesen*) through whose being (*sein*) 'what is' (*das Seinde*) becomes detached from him and recognized for itself.
>
> p.61

But this awareness of what is detached from his immediate realm is a product of 'distance and relation'. 'Only when a structure of being is independently over against a living being (*Seinde*), an independent opposite, does a world exist.'

Man's special kind of existence, with consciousness and the creative capacity to transcend, is a product of *'being for'*. And being for is an act of imagination: 'the making independent of his being . . . is . . . to be understood not in a psychological sense, and should therefore rather be called "becoming a self with me"'' (p.71).

The final paragraph of Buber's essay is magnificent:

> Man wishes to be confirmed in his being by man, and wishes to have a presence in the being of the other. The human person needs it. An animal does not need to be confirmed, for it is what it is unquestionably. It is different with man: sent forth from the natural domain of species into the hazard of the Solitary Category, surrounded by the air of a chaos which came into being with him, secretly and bashfully he watches for a Yes which allows him to be and which can come to him only from one human person to another. It is from man to man that the heavenly bread of self-being is passed.
>
> p.71

It is with this 'heavenly bread of self-being' that English is concerned, not just 'language' – though language is an ingredient of that bread. Again, we are 'beyond the words'.

'Self-being' implies a dynamic of self-realization, a becoming. Psychotherapeutic accounts speak in many different ways of what seems to Rollo May to be an 'ethical principle'. In many areas of thought in psychotherapy it has come to be recognized that the capacity of a human being to develop his own capacities and to deal with others and the world depends upon his experience of relationship with others who are significant to him. If we are concerned with *meaning*, we need to take account of these findings, that the capacity to mean is created in that intersubjective relationship between mother and infant, which is (as Leavis sees, quoting F.J.J. Buytendijk) the first social experience, and so the basis of all the child's capacities to relate to his world, through the instrument of culture.

Culture comes very much to the centre of Winnicott's model of human nature. From his work as paediatrician and psychotherapist Winnicott came to open up many areas of experience which we take for granted. How do we become a whole continuous self, relating to a real world and others, in a meaningful way? What enables these complex processes to develop is the capacity of the mother to 'be for' the child, which is a creative-imaginative act. If we consider the phrase 'to be for' it is clear that Winnicott postulates a special state of the mother's psyche, which enables her to fulfill her rôle in *being for her child*. This is an extension of her personality in a schizoid way, and it would be an illness if it were not for the fact of the pregnancy (*Collected Papers*, p.302). He calls it 'primary maternal preoccupation'.

Winnicott even calls this state in normal life an 'illness' ('I bring in the word "illness" because a woman must be healthy in order both to develop this state and to recover from it as the infant releases her. If the infant dies, the mother's state suddenly shows up as an illness. The mother takes this risk.')

The state of primary maternal preoccupation of which Winnicott writes is not mere normal devotion. There are very devoted women who cannot allow themselves to have this normal 'illness'[1] But most mothers enter into this special state – and Winnicott explores it further by contemplating the 'mirror rôle' of the mother. What does the baby see when he looks into the mother's face? Ordinarily, Winnicott says, 'what the baby sees is himself or herself'. In other words, the mother is looking at the baby and *what she looks like relates to what she sees there*.

This interpersonal reflection is made complex by the fact that, at first, the baby does not experience itself or the mother as continuous entities. Moreover, the baby does not fully recognize that the mother is separate from himself. At first he simply believes she is simply part of him: that is, she is his 'subjective object'. She has to 'disillusion' him, so that he seems to find her (and the world) as the 'objective object'. In this she enables him to complete very complex problems of relating to the world. She helps to create 'the beginning of a significant exchange with the world, a two-way process in which self-enrichment alternates with the discovery of meaning in the world of seen things' (*Playing and Reality*, p.113).

---

[1] 'When a woman has a strong male identification she finds this part of her mothering function most difficult to achieve . . .' (p.300). It is perhaps saying here that much in 'liberation' campaigning seems directed at urging a strong male identification on women. The result could well be serious problems in the next generation. It should perhaps be added that if the mother herself cannot 'be for' it is possible for another woman to do the 'creative reflection': but a child cannot become a human being without such mothering at all.

The denial of the capacity *to be* is a central weakness in our civilization: see, again, Karl Stern in *The Flight from Woman*. The problems are also discussed at length and in their historical context in Harry Guntrip's *Personality Structure and Human Interaction* and *Schizoid Phenomena, Object Relations and the Self*.

These processes, then, belong to separation and union, and depend upon processes not unlike telepathy: 'one can think of the "electricity" that seems to generate in meaningful or intimate contact and that is a feature when people are in love.'

In his account of the mother's mirror rôle, Winnicott is delineating 'creative encounter' in terms very close to those of Buber: processes by which the infant 'finds himself in the other'. He links apperception with perception by postulating a historical process in the individual which depends upon *being seen*. Out of these processes of formative inter-subjectivity culture develops. The growth of those 'mansions of consciousness', the 'world' in which a human being lives, goes with the development of play, of language, and of *symbols*. Culture arises out of 'the potential space between the subjective object and the object objectively perceived, between me-extensions and the not-me'. Winnicott felt there was a need to find a third dimension in which to discuss the origins of culture. Human nature needs discussion in terms of interpersonal relationship, taking into account the imaginative elaboration of function and the whole of fantasy, conscious and unconscious. There is a need to recognize *inner reality* in human experience. But then there is the *third* part of the life of a human being '. . . an intermediate area of *experiencing*, to which inner reality and external life both contribute' (*Playing and Reality,* p.2). These explorations have an evident profound relevance to problems of culture, symbolism and language.

Here one of Winnicott's most important essays is *The Location of Cultural Experience*, also collected in *Playing and Reality* (p.95). He declares that, 'Freud did not have a place in his topography of the mind for the experience of things cultural.'

Winnicott's work represents a radical rejection of Freud's meta-psychology: he recognizes human 'realities' which Freud could not find because he had concentrated so much on instinctual experience and based his metapsychology on natural scientism, even though his analysis of dreams was phenomenological.

Winnicott developed his theories from a number of cases, some of which may be traced in his work. He treated people who were so ill mentally that any promise of 'release' of 'instinct' meant nothing to them. First, they had to find out whether they were human at all: and then they wanted to find some meaning in life.

The phrase he uses, for the baby's 'use' of his mother is 'reaching out', an imaginative act on its part. Winnicott implies that a child's creative emergence depends upon his looking into his mother's mind, to see what kind of image she has of him. So these are imaginative-cultural processes, belonging to the emerging child's creative perception of the world and to *meaning*, and to potentialities coming into being.

This represents an important shift in psychoanalytical theory: 'You can cure your patient and now know *what it is that makes him or her go on living* . . . we have not yet started to describe what life is like apart from illness or the absence of illness.'

There is the universal problem of the meaning of existence:

> That is to say, we have yet to tackle the question of *what life is about*. Once psychotic patients force us to give attention to this sort of basic problem . . . it is not instinctual satisfaction that makes a baby begin to be, to feel that life is real, to find life worth living . . .

Obviously, what a baby takes in from its mother, if she is capable of 'being for' him, is something more than mere milk and comfort: it is a capacity to perceive the world, to love, to develop symbols, culture and a sense of richness in those mansions of consciousness – that which is meant by all the paintings in the world of the Virgin and Child. Winnicott, by this emphasis, brings culture, obviously, to a central place in personal development, in a way that was impossible to Freud. What also interests Winnicott is how

> in any cultural field it is not possible to be original except on a basis of tradition . . . the interplay between originality and the acceptance of tradition as a basis for inventiveness seem to me to be just one more example, and a very exciting one, of the interplay between separateness and union.

Thus, in the origins of our humanness in the interplay between union and separateness of the baby in his mother's care, we may find the origins of that interplay between union and separateness, between the individual and the culture, without which he cannot begin to be human.

In this important essay, Winnicott traces the origin of culture of the child's first symbol, which arises from the first 'transitional object'–symbol, which 'is a symbol of the union of the baby and the mother (or part of the mother)':

This symbol can be located. It is at the place in space and time where and when the mother is in transition from being (in the baby's mind) merged in with the infant and being experienced as an object to be perceived rather than conceived of. The use of an object symbolizes the union of two now separate things, baby and mother, *at the point of the initiation of their state of separateness.*

*Playing and Reality,* p.96-97

Winnicott begins with the baby at the breast, and sees that from this encounter emerges that creative encounter by which the infant 'finds himself in the other';

Perhaps a baby at the breast does not look at the breast. Looking at the face is more likely to be a feature. What does the baby see there? . . . what the baby sees is himself or herself. In other words the mother is looking at the baby and *what she looks like is related to what she sees there* . . . I am linking apperception with perception by postulating an historical process (in the individual) which depends upon being seen: when I look I am seen, so I exist. I now look creatively and what I apperceive I also perceive . . .

*Mirror-rôle of Mother and Family* in *The Predicament of the Family,* Ed. P. Lomas, pp.27-9, also in *Playing and Reality,* p.114.

The individual's emotional involvement with his seeing, then, is a product of the loving relationship between himself and his mother. And more than that, the individual can only find his world meaningful if his perception is based on such a loving experience with the 'significant other'.

At the head of his paper Winnicott quotes Tagore: 'On the seashore of endless world, children play.' He says he believes that:

the sea and the shore represent endless intercourse between man and woman and the child emerged from this union to have a brief moment before becoming in turn an adult or a parent . . . the sea is the mother, and on the sea-shore the child is born. Babies come up out of the sea and are spewed out upon the land, like Jonah from the whale. So now the seashore was the mother's body, after the child is born, and the mother and the now viable baby are getting to know each other.

Pondering this concept led Winnicott to ponder the nature of play, and he came to realize, he says, that play is in fact 'neither a matter of inner psychic reality nor a matter of external reality'. But then, 'if play is neither inside nor outside' where is it? It is in the space between mother and infant – a poetic or philosophical space.

The child's first 'not-me possession' – its piece of blanket, or its teddy-bear or whatever – is its first *symbol*. It is 'a symbol of the union of the baby with the mother'. And in time it belongs to the moment when the mother is ceasing to be 'merged' with the infant, but being *experienced as an object to be perceived rather than conceived of*. That is, the transitional object, the first cultural object, belongs to the moment when perception of the real world, as something that exists 'out there' in its own right, begins.

Winnicott sees the 'transitional object' phenonomen as lying in the 'intermediate area between the subjective and that which is objectively perceived'.

At the same time, the transitional object symbolizes the union of the baby with his mother – and dependent being – as we have seen. This 'separation' is an immense 'originality' in the infant's use of this symbol: but it is an originality only possible because of the 'union' behind it. The cultural implications at large confirm those explored by T.S. Eliot[1], whose words in his famous essay are close to those of Winnicott about the interplay between originality and tradition. Winnicott sees this traditional object symbol as standing at the beginning of the child's life of culture, which makes him a human person, as we have seen. And, as a man, he will use this culture (rather than his 'instinctual life') to explore the 'point of life': 'It is these cultural experiences that provide the continuity in the human race which transcend personal existence. I am assuming that cultural experiences are in direct continuity with play, the play of those who have not yet heard of games.'

Play with the first transitional object, an extension of this first artefact, is, then, if we follow Winnicott, both a way of 'belonging' and of being independent. It is a way of finding that one belongs to a continuity beyond oneself, and yet of feeling a substantial security about one's own continuous existence. One's union with the mother,

---

[1] In *Tradition and the Individual Talent, Collected Essays.*

and with all those with whom one shares one's culture, is that which enables one to feel human, and to feel there is 'a point to life'. Moreover, it enables one to develop and work on the capacity to perceive the world of reality.

If the 'transitional object' (teddy bear or blanket) represents our first symbol of our union and separateness, then it must also be a focus of concern for others. That it is so would seem clear from Winnicott's earliest discussion of the ways in which 'transitional objects' are treated ('Transitional objects and transitional object phenomena', *Int. J. Psychoanalysis,* **34**). Transitional objects are both loved and abused: thus they are used for research (as it were) into the strength of the existential security for which they stand. Such affection is bestowed on a transitional object, and it has great importance in the infant's life. He cannot go to sleep without it. (It may also still be seen in the college student's room at the age of 20!) It stands for the importance of *giving and finding* – and 'meeting'. It stands for ways of guaranteeing that one is 'good enough', and sufficiently capable of reparation, of giving to others, to survive. Of course, from the level of the transitional object, play develops into a rich and complex personal culture, including language. It is then very much more than merely a means to survive as an independent being: yet the elements which come from 'togetherness' remain in it, not least when it manifests itself as an assertion of freedom.

There is another conclusion in Winnicott's chapters which concerns us. His work with psychotic patients brought him to realize that the Freudian model was inadequate. You cannot tell a mad person that he should try to 'release his instincts' as much as possible. He has failed, for some reason, to complete all those processes in infant relationship by which the self and world can feel whole and meaningful. This kind of person cannot begin to live, until he can work on two questions: 'What is it to be human?' and 'What is the point of life?'

Winnicott has thus completely reversed the Freudian view of culture, which was based on 'instinct' theory, with its roots in natural scientism and nineteenth-century functional thinking. He makes culture *primary,* in an existentialist way, because he makes it clear that human beings *cannot begin to live* unless they have sense of their own humanness and *a sense of the point of life. Again, the central preoccupation in our life is meaning,* and Winnicott declares that the capacity to symbolize is employed to work on those two questions. We can apply these observations to any poem or story by a child which we pick up from his desk. Between the shared culture (union) and his own unique dynamic 'formative principle' (his separateness), what is there here that contributes to his capacity to pursue those questions? And because of the interplay between union and separateness, we can see how we must continually bring into the child's world material from his union with all men (Mozart's piano sonatas, paintings by Bonnard, Isaac Rosenberg's poetry, folksongs) to allow his inner world of symbolism to enrich its scope, thus contributing to his inner resource in 'separateness' – the capacity to be alone, and self-reliant: to fulfil himself.[1] As Marjorie Grene insists, in *Approaches to A Philosophical Biology,* the purposiveness of the creative impulse in man, as bound up with his cultural capacities, is a biological reality.

But this dimension of man cannot be studied merely as a fact to be found by the disciplines of positivism. Even at the earliest stages the child's actions will have a symbolic meaning.

Merleau-Ponty shows himself well aware of the body-signs and meanings evident in the naïvest encounters with infancy: 'A fifteen months' old child opens his mouth if I playfully take one of his fingers between my teeth and pretend to bite it.' As Buytendijk had pointed out, this indicates that 'the act of biting has immediately an inter-subjective meaning', and such meaning is only possible when there is encounter.

In truth, the special dimension of human existence from the beginning is the dimension of the *animal symbolicum,* and this is a complex dimension between union and separateness, impossible without intersubjective experience. As Marjorie Grene says: 'The child's first immense step towards humanity, therefore, consists, prior to his first words or his first steps, in his first encounter with another human being' (*Approaches*, p.168).

Marjorie Grene discusses the work of Buytendijk, which runs close to that of Winnicott in its phenomenological investigation of the origins of play and meaning.

F.J.J. Buytendijk is essentially a physiologist and a comparative psychologist, and his concern has been to force adequate conceptual tools for the study of behaviour. He believed that in trying to

---

[1] It is perhaps worth pointing out that the absurd accusation that I am an 'élitist' arises from a misunderstanding of my purpose in drawing on the best in poetry and prose to stimulate creativity. The richest artefacts can stimulate the individual's resources, his own voice, if they are properly related to his need for meaning: here 'union' is used to stimulate 'separateness', towards further originality: hardly an 'élitist' aim!

understand human beings, we need to participate in an existential way in encountering them; otherwise we should have no access to the phenomenon we have set out to investigate. 'Each person chooses his way of being in the world' so we can only know others by an imaginative act of investigating the unique individual dynamic of processes. 'Reciprocity' said Buytendijk, 'is the condition of real encounter': and though perhaps symbolism and culture in the 'space between' are not emphasized by him as they are in Winnicott, yet Buytendijk evidently recognizes this element, because of his recognition of the rôle of speech, and the implications of his phrase 'when two freedoms meet'. One can only speak of a free man, to use Winnicott's phrase, if one speaks of him along with his personal culture, and it is through culture that 'freedoms' encounter one another.

Human consciousness and the ways in which we perceive the world and act in it depend for their origins and development upon complex forms of intersubjectivity, upon 'meeting' and the creative imagination, which 'begin in play at mother's breast'. Looking at the purpose of play in such growth, Buytendijk quotes Merleau-Ponty: 'In order to perceive things, we have to live them.' In this active life with the world . . . things 'show themselves, approach, play games with us – and so are able to encounter us'.

This 'freely chosen loving encounter' is the basis of consciousness:

> The child comes to discover the presence of his fellow man, first in direct encounter, and then indirectly in signals, noises, events, and all the cultural objects that surround him. His own world develops, in its differentiation and its inwardness, as the world, at the same time, of other beings: his awareness of 'co-existence' and existence, of the being of others and of his being himself, develops as a unity . . . *The individual becomes aware of himself in unity with the other.* [1]
>
> Marjorie Green, *Approaches*, (my italics), p.171-2

'Existence', says Marjorie Grene, 'is actualized only in communication.' She is discussing one important problem in philosophical thought: whether we can really 'find' the other. But from our point of view what is of central importance about human development is that

---

[1] Buytendijk, *Das Menschliche, Wege zu seinem Verstandnis*, Köhler, Stuttgart, 1958, p.84.

human 'meeting' is bound up with the development of all our powers: 'It is through the infinite variety of such meeting, that we become human.' Buytendijk recognizes that these potentialities emerge out of play:

> Already in the first play of the nursing infant and in all later variants of this play with elastic, swinging objects, there is a condition of being moved while moving oneself and of moving oneself when being moved. This double activity in play is, as in every authentic human encounter, the expression of a twofold intentionality, that is, we do something, reach out to the other in a grasping gesture, and surrender ourselves in such a way that something can be done to us – we choose activity and at the same time passivity. In this ambiguity of existence, in which doing and suffering, grasping and being grasped rise up out of the ambiguous human behaviour and into ambiguous structure of genuine encounter, in a shadowy and elementary form, is the first erotic play of the moving, touching lips, tongue and hands of the nursing infant.
>
> *Das Menschliche, Wege zu Seinem*
> *Verständnis,* Stuttgart, 1958, p.72.
> Translated by Marjorie Grene in *Approaches*

To this aspect of physical encounter we can add all those complexities of fantasy to which Melanie Klein and D.W. Winnicott have drawn our attention. For instance, as well as the 'ambiguity' of 'grasping and being grasped', there are the ambiguities that arise in the child's mind between fantasy and reality (e.g. the fantasied feed and the actual feed). There are confusions between the 'exciting' mother and the 'rejecting' mother – an ambiguity reflected in his own movement between love (when 'met' and satisfied) and hate (when the mother is not 'there' or does not 'meet' him, leaves him for a moment or rejects him).

Buytendijk sees the elements of surrender and aggression involved. The baby playing with his rattle displays a mixture of adaptive and aggressive dynamics in his encounters with persons, grasping and being grasped, movement with and against, making oneself heard, surrender and liberation. He sees that there is in human encounter something 'surplus' over and above the 'natural' foundation of animal life. In the human case there is not only meeting of things, lures or threats, within the world, there is also something essentially different: *loving* encounter of person with person. In order to understand man we have to take the risk of experiencing and confronting *love*. Moreover, we cannot discuss such a subject as language[1] without encountering problems of love and hate, union and separateness, meaning and non-meaning. Man is a questioning being, the only being, as Heidegger has argued, for whom Being is in question. But he is also the only being whose questions can be put to rest through participation in the world of the mind – a world constituted by the union of persons in mutual understanding of the more than personal. The external mark of such a world's existence is speech; but prior to the acquisition of language the infant must have learned to *be* with others in loving encounter. Indeed without such encounter there could be no discourse (Marjorie Grene, *Approaches*, p.188). This view of language development, again, indicates something much more complex, in a holistic view, than most linguists are capable of grasping.

In the acquisition of language the infant must have learned to *be* with others in encounter:

> Plato held that the necessary condition of rational discourse was the separate existence of the Forms; but he also held that this nontransient Being could be approached only through dialectic, that is, through dialogue. It takes two to make a language; a speaker and hearer, questioner and answerer. *The child's first immense step towards humanity, therefore consists, prior to his first words or his first steps, in his first encounter with another human being.*
>
> Marjorie Grene, op. cit., p.168 (my italics)

Helmuth Plessner is another philosopher and psychologist who has explored this early formative area. His work is close to that of Buytendijk and Winnicott in the phenomenological analysis of the meanings we send across from one to the other, beginning at the breast.[2]

---

[1] These life problems are symbolized in fairy tales and nursery rhymes. I am trying to explore the symbolism of children's literature in other studies, one on C.S. Lewis. See also my account of the work of Melanie Klein and others in *Human Hope and the Death Instinct*.

[2] By 'breast' we mean the mother's care and feeding of the baby, her responsiveness, and body presence. In normal child care the breast is the focus of all this, because it is beautiful, it excites, and satisfies bodily need, and so educates in the capacity for adult sexual love, also.

The first sign of encounter is the *smile*. With its ambiguity of approach and withdrawal, openness and secrecy, the smile marks the child's entry into the intellectual world. Not that the infant with his first smile grasps intellectual concepts, but he has come to the threshold of such understanding, says Plessner (who collaborated closely with Buytendijk). Smiling is the 'miming of mind'. It expresses that distance from natural being and at the same time identification with a new, yet alien being, which constitutes humanity. 'To the smiling infant the other is not a threat but an invitation – *an invitation to find himself in the other* – to reach out beyond himself and be restored to himself at a new level of reality, the level of being human' (*Approaches*, p.168, my italics). These are phenomenological explorations of the processes Buber refers to. So Winnicott, Plessner and Buytendijk, beginning with the baby at the breast, see that from this first experience of distance and relationship emerges that creative encounter by which the infant 'finds himself in the other'.

As Marjorie Grene says, it is not that the child distinguishes 'consciously' or even 'unconsciously' himself from the other. That is just what he does not do. The point is rather that he comes *to* himself, hesitantly and shyly, through the other, in the loving reciprocity which he expresses by giving smile for smile. On this ground of mutuality, and only on this ground, the life of mind, with its impersonal, 'objective' content, can take root ( *Approaches*, p.169).

In these discussions, philosopher and psychologists are only telling us the implications for the study of man of what every working teacher knows.

Many have written in a simpler way about their insights into child development, several of them women of especial insight, like Susan Isaacs and Len Chaloner, well aware that perception depends upon 'encounter', and that these 'begin in play at mother's breast'.[1]

One further observation is important here. Some psychotherapists tell us that, in their experience, there seems to be in everyone a 'formative principle' which impels them to seek to fulfil the kind of person they have it in them to become. Moreover, this capacity for self-realization cannot be discussed adequately unless it is as a product of intersubjectivity, primarily of the mother-infant relationship, from

---

[1] See 'The beginning' in Susan Isaacs' *The Nursery Years*, e.g. 'For the young infant, it comes as a thrilling discovery that things which can't be touched but only seen are nevertheless really "there".' Len Chaloner's delightful book is *Feeling and Perception in Young Children*, Tavistock.

the beginnings in which the mother offers the infant 'creative reflection' of his emerging self.

In every human being there does seem to be a drive towards the realization of the true self: a dynamic which we know to be one of the tacit dynamics behind 'English'. Marion Milner found the concept of a 'formative principle' very meaningful: she speaks of finding this dynamic force in her patients.

> Increasingly in my clinical work I had found myself needing to find what verbal concept in psychoanalytical thinking corresponded with what L.L. Whyte has called the formative principle . . . an organizing pattern-making aspect . . .
>
> . . . some patients seem to be aware, dimly or increasingly, of a force in them to do with growth, growth towards their own shape, also as something that seemed to be sensed as driving them to break down false inner organizations which do not really belong to them: something which can also be deeply feared, as a kind of creative fury that will not let them rest content with a merely compliant adaptation; and also feared because of the temporary chaos it must cause when the integrations on a false basis are in the process of being broken down in order that a better one can emerge.
>
> *In the Hands of the Living God,* p.385

She speaks of

> . . . something that is shown in a person's own particular and individual rhythms and style. Or is the term 'unconscious integrating aspect of the ego' more appropriate? . . . Certainly, some patients seemed to be aware, dimly or increasingly, of a force in them to do with growth, growth towards their own shape . . .
>
> *In the Hands of the Living God,* p.484

This 'formative principle' is a concept Marion Milner takes from L.L. Whyte in his *Aspects of Form.* We may see it, in the light of philosophical biology, as a psychic manifestation of the essential 'something like consciousness' in animals, their *Selbstdarstellung* or manifestation of the self on the surface and their amazing powers to make use of the world (as in migrations) in their 'preferred activity'

(Adolf Portmann). Whyte's work suggested to Marion Milner the 'spontaneous urge to pattern inherent in the living organism'. There are many dynamics in living things which we do not yet understand: for instance, how 'the bee . . . without ever having seen the like, carries in itself the unconscious representation of the hexagonal cell, accurate to half an angular minute'. This is from Von Hartmann's *Philosophy of the Unconscious* (1868) who also said: 'We must recognize the clairvoyance of the unconscious in the purposiveness of the creative impulse as in that of instinct . . .'

The positivist scientist, following the objective paradigm, tries to avoid living with the mysteries: the writers to whom I have referred are trying to understand them, allowing them to exist. The impulse towards self-realization is a primary biological reality in man, and English must take account of this. English is not 'personal growth' in the simplistic way caricatured by the Bullock report: but it is one important contribution to each pupil's search to realize his 'true self', and to assert his human freedoms in the context of a form of relationship. We may end this chapter with a reference to Peter Lomas's *True and False Experience:*

> The true self, I take it, is that which develops from the original being of the child. It is imperfect and ill-defined (because we live in an imperfect and ill-defined world) but it remains roughly true to our innate potential . . .
>
> p.93

This is the problem of life to which English may offer some help in our each attempt to find and define that potentiality, between love and symbolism. We are now, of course, far beyond mere 'language use'.

# Chapter Six

# *English for Meaning*

So English is a discipline of thought: and it has to do with language as the expression of 'whole' experience – that is, all our existential reality. It deals not only with ideas that can be taken and abstracted from our minds, but our bodily feelings, and emotions, our dreams, our unconscious fantasies, our creative powers, and our hopes for tomorrow. So it is a phenomenological discipline, concerned with the phenomena of consciousness. Thus it is inadequate to regard English, as linguisticians and the 'language men' do, merely as a discipline of 'language use'. We have only to utter a word, or even make a silent sign, such as a wink or a pointed finger, to point *beyond* the word or sign, and express a meaning which involves the self and the other, our own body and the world, the individual dynamic psyche and a tradition of culture: the whole being-in-the-world, in time. Any symbol involves many tacit elements deep within us, even feelings in our body life, and our protensions – that is, expectancies in the flux of time, towards ever-opening possibilities and goals towards which we are drawn. English has to do with *meaning*, and 'meaning is an intention of the mind' (Husserl).

Having written that paragraph, I have surely indicated a new perspective for English? Yet it confirms a traditional approach, which is that English is an art. The writers in psychology and philosophy to whom I have drawn attention enable us to feel confident in our reliance on natural powers, especially on elements of 'creative reflection' between beings. Whatever 'rules' linguisticians and those who pursue other abstracting disciplines may find in our use of language and symbols, we use this language and those symbols naturally, by intuition and imagination, as a natural aspect of our emerging growth. We do not need to be given theoretical instruction to use these powers in the first place: the basis of our language use is not explicit. We learn to speak in response to our mothers, from those with whom we are in intersubjective contact, and from our ever-widening cultural inheritance, as our consciousness develops. Of course this is not to say our performance in speaking and writing, as in dancing and playing the piano, cannot be improved by conscious knowledge and training. But the tacit powers of indwelling are primary, and are best improved by fostering confidence in them, and respecting their mysterious dynamics, by *art* and by *love,* by attention to *being,* not by explicit 'instruction in rules and structures'.

In all our thinking, the first thing to recognize is that English as a discipline of thought is part of a process of living in the world which 'comes by nature' (Dogberry was right), and that the powers upon which it primarily depends are intuitive and tacit. To recognize this, and to maintain our insistence upon it, requires a psychology and a philosophy capable of embracing this kind of human reality, the reality of all those processes which Polanyi found to be the basis of knowing. By contrast, mere intellectualization, making explicit, towards 'unbridled lucidity' (as Polanyi called it), can actually inhibit our subsidiary powers (*The Tacit Dimension,* p.18). To say as much is not in the least unscientific. Science itself depends upon imagination, and knows this. In Professor Beveridge's *The Art of Scientific Investigation* there are chapters on *Intuition* and *Imagination,* and he reveals that many scientific conclusions are 'reached' when the explicit attention is absent.[1] Our problem is to understand tacit and subsidiary powers, while also allowing them to operate unscrutinized, and to develop by natural grace, at the centre of the process of learning.

To get our perspective right, then, we need to see English in the wider prospect of those humanities disciplines by which we seek the truth of the world – *including* the sciences.

English is a humanities subject which is obliged to grope towards the truth, in the spirit of Husserl's injunctions to us, to pick up the original impulse in our civilization, and to pursue *something in which to believe.*

Some critics, like Bernard Bergonzi, have criticized F.R. Leavis for trying to make English a 'religion'. But this is to misrepresent the emphasis. English has to do with the pursuit of meaning through symbolism. In the pursuit of Winnicott's two questions, 'What is it to be human?', 'What is the point of life?', the first question belongs to the attempt to redefine man in answer to Kant's last question, 'What is

---

[1] 'Spirit is the power of creative intuition; without imagination science remains sterile', Karl Jasper's, *The Idea of the University,* p.44.

man?'; the second obliges us to continue to assert that we *can* find meaning – as Shakespeare did, even, or not least, at the end of such a terrible confrontation with man's fate as *King Lear;* or the author of the *Book of Job* when confronting tragic despair. English *is* a 'religious' subject insofar as it *must* concern itself with these questions. It is also a creative subject, in which the dynamics of the individual are actually trained, to encourage the individual to explore his own authenticity, and to enrich and foster his effective relationship with others and the world. In this sense, it is a philosophical discipline in the existentialist sense: that is, it is involved in the development of attitudes to life. It is a *moral* discipline, since it engages inevitably with values, because these are bound up with meaning: and it changes us as we study and work.

So, English is for meaning – but not the meaning of words as the philosopher approaches them, in his concern with logic and definition nor is it analytical in the linguist's way, attending to form and structure. The use of words in English is a discipline of meaning in what I shall call a phenomenological way – as a way of understanding what goes on in the human consciousness.

Any genuine investigation of the phenomena of education must recognize that it is rooted in tacit processes; must recognize that what happens in the classroom or university lecture room is a process that depends upon intersubjectivity and subsidiary energies of 'being' including love and 'encounter'. Think of what actually happens in a supervision, for example. I sometimes think, in the middle of a supervision, 'Whatever am I doing? Here I am arguing with this young man above love in *Anthony and Cleopatra*. Who am I to say this or that about the "message" of this play?' One morning I remember being distressed by having read *Anthony and Cleopatra*, unable to find any clear solution to the question as to whether one should feel the protagonists were being true to their best selves when they abandon their political and regal responsibilities for passion: or was the passion the highest existential truth? I had a sleepless night, about this problem; and I really didn't know what to say to my young men, coming in all that morning. I was having a bit of 'moral teething' myself. But then I came to see that what they needed was to be helped to *read the play* and respond in their own way: my function was to help tease out the ambiguities and the ambivalence, the interwoven bafflements, in the poetry. And then say, as a man with nearly 30 years of married life behind him, 'I register this as true about human experience: I know some of this kind of suffering, but I am at the moment overwhelmed by the play, and I cannot say anything clear and straightforward about it. What do you think?' Actually, I found myself helped to understand the play by their intelligent responses, and even from their naïvety and innocence. They helped me with my own problems of wishing human beings were not so complicated, and that women would not misuse their power and their 'riggishness' to destroy others: strong feelings which inhibited my response to the play. In the end, I thought I found, I had let the play work upon me, in a deeper way, than ever before, because, confronted with them, I hestitated to simplify. It is clear that in such teaching we have something much more complex than passing on information or merely improving 'language use'. But this *is* English, this personal relationship in the sharing of meanings in words: this sharing of a great artist's disturbing investigation of 'life', and his capacity to hold complexities in unresolved suspension.

What I did during those supervisions under the heading of 'English' could not be made explicit by any merely rational analysis. The analytical tradition in our philosophy is in this sense an enemy, since it tends to imply the exclusion of Being. As Marjorie Grene puts it, 'He who remains within the clear light of reason goes nowhere and has nowhere to go' ('The errors of Descartes', *The Knower and the Known*, p.78).

The exclusion of all that is shadowy, inward and irrational in our experience of the world would also be an exclusion of all creativity. This is what Blake objected to when he rejected 'Newton's sleep'. A corrective is creative work – painting, dance, drama, or writing. There is a kind of dread which comes over us, when we surrender ourselves to what Straus has called 'creative fate'.

When we face the blank canvas or sheet of paper, we rely on powers which can never be the mere bringing together of explicit forms of knowledge: there is another kind of process, to which we must give ourselves – some primary impulse to create patterns and order (as Marion Milner suggests above, p.116). We bring to bear on our experience a range of potentialities which do not belong to masculine knowledge of the analytic kind but rather to 'female element being'. Because these are female and sensitive, they feel vulnerable, and because of our fear that this may expose us to being hurt, creativity is often painful. All arts involve the pain of exposing ourselves to our own sensitive vulnerability and to the possibility that we may not be able to find the meanings we seek to set against death and nothingness. It is this that makes the confident analytical intellect so hostile to art: the fear that the quest for *Dasein* may not succeed and leave us only dread. On our part, we have to recklessly exercise the creative power. We go on reading and thinking, and suddenly (if we are lucky) 'it all coheres': this view of our kind of processes is quite different from Descartes' idea of 'clear and distinct ideas' that has dominated the West, under the influence of the scientific revolution, and which seeks certainty at a certain cost. The universities are centres of hostility to creative uncertainties: this is why their influence on education is sometimes baleful.

To underline the contrast, we may take Jean Renoir's account of his father's painting:

> He succeeded in taking complete possession of his subject only after a struggle. When painting, he sometimes appeared to be fighting a duel; the painter seemed to be eyeing the movements of his opponent and watching for the least weakness in his defences. He harrassed the subject ceaselessly as a lover harrasses the girl who puts up a struggle before yielding. He seemed also to be on a hunt. The anxious rapidity of his brush strokes, which were urgent, precise, *flashing extensions of his piercing vision,* made me think of the zigzag flight of a swallow catching insects. I purposely borrow a comparison from ornithology. *Renoir's brush was linked to his visual perceptions as directly as the swallow's beak is linked to its eyes.* This description would be incomplete if I failed to point out that Renoir in the act of painting had a wild side to him which startled me several times when I was small.
>
> Jean Renoir, *Renoir, My Father,* (my italics), p.183

There is all the difference in the world between a processing machine, or even a person involved in a processing task, and an individual *totally absorbed thus in the task of symbolizing* – symbolizing as an act of perception, of 'being in the world'. Michael Polanyi uses the term 'indwelling' meaning an extension of the self into the world by a tool, or an intellectual system, or a paintbrush, by which we 'live into' experience and create a life-world in which to meaningfully exist. Jean Renoir's account indicates, powerfully, the tacit 'indwelling' elements which are the foundation of all creativity, and cannot be explicitly commanded:

Sometimes the forms and colours were still indefinite at the end of the first session. Only on the following day was it possible to sense what would come. For the onlooker the overwhelming impression was that the subject, defeated, was disappearing and the picture was coming out of Renoir himself.

Towards the end of his life, Renoir had so perfected his method that he eliminated 'little details' more quickly, and got down at once to what was essential. But to the day of his death, he continued to 'caress and strike the motif' the way one caresses and strikes a woman so that she can express all her love. For that is what Renoir needed: that state of abandon on the part of the model, which would allow him to touch the depths of human nature freed of all cares and prejudices of the moment.

op.cit., p.183

In such a penetrating account of how a painter paints, one gains a glimpse of symbolizing as an embodied process ('all thought is incarnate' – Polanyi). One may see a parallel process daily in a good kindergarten or good English classroom. In creative writing by children there is a parallel wildness, however callow or naïve, at best. But in *any* writing or reading that counts because it is involved and meaningful, there are the same elements – of language, in the sense of 'tonguing'. Renoir made the connection himself: Mary Cassatt said to him: 'I adore the brown tone in young shadows. Tell me how you do it.' 'The way, you pronounce your 'r's', he replied.

Such dynamics make sense to the phenomenologist: the abstracting investigator working according to the paradigms of natural science cannot find them at all.

In referring to the various new disciplines I have invoked, have I been trying to construct a philosophy of English teaching? If this means constructing a philosophical system, then this is something of which I am certainly incapable, and would not wish to do anyway. Yet we must have some kind of philosophy to support our practical work, and our capacity for discrimination.

By 'philosophy' here, it will be obvious, I mean something different from the critical dissection of terms and logic which is the basis of academic Western philosophy today. I invoke Husserl's injunction to philosophy, to pursue something to believe in, and to pick up the telos of Greek thought. However, such an emphasis must seem unfashionable in today's climate, even in education. But, again, we may find support from a distinguished mind. Professor E.A. Burtt declares that one of the worst diseases of our time is 'moral relativism' (humanities projects today even demand the 'neutral teacher'.) The idea that intelligent discrimination between values can fill no positive rôle, says Burtt, is one of the saddest superstitions that have found currency among educated people. In his book Burtt tries to open up a path from moral relativism beyond moral nihilism guided by the vision of a truly ultimate value – a 'value that is universal while making full room for variety, all-encompassing and yet dynamic, free from dynamic pretensions and thus ever open to revision'. (p.xv).

As Burtt himself points out later, the self-correcting process involved in the quest for philosophical understanding will never come to an end – this was Heidegger's opinion. And as for existentialism itself, Burtt seems to agree with Kierkegaard that the true aim of an existentialist is 'not to convert others but to encourage them to embark on a quest for their own self-realization' (p.92). In the work of Viktor Frankl and Abraham Maslow, we have seen that this quest to fulfil one's potentialities is only to be pursued in the serving of one's 'life-tasks'. This raises, in turn, of course, the question as to whether 'society', or one's civilization at large, can provide sufficient opportunity for this kind of fulfilment, and in this our conclusions may be revolutionary: here there are many political implications which are truly radical.

But now it is time to turn to the practice of English.

# III

*English for Meaning in Practice*

# Chapter Seven

# *Teaching Poetry*

Polanyi speaks of the *'ineffable domain'* where the tacit component predominates. By 'tacit' he means all those elements in our being which lie below explicit knowledge, but on which this knowledge depends – the shadowy, unspeakable areas of body-life, personal history, memory, experience, readiness to act, intentionality, feeling for interaction with the world, which we use continually, but cannot fully articulate.

So it is useful to put poetry first in English, because it is a constant reminder of all that is ineffable. This does not mean that what is ineffable may not be discussed. For this, however, we need better disciplines than the weak kind of theorizing that lies behind the Bullock Report and linguistics. We must try to give a phenomenological account of what happens in English, attending to what happens in consciousness, in both teacher and taught. The account is best given by demonstration, and I shall discuss four examples in the next four chapters. First, I shall take some poems by Edward Thomas, to try to show how poetry can create meanings, and how the teaching of poetry can convey those 'existentialist' meanings to the pupil's sensibility. Secondly, I shall discuss creative writing with 11-year-olds, and thirdly the writing of poetry with 16-year-olds, discussing both experiences in 'whole' terms, of cultural response and 'the living principle' of engagement with experience. Finally I shall discuss how the teaching of the novel *Great Expectations* can be an existential act, concerned with true and false self, and true and false solutions to the problems of life. There are, of course, those who do not like this kind of approach to English, or indeed to any of the arts. They believe that English should concern itself only with structure and form, with the aesthetic beauty of works of art, or 'language use', or whatever. They distrust 'moral' or 'religious' approaches. But this is to separate art into a compartment, by a dead and arid aestheticism. When we are deeply moved, to tears perhaps, by Mahler's Tenth Symphony, or by a Mozart ensemble in one of his operas, or are moved by Berthe Morisot's drawing of a child to feelings of deep joy, or are transfixed in anguish (even though we are not Christians) by Bach's *St. Matthew Passion* – what is it that is so deeply stirring us? Are there separate, aesthetic emotions, which are not the same as those which trouble us in bereavement or love? Of course, we are not standing alongside the Cross as an actual Saviour is dying: of course, we are not actually watching the funeral of a fireman in New York, and experiencing feelings of overwhelming gratitude, as Mahler was, at a moment in the composition of the Tenth Symphony. But the symbols of the music (or poetry) create in us meanings which can be related to those 'real' modes of consciousness and body-life in which, too, we have our actual emotional being. And while we may not share Bach's joyful anguish over the death of Jesus, what we do most certainly feel is that human acts and the individual tragedy of every life have a significance which is not swept away by death. When I say tragedy I mean this in a positive sense, for the point of a tragedy is not that the protagonist dies by the consequences of his 'fate', but that in the acts that lead to his death, and in the response of those around him, ultimate *meanings* are created which we may universally uphold against death and nothingness. Thus, tragedy has something to do with time, and being: 'being-unto-death' and the *Dasein*. The meanings created by the work of art about mythical or imaginary events by evoking emotions embodied in a fictitious work endure: and they endure as meanings to have their effect in our real life-and-death existence.

These questions may perhaps be discussed with immediacy and directness here, around some poems of Edward Thomas. If I refer to some poems by this distinguished artist, I may be able to make my points more concretely, and also, because his poems are so simple and direct, I shall be able to show how the general approach I am emphasizing can be put directly into practice in English teaching. Here I pick up from what I said above about *Tall Nettles*.

Discussing the strains within the European consciousness, Rollo May says that in 1914, the human world, in a sense, broke down altogether – and, I believe, our consciousness at large has not yet recovered from this overwhelming catastrophe. Edward Thomas is not, in his poetry, suffering immediate extinction daily, as was Isaac Rosenberg. But Thomas's poetry can only be understood in the face of that Great War, and the menace if offered to the young man, and to the whole society in which he lived. (He died at last, of course, in the trenches, in 1918.) The huge losses of men in the face of the machine-gun and artillery barrage not only threatened death: they also threatened meaning systems, because the individual seemed to count for nothing, since such hordes of men were sacrificed for nothing – literally, as we know from Robert Graves's *Goodbye to All That* – sacrificed for odd stretches of ruined countryside, often only a few hundred yards wide, and lost again next day.[1] To the individual young man, the Great War threatened almost certain extinction. And the more sensitive could detect in it portents of even more terrible forms of annihilation and denial of the individual life in the mass catastrophe, such as we have experienced in our time since. All those forms of collapse of meaning and values which Nietzsche foresaw were inherent in the madness of the Western Front. *On Receiving News of the War*, 1914, Isaac Rosenberg wrote:

> . . . Some spirit old
> Hath turned with malign kiss
> Our lives to mould.
>
> Red fangs have torn His face.
> God's blood is shed.
> He mourns from His lone place
> His children dead.
>
> O! ancient crimson curse!
> Corrode, consume.
> Give back this universe
> Its pristine bloom.

> *Complete Poems*, p.127

It is as if, immediately he heard about the war, Rosenberg realized that he was going to die and the world was going to be overwhelmed by corruption. So, we should look at Edward Thomas's poems in the light of this kind of dread – a dread that is clear from *As the Team's Headbrass*, discussed below.

There is another problem with Edward Thomas, which we understand better today, from psychoanalysis, and that is his

---

[1] Not that in itself this was new: Cf *War and Peace*. The scale and impersonality, however, were different: the machine gun was one technological 'advance' which brought into war a new mass element of stasis and futility.

depression. He would sometimes go off for days walking on the
downs, as a fit of depression gripped him. At the deepest level,
depression marks a failure to solve the *Dasein*-problem. It seems, in
the light of the work of Melanie Klein, to be a state of mind which
arises from guilt, at the possible consequences of one's hate of
the mother as original object in infancy. The infant feels he may have
created an emptiness within the mother's body and being: in return,
there is a threat of emptiness within, a triumph of nothingness. It
seems in a state of depression that love cannot be exercised, and
nothing can be created. What might have been created is meaning, as
established between two human beings who 'meet' and confirm one
another. But in depression it seems that this bridge cannot be
established, and so there can be no meaning in life.

In his poems, then, Edward Thomas is often struggling both against
the overwhelming nothingness inherent in the world at War, and
against the inward failure to achieve meaning, despite the love that
surrounded him, of which we know from his wife's lovely and deeply
sincere autobiographical works. The sense of nothingness haunts his
poems:

> How dreary-swift, with naught to travel to
> Is Time . . .

This is from *The Glory*, and we may as well begin with this poem
(p.64) in which he records the conflict, of realizing that beautiful
things are all around him, but he cannot be happy, cannot get to the
meaningful centre of things:

> I cannot bite the day to the core . . .

He knows the experience of love: he wants something beyond it. The
poem opens:

> The glory of the beauty of the morning, –
> The cuckoo crying over the untouched dew;
> The blackbird that has found it, and the dove;
> That tempts me on to something sweeter than love;
> White clouds ranged even and fair as new-mown hay;
> The heat, the stir, the sublime vacancy
> Of sky and meadow and forest and my own heart . . .

The glory invites him, yet 'it leaves me scorning'

    All I can ever do, all I can be . . .

It seems as if the *Dasein*-problem cannot be solved. He seeks a happiness he fancies fit to dwell in beauty's presence, as if he felt guilty that he was not as happy as the beauty around him should make him. How shall he find this appropriate beauty? In exercising his creative power, what he significantly brings out is a certain kind of attention to the immediate foreground: the immediate, commonplace, natural world at his feet:

>                 Shall I now this day
> Begin to seek as far as heaven, as hell,
> Wisdom or strength to match this beauty, start
> And tread the pale dust pitted with small dark drops,
> In hope to find whatever it is I seek,
> Hearkening to short-lived, happy-seeming things
> That we know naught of, in the hazel-copse?

He seems to be seeking vainly for something he can encounter, can feel, and grasp, so that he can be at home in the universe. Knowing that he suffered depression, I would say in the light of psycho-analytical insights that he is seeking to find the mother's body, and to find that kind of reciprocal encounter between I and Thou which gives existential security: then he could establish a sense of meaningful being. But he is threatened with plunging hopelessly, into heaven or hell: how shall he hold his world together, so that he can feel the happiness he knows should be possible on such a glorious morning?

The answer is, by grasping the short-lived immediate things, and this attention yields the lovely line:

> And tread the pale dust pitted with small dark drops . . .

The dust here is like the dust in the poem *Tall Nettles*, which we have examined as a symbol. There, the dust 'proves' the sweetness of a

E

shower, and here too the dust shows the impression of a spring shower, making its print in the soil. But those drops also seem like drops of sweat or blood, from some anguish of suffering like Christ's. Dust settles over a long period, and so speaks of time and death. But, spotted with the dark drops of a shower, it also speaks of the renewal of life and continuity, of refreshment, and so brings an attachment to the immediacy of the present moment, to 'life'. Often, in Edward Thomas, this grasp of the immediate moment is itself an assertion of being alive, against the threat of being swept away into nothingness, the 'sad waste of time, stretching before and after'. It would be possible, I believe, to show other poets striving with their depression in this way, essentially against being swept away by being-unto-death: Wordsworth, for instance in his lines about the spear-grass on the wall in *The Leech-Gatherer;* Crabbe, with his keen attention to the most humble weeds; and Coleridge in *Frost at Midnight* and *The Dejection Ode.*

When Crabbe is depicting the thistles which 'to the ragged infants threaten war' (but also thrive in the most sterile circumstances); when Wordsworth concentrates our attention on the rising spear-grass, or the bindweed dragging down a row of Margaret's peas, we have images of continuity – of life going on. And it is this earnest of life continuing that helps overcome the depressive's fear that life will collapse or come to an end, because of a failure of the creative process. Depression arises from a fear that the normal methods by which we stay in existence, and by which others stay in existence, must fail. We cannot exist without the I-Thou relationship, and if it breaks down totally, then we are doomed. This is the (depressive) theme of *The Ancient Mariner.* The world is devastated by an offence to the world as Thou: and then comes the ensuing guilt. The crisis comes when, out from the protagonist, streams the life-giving reparative impulse, by which he *loves* the water-snakes unawares. When love becomes possible like that, then reparation becomes possible: the world is restored from the destruction that menaces it from the emotional failure, at the deepest subjective level. The failure of the reparative impulse threatens a loss of meaning, which is why people in a depressed state are so blank (and sometimes suicidal). The restoration of the capacity to love and give can bring a feeling that the world is restored (as in *The Ancient Mariner*) and so the normal processes of feeling meaningful in it can go on: 'peak moments' are possible again, bringing their earnest that life is worth living. In *Frost at Midnight*

Coleridge speaks of how his child's relationship with the world shall not have the sterility of his own childhood, but in *his* world (which is clearly the Lake District) God shall, 'by giving', make the child's soul 'ask'. What he imagines for his child is a relationship between self and the world which is rich with 'creative reflection', and the product of this is not only good and secure relationship, but rich meanings, too.

When Edward Thomas concentrates on lowly corners, what we have in his poem is an intense concentration of *consciousness*. As with the 'pale dust pitted with small dark drops', he attaches his concentration to things clearly seen which yield a strong immediate sense of being alive. The dark drops are like spots of blood, and the very suffering is itself, like Christ's, both a consequence and an earnest of *being alive*. These moments are yet, as in Crabbe and often in Wordsworth, the most commonplace and mean experiences of the most humble and ordinary objects. The deduction seems to be that if these weeds and wretched poor people can survive, then I can: if these can go on tenaciously living, so can I. More glamorous or rich objects might generate problems of envy, for the most terrible aspect of the failure of reparation in the depressive position is envy, which, because of the failure of the processes of 'finding' and love, can threaten to overwhelm the whole world, and reduce it to nothing. Humble things evoke from one's own humility a gratitude simply to be alive, thankful for the smallest mercies.

As he tells us in *The Glory* he can be happiest with the simplest manifestations of life. Yet he sips at that life with a deep and secure gratitude for its on-going tenacity however poor and lowly it is. This relish for intensely meaningful weeds generates the sounds in the poem, the gentle labials (flower/lost) the 'st' sounds, and the alliteration of 'sweetness . . . shower' – which actually takes us back to the opening of *The Canterbury Tales* and that spring of our literature: and to the coming of new life and meaning, as in April.

Even simple poems like *The Glory* and *Tall Nettles* could, I believe, be related to some of the toughest passages in existential and phenomenological writing. (They could certainly be related to the anguish in *Das Lied Von Das Erde*). The new approach to consciousness in these disciplines has brought a new sense of time. Here the chapter to read is that on 'temporality', in Maurice Merleau-Ponty's *The Phenomenology of Perception:* 'Time is, therefore, not a real process, not an actual succession that I am content to record. It arises from *my* relation to things.' Time, in this sense, is the time of the meanings of my consciousness, not an 'out there' process to which I have to abandon my own experience of time. Merleau-Ponty speaks poetically, of 'instances of now'. Edward Thomas's poems are 'instances of now'. A great deal of psychological discussion of time says Merleau-Ponty tries to reduce our experience to a natural science time which belongs to the material world, so that cause and effect can be studied. But what matters to us is the time of the 'I' experiences, and this is bound up with 'lines of intentionality which trace out in advance at least the style of what is to come . . .' (p.416). Here again we have the problem, that certain forms of 'objective' or positivist psychology taught to student teachers may well reduce their capacities to experience intentionality, in their thinking about the self in time. Their 'psychology' lectures may even reduce their capacity to respond to a poet like Edward Thomas, whose poems emerge from his groping at creative intentionality, at possible meanings to be brought into being, from the unprepossessing, from the seemingly doomed, moment. By contrast we need a creative psychology which can make us appreciate writers like Thomas More. This is just what Merleau-Ponty's kind of phenomenology does:

> Husserl, says Merleau-Ponty, uses the terms protensions and retentions for the intentionalities which anchor me to an environment. They do not run from a central I, but from my perceptual field itself, so to speak, which draws along in its wake its own horizon of retentions, and bites into the future with its protensions.

This could be applied I believe, to a poem we shall look at below, Edward Thomas's *Old Man*. We would do well to ponder Thomas's poems alongside some of Merleau-Ponty's observations about creativity in time: 'Subjectivity is not in time, because it takes up or lives through time, and merges with the cohesion of a life' (p.422).

Edward Thomas, faced with loss of meaning, created an immediate sense of meaningful existing, and of 'biting into the future', trying to establish a sense of the 'cohesion of his life', drawing intentionalities out of the moment of consciousness. That sentence may sound angular, but I am trying to bring together a new way of talking in philosophy, and Thomas's simple and direct poetry. He uses the same word, is speaking of 'biting the day to the core'. What he establishes above all, in the body of his work, is the continuity of a consciousness, that 'lives through time', and 'merges with the cohesion of a life' – that is *his* life. And, as with Rosenberg's trench poems, it is the unique quality of that life which is established – which nothing, neither Armageddon nor the collapse of consciousness in our time, can eradicate. In both these poets we have an astonishing existential achievement. (See my comments on Rosenberg's *Break of Day in the Trenches,* in *Lost Bearings in English Poetry.*)

All this can be made clear by a discussion of the poem *Old Man* (p.104), one of Edward Thomas's most successful poems. This poem will help me show what I mean when I say that English has to do with the creation of meaning. Such a poem could not be appreciated in the atmosphere of analytical philosophy: Leavis is right in suggesting that philosophy seminars on such lines would do nothing for English students. By contrast, this poem, while being deeply philosophical in Roger Poole's sense[1], shows clearly that any attempt to set up an intellectual system, or to clarify meaning beyond a certain point is futile, because there is always an area in our consciousness which is inaccessible:

Only an avenue, dark, nameless without end . . .

Consciousness exists only in a body, which has a history going back to the experience of birth, even to pre-birth experience, and to those dark days of early infancy, where many experiences (like birth itself) are gone through, many of which cannot be remembered, yet some of which affect our lives throughout our future existence. Both in these unconscious experiences, and in conscious ones, the 'names' of things, the words we use to explore and express our world, only partially find them, only lamely attach themselves to things, are not the things, so the poem is about the intractability of language as much as anything:

Old Man, or Lad's-love, – in the name there's nothing
To one that knows not Lad's-love, or Old Man
The hoar-green feathery herb, almost a tree,
Growing with rosemary and lavender.
Even to one that knows it well, the names

---

[1] Of each person being entitled to his 'philosophical space'.

Half decorate, half perplex, the thing it is:
At least, what that is clings not to the names
In spite of time. And yet I like the names.

The names condition one's responses to the thing: the thing it is clings
not to the names, however long one has known the plant. There is the
experience itself, which is embodied, and rooted in consciousness and
memory, and this I-the-thing experience is repeated every time one
shrivels and sniffs a leaf.

The poet sinks deeper and deeper into perplexities: he doesn't like
the herb: but he loves it. He loves it, as he loves the nettles, for the way
in which it evokes strong feelings of continuity – and takes him back to
his childhood. That is, it helps him feel the 'cohesion' of his life. Here
love is associated with guilt – there is a forbidding figure, which,
actually, to the child, is himself, but which, in the depths of memory,
is evidently associated with deep feelings of meaning, at-oneness and
the need for significance: and guilt. Using phenomenological
disciplines, I want to try to pursue the deeper meaning at which he is
grasping here. As I do so, I risk disturbing the reader. (In the
educational setting, I would have to be careful about such depth
analysis. I might pursue this investigation of symbolism with under-
graduates, but not with children at school, for instance.)

In this area, I believe that the scent which he finds so evocative is
the smell of the mother's body experienced as an infant, it could also
be, taking in insights from Melanie Klein and Winnicott, the
experience of parental sexuality. The forbidding figure is a parental
figure and emerges from feeling about love. The erotic content of the
name cannot be denied: the 'folk' call the plant Lad's love, because its
feathery flower is like a young man's beard, or like an old man's thin
beard. While this suggests time at the ordinary poetic level, it also
suggests by displacement pubic hair. There is a suggestion of this in
the folk name 'Lad's *love*', and there is a suggestion that this love is
very evanescent and not very well sustained, in its sexuality.

Dimly, in the background to Edward Thomas's fascination with
this plant, then, is the infant perplexity about parental sexuality, and
about the relationship between this and his own love for the feel and
smell of the mother's body. We may relate this to his depression, for
the guilt and dread which torment the depressive individual arise from
concern about fantasies about the mother's body, about her possible
vengeance to be taken by the parents, in response to the infant's

involvement in parental sexuality. Thus behind the poem is a dreadful figure, menacing the unconscious mind with annihilation: in Melanie Klein's language it is the Castrating Mother, or Combined Parents. The 'low thick bush beside the door', in psychoanalytical terms, is the mother's public hair hiding the entrance to the womb: the deeper levels of body-mind experience to which he yearns is full of threats of annihilation, and thus the word 'nothing' recurs, while a sense of nameless dread remains. The dread is of the nothingness overwhelming him from those images, and when he thinks of nothing, and the child thinks of nothing, they are not only unable to bring anything into focus (it is deeply suppressed) but they are troubled by the possibility of nothingness itself, of being brought to nothingness by some nameless threat.

The identification with the child is important, here, because that takes him at least half way back to the source of his fascination with the evocative scent.

But also, of course, it establishes a sense of time that 'arises from my relationship to things' and to overthrow the tyranny of time as it comes to us from natural science. The child is both him in the past, and the child-part of him, now; and then, as the child grows up in his imagination, the child in the future as he is now in the future, in relationship to himself as a child in the past. And what the verse 'does' as well as 'says' is to enact the puzzlement of consciousness reflecting on itself:

> Often she waits there, snipping the tips and shrivelling
> The shreds at last on the path, perhaps
> Thinking, perhaps of nothing, till she sniffs
> Her fingers and runs off . . .
>          As for myself
> Where first I met the bitter scent is lost.
> I, too, often shrivel the grey shreds,
> Sniff them and think and sniff again and try
> Once more to think what it is I am remembering.
> Always in vain.

The word to bring in here, perhaps, is Merleau-Ponty's 'ante-predicative', which indicates shadowy apprehensions we have of things emerging into consciousness, before we can express them in a predicated way; and also Polanyi's concept of 'tacit' knowledge.

Thomas's poem makes it quite clear that we do have important, continuing, and central experiences which we cannot cover by naming, to which names can only 'cling', that cannot be expressed except by the virtually unspeakable. Moreover, these ungraspable and inexplicit forms of knowing ourselves and the world can be centrally meaningful in our lives:

> Yet I would rather give up others
> > more sweet,
> With no meaning, than this bitter one . . .

If, 'English' has to do with *meaning*, then many of the kinds of meaning with which it deals may well be meanings that cannot be expressed, except in art which records the awareness of their existence, without being able to define them. This lovely poem, with all its concreteness of attention is the symbol-plant, is about *not being able to formulate a meaning* which is primary in the man's life:

> I have mislaid the key. I sniff the spray
> And think of nothing: I see and I hear nothing
> For what I should, yet never can, remember:
> No garden appears, no path, no hoar-green bush
> Of Lad's-love, or Old Man, no child beside,
> Neither father nor mother, nor any playmate;
> Only an avenue, dark, nameless, without end . . .

And this avenue not only leads down to the primitive experiences, perhaps pre-natal ones, but it also leads forward, to his death, where the primal unconsciousness ends in the final unconsciousness. The poet thus links the nothingness out of which we come with the nothingness into which we go. And yet, in the poem, he establishes a sense of meaning, because nothing is more human than thinking like this about the unthinkable, and unrealizable, in response to an intense scent, that itself, with the energy of consciousness it invokes, makes us feel tremendously alive. Though the poem is very much about 'thinking of nothing', it has the effect of making us feel significantly alive. It is in this that its *Dasein*-quality lies, for though it contemplates 'being unto death' it also gives us the delights of being perplexed by this predicament. It records the perplexed moment, but just as the child's future is cherished, the perplexity itself is cherished – and this is symbolized by the ambiguities of not liking the plant, yet loving it: liking the names, but find them unsatisfactory; being baffled by the scent, but being less willing to give up others than this bitter baffling one. What the poet loves is *being alive*, and being perplexed by the *Dasein* problem, of what to set against nothingness: this enactment of the steps of the inquiring consciousness, moving through the labyrinths of less conscious, and some unconscious, memories, takes us into the life of the inquiring mind, than which there is no greater gift. While it is very exacting for us to elicit all these meanings, if we teach the poem, children will 'get' them. All we have to do is to read them the poem aloud!

It is unnecessary to emphasize the importance in Thomas's world of love, and the way in which the meaning of his existence is related to love. Take, for example, *The Mill Pond* (p.68). Here again we have a play with time: he knows the girl now, and perhaps he is married to her. She is constantly good and kind, over a long period. But the warning she gave him was about a momentary shower, coming on for a moment one summer day. There are portents of this imminent shower. But these are unheard by him as, carelessly and timelessly, he is 'absent':

> As my feet dangling teased the foam
> That slid below . . .

Her warning made him 'angry'. He was attached to the flowing moment. There are images of momentary things – the flickering wagtail, the pigeons cooing (in alders that 'shiver'), the 'scared starlings in the aspen tip' obviously going away any second. The water is 'teased' and slides away like Time.

But what the poem leaves in us is a sense of suspended time, in the heat, with birds flickering and water sliding, when the self is absorbed in sensuous sounds and feelings (blazing sun, feet dangling in the foam) so that one is careless of reality. The girl seems to realize this, and warns him about the approaching reality – but he is angry. But then he has to crouch:

> Then the storm burst, and I crouched
> To shelter, how
> Beautiful and kind, too, she seemed
> As she does now!

She seems beautiful and kind because she broke through to him, shattering his idyllic dream, warning him about the reality and danger. The poem is very much like some of Thomas Hardy's, being about a momentary experience to which the essence of 'meeting' is embodied: and with that meeting of one with another, a moment of meaning, established in the immediacy of the surroundings and the mood. There is a triumph over time, over its sliding away, and over the menace symbolized by the thunder's boom.

In Thomas's poems, moods are pursued and followed through with such exactitude that he enhances immediately a triumphant feeling of *being alive* in the here and now, despite the underlying themes of sorrow and dread which are often there as well. He is struggling often against going out of existence, and these feelings have the deepest unconscious roots – exacerbated by the doom-laden atmosphere of the time. In the face of these threats from within and without, he asserts the *Dasein,* which is also to say, in my terms, that he asserts 'meaning' which Leavis, I suppose, might put in terms of asserting *'life'. As The Team's Headbrass* (p.29) is another poem that makes all these elements clear: it begins

> As the team's head-brass flashed out on the turn
> The lovers disappeared into the wood.

At the end,

> The lovers came out of the wood again:
> The horses started . . .

The lovers represent continuity, creative life, and the whole conversation takes place against their background, of their creative secrecy in the wood.

The major natural object in the scene is a fallen elm, felled by a blizzard.

> The ploughman said, 'when will they take it away?'
> 'When the war's over.' . . .

So, while the lovers pause momentarily in the wood, and the ploughman pauses momentarily to talk to the poet, there is a longer pause – that of the suspension of normal life, until the end of the war. The poet sits in the crest of the fallen tree: an image just enough to suggest the topsy-turvy state of the world. And again we have contrasts of time:

> One minute and an interval of ten,
> A minute more and the same interval.
> 'Have you been out?' 'No.' 'And don't want to, perhaps?'
> 'If I could only come back again, I should.
> I could spare an arm. I shouldn't want to lose
> A leg. If I should lose my head, why, so,
> I should want nothing more . . .' 'Have many gone
> From here?' 'Yes'. 'Many lost?' 'Yes, a good few . . .'

Of one of his mates, the ploughman says, 'if/He had stayed here we should have moved the tree.' 'And I should not have sat here':

> 'Everything
> Would have been different. For it would have been
> Another world.'

Again, we have an intense concentration on the actual living moment, while undercurrents beneath are full of madness and dread, as manifest in that 'I should want nothing more . . .' Yet even in this same poem, there is both a *Dasein* quality, the fact of *being there:* and the intentional – a pointing forward, to the lovers' future, to the tree being moved at last, to the possibility at least of another possible world. And another quiet contribution to the record of being alive: as Merleau-Ponty says, 'We have been concerned with gaining an understanding of the relationship between consciousness and nature, between inside and outside ourselves' (p.427) – and it is exactly this kind of philosophical exploration of the nature of being towards which Edward Thomas contributes.

I have been writing in the last few pages for my reader who is perhaps a teacher, or a student teacher, or a lecturer in a college or department of education. But is it possible to communicate the 'existential' qualities of such poetry to pupils? This is, of course, a problem each teacher must solve in his own way. But because we recognize and accept the tacit elements in English, all our exegesis should enable us to feel more confidence, that all we have to do is to read the poem to children and, by asking a few simple questions about meanings, help them to possess it, as a work of art. A child who is thrilled or moved by a poem of Edward Thomas's will possess, 'tacitly' at least, something of the existential issues I raise imperfectly and explicitly in this chapter.

# Chapter Eight

# *Poetry from Eleven-year-olds*

On a fine winter afternoon, while writing this book, I go to spend an afternoon teaching my small son's class in Stapleford Community School. His teacher has asked me to read the children my own poems and then to try to get them to write poems. They have had a visiting poet before (Edward Storey), and they wrote poems for him. But they have never spent a whole hour concentrating on writing a poem until now. This we are going to do, after break-time. I am very nervous, and I read them a selection of my poems and lyrics, including *Bowling for a Pig*.

Here I shall quote some of the poems which I read them, and then discuss the poems they wrote for me. I shall try to say what good this afternoon of 'English' was. The lesson was the kind of thing that goes on day after day, hour after hour, in school. My good fortune is that I can stand aside and look at my two hours' teaching like a novelist – and, I hope, like a phenomenologist. If I do so, what emerge pre-eminently are the tacit elements: the elements which could never be reduced to the explicit validations of the positivist psychologists and linguists. My experience makes sense in relation to many of the general human observations in *The Bullock Report:* it makes no sense at all in relation to the Report's proposed courses in linguistics and language learning, or its attempts to pin down 'English' to the intellectual analysis of the linguists. I am concerned with the criss-cross of utterance between us' and the free play of imagination, beyond the words.

Let me start, indeed, from the artefacts as I have them. Where do the poems exist? I have a bundle of pieces of exercise paper, on which are written two dozen poems. They are the outcome of the lesson. What else remains? What remains in the children's memories (and mine) is a recollection of that afternoon when Mr. Holbrook (who is Tom's father and lives up the hill) came and talked to us. When I meet anyone from class JE, they smile, or look at me in an inquiring way: and this smile or look means, 'I remember you. You read us your poems. I laughed at one, but it turned out to be sad. Then we wrote poems. Do you remember it? I'm Janice Crofton.'

All that is conveyed in a flash of facial recognition, a flicker of the eyes. And if I think of the human encounter, in all its complexities, I am on the way to writing a book. A novel could be written around this one afternoon. This would require an account of the village, which is both an old traditional farming village with a strong sense of community, and also a suburb full of very well-off, professional, middle-class people, most of them working in Cambridge. It would require an account of the school, which is an extremely good one. Actually, the best way of indicating this would be a description of a single public occasion, such as a Maypole dancing put on for parents, which I have just seen. The infants and 'primary' children sat round in a square, with the teachers among them, and a few parents in a row. It was a warm day in May. The bodies of the children were relaxed, and the general feeling was one of peacefulness, of being at home. They were fidgety and lively, of course, but it was astonishing that a hundred children should sit so happily at ease, to watch with interest the dancing teams weaving in and out of their ribbons.

There was no trouble. While I was there not one child had to be 'corrected' or admonished. The teachers, who were also relaxed and calm, talked among themselves, or to the children. When they did, the conversation was about the weather, flowers, vegetables, dancing, the last concert, the swimming pool and other school events. The children spoke respectfully but intimately to the teachers, and smiled or winked cheerfully to their parents. The entrance of the dancing teams and the music was stage-managed quietly and without shouting or bossiness of any kind, by the headmaster, a middle-aged Yorkshire-man of great patience. The keynote of the afternoon was a great feeling of calm, even though here were a hundred lively small children, watching the vigorous teams of dancers. Among these were a handful of girls who were already becoming young women: yet they were still totally absorbed in being children, dancing as children, displaying on their faces a trustful innocence which echoed the fatherly care and attention on the faces of the men and women teachers. To watch them was to watch a community whose contribution to 'society' is immense – by ineffable dynamics. There was a concern on the part of the dancers to please and amaze (as when the ribbons were all wound up –

would they ever unwind?). The audience was deeply engaged in responding, in pleasing the dancers by their attention (and their happy applause). The air was full of care and affection: nothing disturbed the sense of belonging, of human meeting. It was an enrichening experience for us, the parents, and stood for everything that may be set against the destructiveness and inhumanity that fills the news pages and television screens today.

To say as much is to open up these things we take for granted, like the very good school which these teachers have created.[1] When there is so much talk of a decline in educational standards, here, as in so many schools, we have the highest possible achievement in the State system – drawing out in the child a rich sense of human value, and great effectiveness. My two hours took place, then, in the context of all this, and of the school's excellent English teaching.

At first, I was a nervous middle-aged poet, 'Tom's Daddy', in his best suit, come to read his poems. Gradually I could feel, the children liked some of the poems, especially *Bowling for a Pig* and a funny one about a railway porter who dreams of saving a ship by being a courageous and efficient radio operator. But I made a mistake in playing them some songs of mine set to music by a young Swedish 'folk-pop' composer: the mechanical operation broke the 'spell'.

After a while I began to enjoy myself, not least because of that magic: the teacher casts a kind of spell over the children. I was aware of that as I exercised my powers to cast it, and I recognized it as a version of the state of 'primary maternal preoccupation' which develops in the mother, to enable her to respond to her baby's emerging self and the potentialities of the self. The form teacher of the class I was teaching sat there exerting her spell over them too – a handsome married woman, she radiated happiness and sympathy from her smile. She can be stern: but the atmosphere she establishes is one of calm security – and trust. So, I can work very quickly in this atmosphere – moving rapidly towards my aim.

I begin by reading the children a number of poems and passages from *English in Australia Now*. Deliberately, I chose poems written by children who had not written any poetry before. Moreover, they illustrate how children can organize words with simple directness to be very effective – effective, however, in communicating subjective experience. 'Communicating' isn't quite the right word either, because the poems bring experience to life in us:

---

[1] Stapleford Community School, near Cambridge.

> Old shoes
> that live on shelves
> are usually eaten
> eaten by the moths in deathly hush
> at night

What is this about? Mutability: all the time, things are gradually decaying, wearing away. The child is aware of this, and is dreadfully troubled when it finds a maggot in a peapod, or a hole eaten in a woolly cardigan in the clothes cupboard. Moths don't in fact eat shoes: and shoes aren't 'usually' eaten. So, the poem is a dream fantasy – the literary parallel is that strange central episode in *To The Lighthouse:*

> So with the house empty and the doors locked and the mattresses rolled around, those stray airs, advance guards of great armies, blustered in, brushed bare boards, nibbled and fanned, met nothing in bedroom or drawing room that wholly resisted them but only hangings that flapped, wood that creaked, the bare legs of tables, saucepans and china already furred, tarnished, cracked. What people had shed and left – a pair of shoes, a shooting cap, some faded shirts and coats in wardrobes – those alone kept the human shape and in the emptiness indicated how one's hands were busy with hooks and buttons; how once the looking glass had held a face . . .
>
> *Everyman* edition, p.149

The teacher who has read Virginia Woolf will recognize that the child who wrote 'Old shoes' is pondering the passage of time in a poetic way. Once upon a time the shoes were 'filled and animated': now they 'live on shelves': the word 'usually' picks up an ambiguity from the word 'live'. The child remembers the mother's voice, perhaps, using the word 'ironically': 'what usually happens when you come in is that you leave your muddy boots outside the pantry door: usually I fall over them!' So 'usually' here has an ironic quality: 'if you leave shoes in a cupboard, what usually happens is that they begin to decay or get merged into the flux of disintegration'. Mutability is *usual*, and when *use* is at an end, another *usual* process begins (that is a quite commonplace process begins) of things returning to dust: things become 'furred, tarnished, cracked' – 'faded'. These processes go on, in the 'deathly hush' of night.

> . . . Will you fade? Will you perish? . . . Once only a board sprang
> on the landing: once in the middle of the night with a roar, with a
> rupture, as after centuries of quiescence a rock rends itself from
> the mountains and hurtles crashing into the valley, once a fold of
> the shawl loosened and swung to and fro.
>
> *To The Lighthouse*, p.150

Those who are hostile to my kind of attention to such a small poem
accuse me of finding 'too much in it'. But I am convinced by the
rhythm, by the arrangement of the words into their lines: for this
reason, I reproduce the poem in facsimile in *English in Australia Now*,
to make it plain that this *art* is no accident – there the poem is in all its
innocence of scrawly handwriting. Rhythmically and in its 'form' it is
perfect.

But my attention is beyond the words. What I am attending to is the
child's act of consciousness. He or she is aware that the world in which
we bodily exist is continually in flux and decay: stealthily, things
almost steal away from us, in the deathly hush of night. This
disturbing truth of quotidien existence is explored by symbolism, in
such a child's poem, in its simple way. The child is on the way to

> Lay not up for yourselves treasures upon earth, where moth
> and rust doth corrupt . . . Take no thought for your life, what ye
> shall eat, or what ye shall drink; nor yet for your body, what ye
> shall put on. Is not the life more than meat, and the body than
> raiment?
>
> *Matthew*, 6, 19-25

That is, the child is on the way to understanding the Sermon on the
Mount: and in the area of asking those existential questions, 'What is it
to be human?' and 'What is the point of life?', through the word. This
first small poem is an act of entering on a whole field of philosophical
inquiry, into the nature of existence in time.

Our age, of course, is very frightened of such inquiry, since it
attaches the point of life to everything that Christ rejects in his
Sermon! It translates this Sermon into polite committee language, to
emasculate it, as in the *New English Bible:*

> Do not store up for yourselves treasure on earth, where it
> grows rusty and motheaten, and thieves break in to steal it . . .

therefore I bid you put away anxious thoughts about food and
drink to keep you alive, and clothes to cover your body. Surely
life is more than food, the body more than clothes?

*New English Bible*

Why alter the original work at all? Because the present age must
avoid the dreadful force of that 'corrupt'. In the modern version, the
disadvantage is that earthly treasure 'grows rusty' and motheaten! So
tenacious is our hold on materialism that the implication is that this
must somehow be stopped – the language does not now allow any
recognition that *all* wordly possessions must *absolutely* become
corrupt. 'Take no thought for your life' does not suit the double-
glazing and the Slumberland mattress: how could suburban people go
home to their comfy homes after hearing the Authorized Version
passage: 'is not the life more than meat and the body than raiment?'
The absoluteness has an ultimate existential force: what matters is that
which transcends bodily existence: 'take no thought for your life' today
means more than *getting rid of anxious thoughts,* as in therapy. But
what Jesus was trying to do was to get people to confront the *Dasein*
problem – the need to find a meaning that transcends all concerns with
food, clothes, treasure, decay or death. In the old Bible's emphasis we
move beyond anxious thoughts to existential dread, and towards a
sense of ultimate meaning that can triumph 'even if the world ends
tomorrow'. The New Bible dilutes the message, and removes the
ultimate element from its injunctions.

So far, I have discussed only five lines of a child's poem. But I am, I
hope, beginning to unfold the 'tacit' elements surrounding and
underlying what I call 'English for meaning'. In reading this poem to
the class I was doing many things all at once:

1.  I was showing by example how to speak poetry well and
    clearly – expecting others to hear and respond. Thus I was
    demonstrating effective language use, in intersubjectivity.
2.  I was showing my respect for the utterance of a child,
    hoping that this would establish me as an adult who was fit
    to accept their poems – that I was to be trusted.
3.  I was showing that what I was concerned with was
    symbolism, and the creative exploration of experience in
    such ways, not least by *words.*
4.  I was conveying to them that I was as much concerned with

the strange and shadowy areas of awareness, of the subjective realm, of dream and fantasy, of death, time,
nothingness and existence.

5.  I was conveying to them that I was not interested in
    impressing my taste upon them, or 'teaching them poetry',
    or training them to write, in some prescribed way, or being
    'élitist' or 'paternalist' (though I may have *paternal*, which
    is a very different thing.) What I wanted was to hear *their
    voice*, the voice of the emerging 'formative principle' of their
    true self dynamics. And I showed this by attending respect-
    fully to the voice of the child who wrote that poem:
    attending to the *meaning*.

I was probably doing many more things, of which I remain
unaware. Nothing I said or did has anything to do with explicit 'rules'.

This approach of course is well-documented in *English for the
Rejected*: each child discussed there displays an emerging voice, which
is not mine, nor imposed by me, though it emerges in the context of
my respect and expectancy.

Now I turn to the second poem I read the Stapleford children:

> Door chime
> Quick and powerful
> Aroused my fear of them
> And as I waited
> powerless
> They came . . .

In the facsimile, the careful placing of 'powerless' is clear: the first
word that came to the child writing, crossed out, was 'quietly'. How
much more memorable, this simple poem about nameless dread, than
the sensational photographs used in 'English' textbooks today,
showing riot squads or dead bodies in the street, by which the child is
likely to be overwhelmed with violent and shocking images.[1] What
matters after all is the child's capacity to come to terms with the world
of terror and pain and to place the dreadful aspects of experience in

---

[1] Looking through a series of such books I was quite stunned. In one there was actually a
series of pictures showing a Buddhist monk burning himself to death, while many other
pictures were quite devastating to the sensibility. One is left wondering what kind of
English teacher supposes it is beneficial to the imagination to use such images rather
than, say, the quiet poems of Han Shan, or Walter de la Mare.

such a way that they do not reduce his powers of living. He should become a stronger rather than more vulnerable, at the hands of the English teacher.

So, in reading this poem, I am conveying to them that I cherish the capacity to confront a fear, and hold it in place, as it were, for here the careful form of the poem holds the dread at bay, not least by the careful rhythm. I am also conveying to them that poetry deals with archetypal and universal experiences beyond the mundane. They would perhaps have less difficulty now with (say) this poem:

> *Dawn*
> Not knowing when the dawn will come
>     I open every door;
> Or has it feathers like a bird,
>     Or billows like a shore?
>
> Emily Dickinson

After the two poems, I read them a piece of prose, to show that I wasn't just expecting solemn and deep things – sometimes the piece one writes can be just a good entertaining yarn, to amuse others:

> *Family Matters*
> When I was three or four years old my mother on SATURDAY night always use to cook SPAGETTE and one night I took a string of spegete and put it on my desert spoon and flicked it at my dad's face and it landed on his nose he got angry and chased me into my parents bedroom and which side he be on I be on the opposite side. I ran to my mother and not behind her and then she turned against me and told me to go to my room so I did so. I loved climbing so I tried to get up on my wardrobe but it fell on top of me so I cried and my dad came in and put it straight and he told me to do something so I went to the bathroom and started to cry but nobody came in
>
> So then I went and watched a cowboy picture and the bad guy was shooting the good guy so I took my mum's best vase and through it at the tele and I don't remember any more and I don't think I like to.

And then I read another piece which was organized in its sequence rather more like poetry:

A Voice Boomed Out (p.79)

'All right who did it,' a voice boomed out
'Who ate that 2lb chocolate?'
Silence fell
No one stood up no-one murmured a word
One had a guilty conscience
One in a family of six
It did not want to murmur
It did not want to say
It did not want a thrashing –
So it began to pray
It sat in its seat so quiet
It did not want to say
It knew that if it was found out
Today there would be a fight – a big array
Of tears and shouting . . .
It just sat and hoped just hoped and prayed
That it would not be found out today.

And then, to put into the atmosphere a recognition of the 'tacit' elements of the human psyche, as from folksong, I read them the poem by a Greek girl in Australia, Julie's *Would I meet you Again:*

My thoughts . . .
They are coming back again
With meaning something,
And wishing at the same time,
Under trees and rocks,
I am looking for you,
Youliana.

Dry rivers
Are wetted from the rain
Would I see you again
In some dreams
Like you're alive again
With all your clothes torn,
And through your fingers
Red lights shining.

Are you alive?

Or is your heart cold?
    Youliana
The night is so dark
I can feel your heavy steps
From underground.
    Youliana.

Near some dead fire,
With white hair on your head
And wrinkles on your face
You'll wait for me,
    Youliana.

I told them these were the best poems by children I brought back from Australia. Then I said to the children that we would now have a quiet half-hour, during which they could write their own poems, on any subject. The only things they asked were whether they were to write on paper or in their books, and whether they were to write on both sides of the paper.

There was no discussion of poetic 'technique': there did not need to be, for my examples made it clear how words could be used with great effectiveness by children, some of whom had never written poems before. There was no explicitness about 'poetic words', or the 'special use of words in poetry', or about rhythm – these points being made tacitly by the poems I had read. He who hath ears to hear let him hear! So, what I had created in the first hour was an *expectancy* on my part, a readiness to receive: and an assertion of my own trustworthiness – or so I hoped.

When I collect up the little sheaf of poems at the end I wonder, what more could anyone do? At the time there is the 'great debate' on education, and everyone is expressing concern about whether children are being taught a sufficiently 'standard' good English, to enable them to cope with our sophisticated technological world. If this school is representative, there is no problem: the poems I took home were all excellent examples of fluency. And if children can write *poetry* as well as this, we need have no anxiety about how they cope with the 'language demands' of commerce and industry: that is, 'prose' will be no problem.

What 'language learning' could generate a better flow of English well-used than my 'open-ended' poetry lesson?

Take the first poem I pick up:

> The volcano erupts
> A loud steady roar, audible for miles,
> The ash covers the land and sky like
>                     a thick, wooly robe
> A red flow pours down and cocoons the
>                     village
> In a thick layer of rock for ever,
> The noise dies down
> A few more rocks and ashes
> Then silence.
>
>                               Tony Sinister

He spells one word wrong, *woolly*, but he uses correctly and spells correctly *erupts, audible* and *cocoons*. His vision of a Pompeii disaster is vivid, and he used rhythm to convey the shape of the dreadful event. What more could one ask for? *This is simply good English.* From my point of view, in many of the poems there is not a word out of place.

> *Old Man*
> Old man slow as a snail:
> he scuffes his shoes on the path
> still hands cluch on to his stick
> he shivers in the cold
> an owl hoots, sends a shiver down
> his spine
> His wrinkled face battered and sore
>
>                               Derek

It is simple and direct: 'scuffs' is an unusual word; the physical distress is imagined in a 'felt' way. There are spelling mistakes, which, of course, we correct in the editing. But from a 'literary' point of view, the poem has a succinctness and clarity which make it fit to be put beside a poem by Li Po or Han Shan. It has the vividness of simple direct Chinese poetry, and its 'language use' is as good.

Some poems showed a bolder display of imagination: here, for instance, is a poem which captures the experience of waking up:

The crack begins to open
Ominous in dark light.
Then, suddenly a tiny glimmer
Like an egg cracking but,
No noise.
The warm air becomes
A shivering stillness
The crack[1] becomes longer

Bending in an escaped ray from the sun.
More shining stillness and,
A spine chilling fear.
Tickling up your back.
Your eyes begin to blink in terror.
The crack is now . . . is
Blackening your brain
Like a nightmare over and over again.
Slowing like a torture chamber menacing.

Comes a wrinkled wruffled hand
Each vein sticking out, it's ghastly
The crack is now an opening to your bedclothes
And the hand is holding a wet flanel
*Ready to pull you out of bed.*

Michael


Some lines crossed out towards the end read

The crack is opening to a cliffside
And the hand is the early morning waker
And your loving parent called a mother
Ready to pull you out of bed.


So, it's spoof in one sense, to involve us in a nightmare image – but then it turns out to be a waking-up image just before Mum hauls him off to the bathroom. But how effective, all the same, is the description of the way the light breaks into the torpid consciousness of sleep!

---

[1] A fascinating alteration here: the boy wrote 'apperture' (aperture) first – then crossed it out and substituted 'crack' which is better (plain) English. The cynical might say it was because he couldn't spell aperture, but I am pleased to think that he thought (from my examples) I would prefer 'crack'!

Perhaps we recall

> . . . Sponges kiss my lichens away.
> The jewelmaster drives his chisel to pry
> Open one stone eye.
>
> This is the after-hell: I see the light.
> The wind unstoppers the chamber
> Of the ear, old worrier
>
> Water mollifies the flint lip,
> And daylight lays its sameness on the wall.
> *Poem for a Birthday,* Sylvia Plath, *The Collosus,* p.87

We can be certain Michael never read that! But notice how exact and excellent is Michael's use of words: 'ominous' used correctly; 'suddenly a tiny glimmer/ like an egg cracking but,/ No noise'; 'A shivering stillness' – a good phrase for the particular atmosphere of certain nightmares. The child's poetic feeling for the texture of languages is clear in his mis-spelling 'wrinkled wruffled', in which he is expressing himself as Hopkins expressed himself in the lines

> This to hoard unheard
> Heard unheeded, leaves me a lonely began . . .

That is, the child is involved in the textures of words, in the alliteration and in the muscular 'feel' of them. So, again, we have a poem of exceptional literacy, which (incidentally) speaks of excellent English teaching in his school. But this literacy is also the product of well-trained imaginative capacities – and a capacity to investigate *consciously* the phenomenology of consciousness itself. (Crossed out are the lines of a second poem which Michael didn't have time to get into:

> Is my brain working
> Can I think . . .)

Everything one attributes to man as *animal symbolicum* is there in the child at the age of 11. In Michael's poems one grasps his awareness of his own mind, and of his own predicament as a being-in-the-world. And because of the kind of poem I chose as a stimulus, we find these children in touch with metaphysical questions, as older people are often not. Take these three poems, for instance: uneven, childish, but yet elementary explorations of themes of the kind pursued by philosophers such as Gabriel Marcel, Viktor Frankl, Bugental and Jaspers. Janice is confronting the universe of the Second Law of Thermodynamics:

### The Time

What is in the future?
What was in the past?
What is in a million years' time?
How long will the world last?
We may know what was in the past.
But we won't know what is in the future
The sun may never go in again.
All we know is that the sun may soon shatter.

It's getting smaller and smaller every day
In a hundred year's time or more it will
            break up in tiny pieces.
No-one will survive:
Everyone will die
Man will have to start creating again.
O, I wish I knew more about the future.

Janice Crofton

Of course, she is a child and the logic of her poem is a bit inconsistent, as in 'The sun may never come out again.' Again, we might feel we should challenge her allegation that the sun is getting smaller and smaller. Perhaps she has had an overdose of doomwatch and pollution anxiety? Her preservation of her intentionality is delightful. Perhaps her poem was triggered off by 'Old shoes' above? But altogether what pleases me is that a girl of 11 should be thinking about the universe and time as a great mystery, for an hour, in an English lesson, that March day.

### The Future

Always expected,
Never here,
Crawling up slowly in the rear

Over the horizon
Just out of reach
My dreams let me go there,
Telling me of robots and
Huge machines:
Maybe death, maybe life,
What is the future?

### Machines

How mankind relies on machines,
With his computers and other what-not.
Without the old box, or our dear TV,
Many people would be very bored.
The few that can do without machines –
The toaster, tea maker, the fridge and radio . . .

Of course, many of the poems were simply child-like: appropriately so:

### The Animals' Party

The lion was having a party
For everyone.
The tiger wore his new top hat,
The rabbit had a coat.
The cat wore an apron
To keep her new frock clean.

Everyone was waiting,
Waiting for five o'clock.
Waiting for the mouse
And her family to come.
The elephant yawned and went to sleep.
Then they came dressed their best
With bows around their ears.
The party began,
The food was delicious
Milk for the cat,
Cabbage for the goat
They all gave their presents:
Buns, soaps, chocolate, sweets.

The lion said, 'Let's dance!'

The cat danced with the tiger.
The hippo with the snake.
They all danced the polka
Until it was late

The homing presents
Were all kinds of things.
Juices of the fruits, cakes,
Buns and pens.
The animals were very sad
That the party was over.

                                                    Judith Yarham

Of course, we may say (in our learned psychological way) that the animals are 'part-objects', symbols of aspects of human make-up: she tames them by making them into children, with 'bows around their ears'. But there is a sense in which even such a childish poem is asking the question, 'What is it to be human?', and its totally adequate language and structure go with this fascinated look at experience in life, like parties – and the end of the party.

Even the most ordinary, 'average' pieces explore the experience of the moment in all its outer and inward reality:

   *Stillness*
There was not a murmur
In the classroom.
Pencils and pens working away
Otherwise there would be no play.
People looking at their books
Bumping their pencils or pens
Against their teeth in
Order to get the vital answer.
Then one girl said
Aloud knocking over her chair
'Finished Miss, can
I go out to play
I've finished all my work
Miss?'

All the others groaned
And got back to work . . .

. . . Suddenly, crash, clatter
No end: chairs moved and
Everyone rushed up
To the teacher's table
Putting their papers on
Her table then they
Rushed for the door
. . . Bang went the
Door it was quiet again
In an abandoned classroom.

                                                              Christopher

In every poem there are happy phrases, often original: 'the vital
answer', 'an abandoned classroom': what strikes me is the phenomenological exactitude, the ability to *render* the 'now':

> *The Teacher*
> There she sits, at her desk,
> With piles of books like a round nest.
> Her eyes look round, looking for someone to pounce on.
>
>
> She stands up
> And starts to walk towards me.
> I shut my eyes as tight can be.
> I hear her, coming closer and closer.
>
> She stops! But then walks on past
> My desk, and back to her seat.
> She picks up her pen and starts playing
>                         with it
>
> Then she puts her head
> Slowly very slowly down.
> The room is now silent.
> All you can hear is the sound of 36
> Pencils scratching away.
>
>                                                          Hilary

– an archetypal picture of the classroom, expressing respect for the
adult, tinged with apprehension.

Poems like the two that follow seem to me simply completely adequate. There is nothing out of place, in their record of perception, their description of the world in its various forms:

> *The Tree*
> The tree it stands,
> Tall and solemn
> Its branches reaching up
> Into the stormy sky.
> It creaks and bends,
> Its roots spreading
> Across the forest floor.
> Its leaves are fluttering
> Here and there,
> Boughs bending and bowing.
> Swaying and creaking
> Twigs snapping
> Clutching roots.
> Squeaks and creaks.
> The storm is over:
> The trees begin to calm,
> The ivy crawling up
> The rough trunk.
> Masses of branches together
> Slender and twiggy.
> Buds and blossoms appear,
> The leaves rustle in the breeze,
> The branches hardly moving.
> Clumps of moss cling on.
> The tree whistles and calls in the breeze.
>
>                                                        Claire


> *Someone Old*
> His hair grizzled,
> His skin wrinkled,
> His eyes a bluey green.
>
> Not very steady
> On his feet
> And can't hear too well.

He has a favourite chair
In the corner, tucked away,
Near the nice warm fire.

He's kind and thoughtful
For his age,
And very easy to please.

Carolyn

But there were surprises, at both ends of the range of ability. One child, whom I knew very well, produced a sudden exceptional vision of a classical goddess:

> *A Mythical Fantasy*
> Athena, a god of great beauty
> Standing high, a gold-bronze statue
> In the sunny square of Athens.
> Wondering at her great beauty
> I imagine serpents round her spiked helmet
> And her jewel-embedded shield.
> In her other hand
> Her gleaming spear
> Sloping to her gold shod feet
> Her solemn face looking down
>
> As though disapproving
> At the camera-clicking tourists.
> In the background, the high columns of the Parthenon.

Thomas

Wherever did this astonishing image come from that Tuesday in Stapleford? I think that what he saw in the poetry we were reading and writing was an embodiment of civilization – which he himself recognized as embodied in Ancient Greek culture. He was as surprised by his poem as we were.

But even a much less able child created a vivid character, who spoke with his own voice from the dramatic imagination.

Read all about it!
As a sandwich man walks up the road
He shouts the news, ringing a bell and shouting
Read all about it!
All the old ladies stand by their door,
Ethel and Dot stand and natter
But at the end of the day he meets
                    at the S.P.S.
And has a cuppa.
But this brave man has to go out in wet or dry.

So next time you see him you should say,
'There's a brave man':
Do you think of me as you drink your cup of tea.
I do not want charity:
All I want is a new rain coat!

Colin

So, in one afternoon in the classroom, we collect as many unique, individual voices as there are children in the class. Everyone has done something adequate with words: many have excelled. But they have excelled not only in 'language use': their response points beyond the words. Much of what they have written is metaphysical: certainly existential. Little we have done has anything to do with the kind of explicit attention to language of the linguists and Bullock. I have done nothing at the level of 'rules' or theories of 'cognitive development'. It has all been tacit, to do with forms of mysterious indwelling, exploring the experience of the 'I' in the world. It has all been English as an *art*. Winnicott's questions have been pursued through symbolism without one word of philosophy being spoken, and aspects of human life such as waking consciousness, Time, disaster, party fun, age, stillness, and civilization, in genuine poetry. I leave the school with a deep sense of satisfaction, because I find confirmation there that human beings gladly seize such an opportunity because their primary need is for meaning, and that children as naturally endowed with poetic capacities respond eagerly to a poet.

Nearly everything I have said about this afternoon of teaching is missing from the Bullock Report!

*Chapter Nine*

# Creative Writing at Sweet Sixteen

---

If we examine the phenomenology of teaching English to adolescents, the whole matter becomes enormously more complex. It is better understood, however, in the light of a holistic philosophical anthropology than by the abstractions of linguistics and over-simple concepts of 'processing experience' from empirical psychology.

Recently, I lived for a week in a remote small stone house, a mill-owner's house, in a deep cleft in the Yorkshire moors, with 16 girls aged 16 who wanted to write poetry. I was one of two poets engaged to teach them. The experience must be discussed as a whole experience, not just as a question of 'language use'. Each night I slept less and less, as I became increasingly disturbed and perplexed by our relationship with these young women. At the same time we were charmed and delighted. I survived, in the end, quite well, I thought: and in the next week I duplicated a thick bundle of their writings. I am now trying to stand back, and draw some conclusions from this experience, which I found painful as well as deeply satisfying. Many things are in the world that weren't there before: their poems, my conclusions.

The house, Lumb Bank, belongs to Ted Hughes, and he has leased it to the Arvon Foundation, which runs poetry courses there. Small groups of adults may go to either of the two centres run by the foundation, to live together for two days or five days, cook for themselves, wander about the countryside, write, paint, meditate, and discuss their work with others, and with two tutors, who are usually poets or writers. There are evening readings, performances of folk-song or small-scale drama, and at the end of the course the 20 or so members of each course read from their own work, over a glass of wine. The other Arvon Centre is at Totley Barton, in North Devon. I went there once to read my poems, and found a sympathetic young audience: but the meal was terrible – the 16-year-olds had no idea how to cook rice or how to wash lettuce: the salad was gritty and the rice was piled in gluey balls. Everyone thought it was fun, and the members of the course tore my poems to shreds.

So, I was nervous before I went to Lumb Bank, to be closeted for a week with 16 girls aged 16, in charge of their own catering.

Lumb Bank is near Heptonstall. Ted Hughes's sometime wife, Sylvia Plath, is buried in Heptonstall graveyard: on her dull, ugly, grave, a few places along from the grave of Hughes's mother Edith, runs an inscription: 'Even in the heart of the fiercest flames, the golden lotus flower may blossom.' I only visited this grave on the last evening, on the way back from Hebden Bridge with bottles of vino da pasto. It was a depressing experience because the graveyard is so untidy and hideous: to open the graves the sexton has to use dynamite. On the overgrown grave was a funny metal pot 'where the person's navel would be'. The soot, the drab stone walls, the blackened trees, the grubby grass – all spoke of nothingness. Alfred Alvarez implies that to choose suicide 'made you free'. Nothing could be less free, I thought, than being sunk in that sodden and wretched spot, while the reference to the golden lotus seemed to me futile. In the face of the overwhelming collapse of values and meaning in our society, what possibly could be the point of running little poetry courses?

To cheer myself, I could place a proof copy of my book *Sylvia Plath: Poetry and Existence* on the windowsill of the Course Common Room. I don't think any of the girls read it. But my collaborator on the course, Philip Callow, did, and we had a good deal of discussion of questions of the arts which some of the girls overheard, at least. They could understand that what we were there for was to uphold meaning against so much current destructiveness. I began work with Ted Hughes's lovely poem *Full Moon and Little Frieda,* to which I shall refer in a moment. By that poem, I wanted to celebrate the power of consciousness, against a bleak universe. I was not helped by the prospectus I found there from the Birmingham 'Arts Lab.', 1971, for reasons which I will not labour here: sufficient to say it seems to me questionable to associate the arts in young people's minds with such depravity and such insults to humanness.[1]

---

[1] See *Education, Nihilism and Survival,* Darton, Longman and Todd, 1977. On a later visit to Lumb Bank I studied the books and journals more closely. Some, like those by Adrian Henn and Nell Dunn, seemed to me ugly and crude, while a section of 'erotica' in an issue of *Transatlantic Review* seemed to me as brutal and inhuman as any racist tract. They were unsuitable for young people, certainly.

The young women from Accrington College of Further Education with whom we worked were in fact, really rather old-fashioned girls, from warm, good, traditional homes. They were pleasantly childish, and didn't mind being childish: I shall discuss my problems with them later, but it is clear from simple pieces of writing they did that they mostly came from homes with strong positive values, and were refreshingly unspoilt. Most of them wore little or no make-up, and they were enthusiastically domestic. Alison, the housekeeper, said it was the neatest week she had known. The girls cooked very well indeed. We ate chops, *Boeuf Stroganoff,* boiled gammon with pineapple and chicken casserole, all beautifully prepared. They worked with fresh meat and vegetables cutting it all up themselves, and they served the meals with that nervous excitement that comes from a real creative interest in what you are doing. Much of the conversation in the kitchen was about 'Mum', and one knew the rich Lancashire home background was securely there, behind the puppy-like energy, the concentration , the know-how, and the evident joy. Here is one girl's impression of her journey to Lumb Bank:

### *Lumb Bank – A first Impression*
### Christine Hansen

Tall, red chimneys belching black smoke, polluting the blue sky of spring, the centre market place – a hive of activity of huge blue and red Lydburn Corporation buses standing motionless, waiting to be filled with weary shoppers, anxious to get home and put the tea on.

Accrington College, pleasantly situated away from the belching chimneys and anxious shoppers, but a tiresome, boring walk from the Town Centre. The college is noisy, but cheerful; pleasant, and yet industrious. Five o'clock is a haven, when lessons and the mad dash for the Town Centre and the bus home, which waits for no man, begins. The bus journey is tiresome, relived a thousand times in a life-time, but nothing changes, everything remains the same old dirty, grimy, noisy town.

The packing is almost finished, checking off on my list, I find that everything has been somehow squashed into the bag, and it waits in a corner of my bedroom perhaps wondering, like me, what kind of place we will be going to tomorrow morning. Fussy

Mother comes bustling around, kindly interfering. 'Have you got everything, dear? What are you taking that for? Are you sure you've got your toothbrush? Don't forget what I told you, remember your manners, don't go wandering off on your own, don't get involved with any strange boys, don't go to bed late, don't get up late . . .'

I begin to look forward to going away, even if I don't actually write anything creative, at least I've been away from college!

Monday morning arrives; what a let-down to find that we're not getting off until three o'clock! That means lessons until then. My bag seems much heavier with every uphill step I take on the way to College. I wish some kind lecturer would stop and give me a lift up to college, but nobody does and I arrive there with a red face, puffing and blowing, and everybody in the Common Room laughing at me.

The morning seems to drag, and the first two hours of the afternoon seem an eternity. Three o'clock finally arrives, and Helen and I think we have been left behind, because we can't find anybody else. Humping our bags, we run out only to face a laughing Mrs. Lea. She tells us to hurry up, and virtually throws us into the already overcrowded mini-bus along with our luggage.

Sitting cross-legged on a seat, facing the wrong way, and wedged between suitcases, haversacks and bodies is not very comfortable: trust me to sit like that anyway.

There are cheers for Mr. Bentley cannot start the mini-bus, and after several attempts and sarcastic comments later, we are on our way. Perhaps the best part of the whole journey for me is waving goodbye to the staff, and leaving them behind for a whole week.

The two map-readers in the front of the van confidently tell me they know exactly where they are and the innocent driver carefully follows their directions. We got lost – well, not exactly lost, just took a wrong turning and lost our bearings completely! We baffle passers-by by asking them the direction to Lumb Bank, and we begin to wonder whether they are deaf and dumb or both.

By this time, the mini-bus is decidedly worse for wear, the brakes are smelling of burning rubber and everyone is laughing and joking, trying to cover up their uneasiness. The driver swears under his breath as he sees the narrow steep track which we have to descend to reach Lumb Bank. Everyone straining their necks, trying in vain to catch a glimpse of the house, and everyone seems to be uttering 'Oh, look at that view, isn't it fantastic. I'm glad I came now, aren't you? I can't see the house yet; oh, there it is, it's nice, isn't it?'

Mr. Bentley puts on the handbrake, and we all fall out of the mini-bus engulfed in an avalanche of luggage. Before we know what is happening, we are being ferried along a corridor and told to come down for tea when we are ready. Friends cling together, and dive into bedrooms, bagging their own territory, and healthily flinging open windows to let in the cool breeze. The sun is shining, the air is warm outside, the atmosphere inside decidedly friendly. We are told to make ourselves at home, and so we do just that: the gannets dive into the kitchen, cutting door-steps of fresh brown bread and making a mountain with delicious cheese. Shoes are kicked off and flung into a corner of the room, nobody cares. It is such a beautiful day, the scenery is wonderful, the atmosphere great and everybody agrees that they are glad they have come.

It is such a contrast from grimy, depressing Accrington, that everyone lets themselves go. We decide to explore, and, reliving our childhood, go galloping down the almost vertical green fields to the woodland below. Our biology teacher taught us how to appreciate nature, and so we bend and marvel at the wild flowers, growing discreetly among the grass. We have never seen flowers like this before, small, delicate and beautiful, purples, blues and yellows; soft colours, contrasting sharply with the rather harsh, bleak countryside around us, but nobody really notices the cruel outlines of the wooded hills.

I try, unsuccessfully, to catch a large spider, but it just will not go into my tin, so I decide to leave it alone, and we spend a few fruitless minutes trying to find insects which would interest our biology teacher without success.

The climb back to the house is steep, but we do not notice it, we are too busy looking around, with an awful wonder at the beautiful countryside.

The smell from the kitchen reaches our nostrils before we enter the house; mouths water at the thought of food, glorious food. Walking up the hill has given us an appetite, and we rush to the table when the bell rings for dinner. Introductions are made; rules are laid down, what few there are, and then the evening is ours!

Thick jumpers are exchanged in place of thin T-shirts, and we start the walk; we don't know where to, we just walk and walk and talk. Before we realise it, we have walked into the next town, but nobody cares, we are free, experiencing a new type of freedom, and enjoying it! We don't even notice the climb back to the main road, and then, suddenly, we are back. The fire burning in the sitting room is homely, soft music is playing in the background, and someone is softly strumming a guitar; we are home.

First impressions of Lumb Bank have been pleasant, peaceful, friendly, warming, cheerful, but although they may live on unnoticed through the week, they may never be forgotten.

This piece is delightfully naïve, and full of indirect information that is astonishing to me – like the girl's admission about wildflowers, and the revelations of the newness of everything, even of being away from home for the first time. The clarity of her English is evidence of good teaching.

The girls' attachment to the world of 'pop' was but a thin veneer over this natural soundness. Of course, they assumed the fashionable ways of lounging about with the record-player in the background. They seemed to like the false manipulation of feeling offered by the 'pop' record: but the piece of music they picked up pre-eminently was a primitive American hymn, *Babylon,* from a record (American Pie, Don Maclean, United Artists, Vas 29285B, side B). They sang it in parts with great sweetness and tenderness to their guitars, at all times of the day.

Among the poems they left lying around were some that they might have thought were like 'pop' lyrics: but they were also very much more sincere and closer to 'our' kind of poetry.

### A Silent Wish

A silent wish
Sitting alone in my room
watching, waiting.
for the first glimpse of the moon

listening, watching
the day turn to dusk,
how quiet the evening lies.

Looking far over the hills,
Watching, waiting
for what I will never know.
listening, watching
white clouds on blue sky
the land all lying serene.

Shining, the sun on the hills
listening, watching
for the moon to arise
and rule over dark night.

Anticipating, cows in their grass
watching, waiting
To be called to their home,
listening, watching
for someone to come
to lead them to their shippen.

Still I sit in my room
watching, waiting
to be called and disturbed
listening, watching;
hoping noone will come,
leave me alone with nightfall.

(Author unknown)

No doubt adolescent girls are always silly little kitties about men. But the behaviour of some of these unsophisticated young women in the pub in the village startled me. In this sphere it looked as if the influence of 'pop' had corrupted them because their professional style with the local lads (one of whom even had a little paunch) was utterly inappropriate to their age and stage of development. One girl playing court to the Heptonstall version of Mick Jagger was one who told me her mother brings her her breakfast in bed every morning, and will not allow her to do any work in the house, or cooking: when she is married will be time enough for that, mother says. The contrast between child and pseudo-sophisticated adult may well have been a matter of appearances: but the appearances were distressing enough.

Over supper on the evening they arrived I talked (fresh from
Maslow) about the deficiency of meaning and value in our society. I
talked about the blankness of the environment, and the way it dwarfed
the individual. Many philosophers and psychologists (I said) now
recognized man as the *animal symbolicum*, and believe his primary
need to be for *meaning*. People wanted to know what meaning their
lives had, and they applied themselves to this question through
creativity. This began between the infant and his mother in play, and
later became a complex process of exploring the world and the self
through symbolism. By this activity (to which poetry belongs) the
child asked about the nature of the self, his own identity and the nature
of the world he lived in. Through culture, the human being seeks,
through imagination, to find his potentialities, and to contemplate his
life-tasks. People needed more opportunities for this kind of attention
to inner needs and self-fulfilment. Our course (I said), being isolated
in a beautiful quiet spot, was intended to help prompt this kind of
quest in them. I read them some pieces of writing by children from my
books – the 'limbering up' exercises about 'Apples' and 'Fire' from my
*Children's Writing*, and poems by young people in search of a sense of
identity and meaning, *Snakes and Ladders* and *What am I? (Children's
Writing*, pp.22-23; 24-25; 36; 69).
Next day we gave them some 'limbering-up exercises'.

In the techniques I used to prompt creativity, my central concern
was to establish trust in the face of the cultural background outside in
which (as in the cinema) trust has been for them so often exploited.
Obviously, 16 is one of the most difficult ages to deal with in fostering
genuine creative work. The confrontation with adults is beginning,
and the young person yearns for the adult world, though still a child in
many respects. So there is a bewildering conflict of emotions, difficult
enough to deal with, let alone write about. So, there is a need to make it
clear that one is a fit person to be given creative work, and that one
understands the conflicts, pains and insecurities associated with it. We
had, in some way, to get through to the child. The 16-year-old pseudo-
adult, with her veneer of 'pop' and film sophistication, might find it
difficult to be sympathetic to the middle-aged poet. She accepts being
chatted up by the village Lothario: but is wary of a man who is much
more like Daddy. The problem was to step into the father's role
without challenging the assumed 'public' self. Girls are perhaps more
able and willing than boys would have been to express emotion, and to
encounter problems of being, but only in a situation of trust. It seems

clear from the girls' poems that entering into creative work meant exposing their vulnerability, and so that they had to summon up defences, and harden themselves against possible consequences. Having found themselves able to do that they didn't mind being childish, and writing about deep feelings, as we shall see.

So, what I felt we needed to do was to establish a certain 'arena' in which the work could be done in a detached way – in which genuine creativity could happen, involving the area of the shadow, the unconscious, the unknown. So in my opening remarks I spoke deliberately of how our world ignores and underestimates these powers. But I spoke of these and of sources of potentiality, and said that I hoped they would find new qualities in themselves, by writing, and a sense of identity which might suggest new strengths.

When it came to practice, my emphasis on the unconscious became evident by my choices of Varèse's piece of music, *Ionization,* the value of which is that it cannot be responded to in any literal way. It is completely unexpected in its idiom, and speaks about our world from the depths of the shadow. Yet it makes an organization out of the strange noises, bringing them to a final submission in peace.[1] My other introductory stimulus was a fairytale in which, through various vicissitudes, a girl, who has been sold to the devil by her father, regains her powers by the love of the king who marries her. She has her hands cut off, to appease the devil, by her father; but in the end, through her quest for new gifts, and the king's love, she regrows her hands. This, I thought, was a good symbolization of the transformations one has to go through, in order to cast away any inauthenticity imposed upon oneself (the silver hands), to grow potentialities that are absolutely one's own. In choosing this I was again trying to speak to the deeper understanding of the girls, and to gain their trust, as someone who might 'reflect' their utterances, and be positive in response to them. I was also trying to present a symbolism of seeking authenticity, in the existential sense, beneath 'supplied' characteristics and an imposed identity.

In some of the poems which the girls subsequently wrote there is, it seems to me, a remarkable recognition of the way in which, in genuine creative work, one 'speaks better than one knows' and is, as it were, 'taken over' by powers beyond immediate conscious control, by tacit and subsidiary powers. George Eliot and D.H. Lawrence, of course,

---

[1] See a report on younger children's responses to music in the present author's *The Secret Places,* 1967.

have spoken of such feelings, so vividly expressed here by Vivien Muir:

> Poetry runs flowing, flowing down my
>     arm and out of my pen.
> The lines bemuse and baffle me,
> Is it me writing? or has someone
>     taken my pen in control?
> Perhaps that's right?
>
> *Poetry Runs Flowing*

There is a kind of penalty, for submitting oneself to creative effort. It is satisfying to write, but also disturbing, because it raises real questions of being and meaning, which the soul has to work on, once they become articulate. To take part in creative activity in a group is highly artificial, and the conflict opens up the question of one's loyalty to the group: is it stifling? So in this one girl's work there appeared a parallel puzzlement about her relationship to those around her. The course aroused discontent, and she awoke to a feeling of being imprisoned in a kind of tameness. This I would link with the overall philosophical problem, found in many poets, of feeling unable, in our too literal world, to really enjoy the imaginative act, with confidence in its value. She records this painfulness of creative work, the special pains of pursuing *meaning* in a humanities discipline. We hear in this girl's work echoes of the same kind of coplaint made by Han Shan, or Gerard Manley Hopkins, who wrote:

> I wear –
> y of idle a being . . .
>     This to heard unheard,
> Heard unheeded, leaves me a lonely
>         began
>
> *Sonnet 44*

This student wrote of a sense of paralysis:[1]

> Stuck in the hole of discontent
> Where I can do everything and nothing,
> For I need to walk, to think, to dream,
> But I am stuck . . .

---

[1] See my discussion of Robert Lowell in *Lost Bearings in English Poetry*.

> My spirits walk the high moor tops,
> And I sit here alone
> And wander with my mind,
> For I am stuck . . .
>
> Free me from this watered cage . . .
>
> Vivien Muir

In another sense, this is the expression of the weariness of adolescent slothfulness: a necessary, but often painful, stage of growth. Interesting, too, is this girl's comment on her companions' assumption of the poetic mask, *See The Poets:*

> Perhaps I also look poetic
> My face stuck on with glue
> And they talk of depressing poems,
> And I record . . .

In this poem she expressed the inauthenticity of writing poetry to order – an artificial exercise at the best of times. This annoys her, yet enables her (paradoxically) to write a good poem. In such puzzlement, I believe, we can recognize that a genuine engagement with creativity was going on, though, of course, it is all well 'beyond the words', in the area of biting into subjective experience, of finding 'being' and 'authenticity' in an atmosphere that was really artificial.

We should, perhaps, remind ourselves of the perplexity of 'teaching creativity'. Creativity is an activity which of its very nature belongs to the inexplicit. It is possible, as Marie-Louise Von Franz says, to harm people by being too explicit, in psychotherapy (she is a Jungian therapist):

> By grabbing their own fantasies and pulling them too eagerly into the light of consciousness and by interpreting them at once with too much intensity, many people destroy their secret inner life.
>
> Creativeness sometimes needs the protection of darkness, of being ignored, that is very obvious in the natural tendency many artists and writers have not to show their paintings or writings before they are finished. Until then they cannot stand even positive reactions. The passionate reactions of people to a

painting may, even if meant in a positive way, entirely destroy
the chiaroscuro, the mystical hidden weaving of fantasy which
the artist needs. Only when he has finished his product can he
expose it to the light of consciousness, and to the emotional
reactions of others. Thus if you notice an unconscious fantasy
coming up within you, you would be wise not to interpret it at
once. Do not say that you know what it is and force it into
consciousness. Just let it live with you, leaving it in the half-
dark, carry it with you and watch where it is going or what it is
driving at. Much later you will look back and wonder what you
were doing all that time, that you were nursing a strange fantasy
which then led to some unexpected goal. For instance, if you do
some painting and have the idea that you could add this and that,
then don't think, 'I know what that means!' If you do, then push
the thought away and just give yourself to it more and more so
that the whole web of symbols expands in all its ramifications
before you jump at its essential meaning.

*The Interpretation of Fairy Tales*, p.77

– hence the importance of establishing a 'third ground', treating
fantasies as if they were literary works in 'English', which, of course,
they have become by the time they are written as poems.

We, the tutors, were disappointed that so few of the girls sought us
out, during the freer, later part of the week, to discuss their work, or
poetry in general, individually. On reflection, this may have been
because of the way in which we had established what James Britton
has called the 'third ground', in which creativity can be safely engaged
upon. We did have some very interesting talks, in the smaller group
tutorials, about their education and their work. One particularly
serious deficiency in the education of young people today is that of this
very investigation of meaning, on which we were engaged. There
simply isn't 'time' to be properly educated, that is, say, to read the
Bible (*Authorised Version*) without knowledge of which English
literature, English history, and modern civilization cannot be
understood; to read Greek tragedy; to discuss general education in
English and the humanities. And although it was clear that their
English teaching was good, the girls complained that they did not have
enough experience of pondering the nature and purpose of life in their
'liberal studies' work.

The whole problem of fostering creativity depends upon

maintaining a distance, and yet allowing for a kind of intimacy. The girls actually gave us poems and passages which might well have been used, by any unscrupulous person, to hurt them – even private love poems, which some of them poured out because they were separated from their boys. Yet no-one objected to anything being 'published' and discussed, apart from one jokey poem they wished to reserve an open reading at the end of the course, about the Warden.

The 'third ground' on which confidence could be exchanged was established, by the poets reading poems of their own. Phillip and I read out at early sessions material we had chosen which we hoped would transmute the personal into the public world 'out there', so that individual experience could become suspended in 'the criss-cross of utterance between us'. Thus the common phenomenological record of experience could be shared. Often what was shared and known in this was never uttered clearly, and perhaps could not be made explicit at all. But under all the 'fluttering' (as one student called it) there was a tacit assumption that certain deep matters about life and death were being explored, often in a way rather like Emily Brönte's 'exercises' in states of feeling, but in a way that was useful, as I believe, for young people. Here, for instance, is a characteristic, satisfactory, sound poem written on the course:

*Abandoned Church*
I too lived once,
I had friends and lovers,
I knew birth although I was full grown,
I grew older and the wonder of creation
Was replaced by commonplace.

Still I had lovers.
I knew their sorrows,
Joys, hopes, pains.
I aged slowly
Their hair turned grey. Their step faltered
Still I remember them from their youth
And now they are with me forever.

I grew too, my façade
Also cracked. Yet I was sturdy until
They ceased to care.
I am the grave I cannot share.

Susan Broadhurst

Another aspect of the relational problem is that one must allow for the secret, private and 'incommunicado' areas of the attention to meaning. I have been accused, in the past, of 'amateur psychology' – often, I suspect, by people who wish to deny the whole area of emotion and the unconscious altogether. For us, it was a question of respecting the tacit and mysterious: let them contemplate and write; leave them alone; encourage them to be quiet, on the moors, in their rooms; and allow them to keep their contemplations and writings unknown and unseen if they wished. So, much of the time we, and they, did nothing: Phillip Callow and I remained in the background as 'examples', as people 'available' if wanted. So we allowed for that essential privacy without which trust and genuine reflection are not possible. This opportunity was taken by several girls, to write expressions of their incommunicable selfhood:

> I want to be left alone
> Alone on the left of the picture.
> But what about life?
>
> . . . Leave me,
> Leave me
> Can't you see?
>
> On the left of the picture.
> Yes, I can see
> Leave me alone
> Picture me here.
>
> Jeanette Winterson

Interestingly, this girl would have been supposed, from the outside, to be the most sociable of all. Others exercised themselves in cherishing secret depths:

> Dark Lady
> Satanic eyes filled with secrets . . .
> . . . deep as a long black pool
> Of swimming fishes. Dark as the deeps,
>     secrets on her lips and in her eyes . . .
> . . . beautiful, dark, alone . . .
>
> Maria Levy

In a college or school it is very difficult, in the continual chatter of social life, to experience and express such inwardness. Daily life in college is over-organized. At least we managed to break away from that. We hoped the beauty of the Lumb Bank surroundings, and the freedom the girls were given, would enable them to become aware of the private, 'interior' aspects of their existence as part of the education of being as well as the communal and relational aspects. The pleasant account of their arrival quoted above suggests that they were even looking forward to opportunities to be alone and 'secret' in such ways.

They explored Lumb Bank, which hangs on the side of a deep cleave going down to a river. On the other side of the declivity rises a moor with crags, and along the valley are old stone factory chimneys rising about the ruin of ancient silk mills. Not everything was still and quiet, because a mechanic was manufacturing 'pop' loudspeakers down in the valley. So the night air was often throbbing with this hideous ostinato – the same dull, unremitting rhythm of exploitative music that was to haunt us all the week in the background. Where can one get away from it?

On the first morning we gave them some general warming-up exercises. First, we discussed *Full Moon and Little Frieda.* I pointed out that in this Ted Hughes sees how the child's act of consciousness – naming the moon – redeems the universe. She grew out of the moon, the universe made her: now she is delicately aware of the moon, and calls it names, thus humanizing it, and transcending the boulders and blood. We also discussed an adolescent's poem, *The Marvellous Invisible Circus,* in which the whole world is seen as a game, or dream. I read the strange poem by an Australian 14-year-old Greek girl Youliana (quoted above, p.149). The girls were not good at discussing poetry, but they were quiet and attentive, and were obviously responding: they liked Ted Hughes' tender feelings for his little daughter, who is seen in a landscape with webs that are 'tense for the dew's touch'. The poem is full of expectancy, like the lifted pail, whose trembling surface 'tempts' a first star to mirror itself in it.

I chose *Full Moon and Little Frieda* because of its images of inter-subjectivity, its 'mirror' element, its 'intentionality' – the presence of the child and her wondering perception gives the whole universe a quality of feeling that something new is going to come into being. So, the poem redeems the bleak universe of modern science – which is the hopeless universe of Hughes' nihilistic and malevolent work *Crow.* We next moved on to some actual writing in response to a stimulus. I used first that piece of avant-garde music of the 'thirties, Varèse's *Ionization*, because I knew it to be successful as a stimulus with schoolchildren (see *The Secret Places, Intreating Iron Wire*). These girls liked it, and this piece of music touched on the unconscious area of fears, forms of awareness of chaos, aggression and existential dread.

To be away from home for the first time is, for adolescents, often more of an anxiety than an adult realizes. They had been introduced to a number of adults whom they did not know. They didn't know what these adults might do to them – so a degree of virginal defensiveness emerged. They didn't know yet if they could trust us: they felt they had to impress us.

And then, during the first morning, there was a thunderstorm. Some had been down to the river, finding the bank steep and the river swollen by rain, rushing harshly between boulders. All these produced responses to Varèse which spoke of anxiety beneath the self-possessed exteriors:

> *Effect*
> A thunderstorm on a dark night;
> Battle-drums.
> The sound of flung shells and mortars,
> a dance
> The dance of life;
> Now happy, now sad.
> The tragi-comic writhing,
> Banging, weaving, stepping in and out.
> Chaos
> All worlds moving towards each other,
> Now harmony now opposition –
> The dance moves on
> To new dimensions,
> And fades into the distance.

J. Henderson

> *Response to the Music of Varèse*
> City traffic never ceasing
> Incessantly whirling round and round
> The sun beats down on the pulsating city
> Frying the drivers in their glass-meat cages

People never cease searching
Forever their minds wander round and round
Constantly turning from one to another
Never resting nor never still.

With some, however, the percussion music generated fiercer feelings of violence – and some of this tumult seemed to emerge from experience left unresolved in the sensibility; because of certain references it was clear this came to them from television.

*Response to Music 'Ionization'*
The oriental maiden
dances
Hands delicately posed – painfully expressive
Costume glittering.
The oriental maiden
Dances
Dances on the kitchen linoleum floor
The kitchen clatters clanks
shuts, bangs,
Bubbles over briskly.
The Chinese girl
dances
Dances to the table
Dances to the cupboard
Dances to the drawer
Dances to the sounds – of war.
Well Kojak never made those sirens screamy
                              like these do
And Zena never made those eggshells smash
                              like these do
Clatter crack on the kitchen floor.
The Chinese girl listens to the voice of war
'We'll take them on the beaches'
The oriental kitchen warfare continues
                              in its richness
Clack and clang
Dance and bang
Break and bomb
Thunder and snow.

The egg-timer – rings
The siren – screams
The thunder increases, then ceases,
Increases, decreases and smashes to pieces
The oriental kitchen.
The end of the oriental kitchen war

                                                                    Diana Barnes


What strikes me about this is the feeling that violence has been thrust into the domestic life: it has become jokily familiarized (as Vietnam atrocities are thrust into the kitchen). Because of the strange juxtapositions, the child does not know how to respond. Should she respond with a giggle? Is it a joke about Kojak on TV? Or is violence a serious problem? Unable to get it all into perspective, she makes her protagonist simply dance like a child. In others, more extreme violent images were aroused:

        *The Blast*
The noise was horrifically sickening
Everywhere were shouts and screams
One colour stood out above all the others
The ground was red
The clothes were red
There was a smell of burning skin and hair –
Then silence . . .
The screaming and shouting stopped . . .
Then – sirens from every direction,
Police cars, fire engines and ambulances;
Confusion, utter confusion!
The time passed slowly:
The injured were taken away,
And silence fell again.
Perhaps a protest march would have
been better.

                                                                    Gillian Briggs


And in some of the writing emerged intense images of violence which were unresolved, and quite startling in their specific, malicious nature:

*Poem written in response to Music*

Motorbikes!
Motorbikes again!
They, complete with yellow, hornet-helmetted drivers
Buzz and break into my sanctitude
Hot, crimson, pink as my jumper
I am exploding. Stilly, silently, softly
**Then they die**
Only the noise of triangles and drums
**Then they turn**
Again
Back, round, up, down,
They are back to torment me –
They do it on purpose
'I'll murder them!'
'I'll tie a wire from ash to pine-wood fence!'
They, gloating come alone
Zooming, roaring, mocking me
They crash – wham!
Crushed like rotten apples
Under father's fast footsteps
Between Previn's pointed pearls,[1]
The Jaws of the clashing rocks
Through the gate to the golden fleece.
How can I concentrate on cases?
Yes, cases, not suit-cases, the case of myself
But cases
'I'll get them!'
I'll grab a knife
I'll open the door
I'll throw myself down the garden
But by the time I've found the catch,
Unscrewed the nuts and bolts,
lifted the lever –
Too late – or is it?
Anger gone – or has it?
But they have
So it is and it has . . .
For the moment.

Elaine Halliwell

---

[1] Previn is the name of her dog and the pearls are his teeth.

This is a strange, nightmarish vision: and it was written by one of the gentlest and most old-fashioned of the girls – a girl who wants to go to the university to read Classics. It has those qualities which one occasionally comes across in children's writing in the last 15 years or so, that seem very different from anything found before so much exposure to television violence. It isn't the violence so much (because there is plenty in folk tales and other traditional sources, of course). It is the *unabsorbed* nature of the violence, and the deliberateness of the impulse to counteract some menace that is felt to be in the air. Not long ago the English examiners at Cambridge University reported an obsession among students, that 'they' in some way were 'getting at them', getting into their minds: there is a strange paranoia to be found in the minds of young people today.

I believe this kind of phenomena is the consequence of the exploitation of paranoid-schizoid themes in the mass media, to hold an audience. Commercial producers (as in *The Exorcist* which film contains subliminal images to play on deep subconscious fears) have learnt to employ very frightening images – and these imply that the world is full of threats, and malevolence – and you are empty, vulnerable, and without resources to deal with these menaces. Every day children are exposed to hours of such trivial paranoid-schizoid images – with no resolution, no creative engagement with hate, dread or fear. As in James Bond films, the only solution is to toughen oneself, be aggressive, and attack before one is attacked: a dangerous proclivity.

So this girl feels threatened by young men who have adopted the black gear of the motor-cycle group, and who threaten to violate her world. There are groups of youths like this, and they do threaten and attack people and commit rape. (Group rapes are now apparently depicted on record sleeves of 'punk' rock.) In her imagination the girl relies on her own murderousness, her father and her dog's teeth; her counter-measures take on an almost apocalyptic force:

> The jaws of the clashing rocks
> Through the gate to the golden fleece . . .

And it seems that the male aggressiveness in her world and in herself actually threatens her peaceful attention to the classical language she is learning: and she quibbles in an odd way about 'cases': cases of verbs, and the case of herself. The rather hebephrenic confusion is characteristically adolescent: but it also belongs to the special kind of confusion brought by a paranoid-schizoid culture. Just as the writer of the poem about the oriental girl cannot fully enter into her gracefulness, her being, so this girl cannot find her way to a happy engagement with learning and the classics. In both, the music of Varèse evokes an awareness of aggression and hate. But there is confusion between real negative emotions and those of television fantasy. The author of the poem about the oriental girl realized that the feelings of fear and hate in her aroused by Varèse's strange sound are more 'real' than television fantasy which is (by implication) calculated horror. So Varèse's must belong to something real she sees on television, that is, the Vietnam war. While one side of her strains towards grace and beauty ('Murder and snow') another side is obsessed with disintegration ('increases decreases and smashes to pieces': 'break and bomb') I believe the unresolved nature of these first pieces of writing expresses an inability to hold things together, especially where the writers have been disturbed by images which perplex them, so that they don't know whether they are negative aspects of themselves, or destructive elements in the world outside.

The problem of finding a perspective into which various experiences can be brought, is a characteristic adolescent one (see the poem *Snakes and Ladders,* in *Children's Writing*). The author of the poem about motor bikes is surely trying to find a way of establishing harmony among her subjective experiences. The music of Varèse has certainly evoked in her the dynamics of the animus: the menacing, hornet-like, phallic 'driver' – against which she turns murderous. I was startled that such a gentle girl should have a fantasy of stretching a wire across the road to decapitate a motor cyclist: it's the kind of thing we thought about in the war, but even then it was considered a dirty trick. It surely comes from some outside source, is a 'supplied' fantasy?

I believe that the imaginative life of children is distorted today by the meretricious inculcation of fear and hate, through the 'media'. By a constant flow of such material a desperate, self-defensive side of their own nature is aroused, and their 'sanctitude' is menaced. They seize upon the cruellest forms of 'false male doing' to defend themselves, but do not have the resources to resolve the violent images thrust into their minds by the abuse of cultural trust. So these images remain unresolved in the memory. This shy girl feels enormously embarrassed by the way the music has evoked her (largely unrecognized) male assertiveness, to which these accumulated hate-fantasies accrue: 'Hot, crimson, pink as my jumper' (she blushes easily). She summons up Daddy and her dog's teeth to support her own defence measures: but these are desperate in their extreme reaction to the fear evoked. By her quibbling references to 'the case of myself' she shows she is concerned with holding together disparate elements in the identity which she fears (at least in this nightmare) to be threatened with extinction. In the end she hopes to actually dismantle the nuts and bolts of the automaton-animus that seems to menace her: yet this itself seems inhuman, a mechanical monster.

It seems to be one of the characteristics of our age that people's minds have become obsessed with images of hostile functional entities which seem to threaten to 'take us over'. 'Science fiction' (which should be called 'mechanistic fantasy') is full of them. These are symbolic embodiments of our philosophy of life, the feeling that we are 'bundles of instincts', being manipulated by outside forces (of economics, of politics) or inside forces (the *id* or 'biological needs'). Nothing could be more dangerous than deepening such paranoid feelings, since they destroy creativity and intentionality, and tend to distort people from their true need to find meaning, towards mental rage or a desperate impulse to withdraw completely from the world.[1]

This poem, also written in response to Varèse, seems to be a poem of withdrawal, into death, because the violence of the world is too unbearable:

>     *Impressions Made by the Music*
> Pain,
> Stabbing, biting, cruel,
> Needless pricking, axes smashing,
> Body convulsed in scarlet pain,
> Torment,
> Ebbing, fading, dying –
> Brings relief –

---

[1] At a later course at Lumb Bank (1979) it proved impossible to wean the 16-year-olds either from 'pop' or their nocturnal black magic. They were cooperative at formal sessions, but reverted to 'pop' as soon as our backs were turned. At night they held seances, yelling and shouting until five a.m. and showed a total disregard for adults, despite repeated reasonable requests. They displayed an inability to find the reality of others which I found overwhelming. In terms of the writing done the course was successful: but there was a radical failure in the imaginative sense of the existence of others, with whom one was collaborating. For an account of another course (1978) see *Critical Quarterly*, Summer 1979.

Suddenly returning,
Eyes flashing, face screwing
Body writhing, wriggling,
Screaming for help . . .
Painful
Ebbing, fading dying –
Brings relief –
Torso falling, skin shrinking,
Life flashing, eyes crying,
Devil reaching, flames licking.
Death bell tolling . . .
Ebbing, fading, dying,
Finally,
External peace

It should perhaps be added that not all responses to Varèse were violent: here is a peaceful one:

#### Dusk

Walking, arms entwined, through the cathedral ground.
The night creeping up on us, the stars peeping down on us
The bright lights from the boulevard at the end of the path,
Falling blossom surrounding us, blanketing the floor.
The pink fluffiness of the flowers
Illuminated by faint lights in the cathedral
Which filter out through the stained-glass windows:
We laugh and our laughter drifts away,
Like the blossom on the breeze,
We smile and our smiles stay in our hearts.

Tracy Haworth

These exercises established, I think, that we could explore all kinds of experiences and emotions, in a 'third ground' way. We, the tutors, were trustworthy, it seemed. Now, of course, followed the difficult and complex problem of trying to judge the poems that were written.

This was made perhaps even more difficult by the very engaging naturalness of the girls, itself. They seemed so innocent. One girl, very extrovert, very playful, given to wearing flamboyant headscarves and performing somersaults in the sitting room, wrote two poems which startled me because they seemed to be about her own heartlessness.

Yet she was quite happy, with that marvellous innocence of 16, to have
her poem *The Stone* discussed in open seminar:

### The Stone

The stone is coarse and hard
It stands erect and bold
The stone has no feelings
And when touched was all so cold.
The grass and flowers around
Dance and waver in the breeze
Their colours are bright and pretty
They do their best to please:
But when a storm arises
And the elements are wild and strong,
The delicate things of nature
Will not survive for very long
And when the storm is over
And the sun is in the sky
It can be seen that all around
How quickly these things die.
But on looking a little closer
We see the stone is there
As nothing ever hurts it
And for nothing does it care,
On looking at this stone
A reflection do I see
This hard unfeeling object
Is really only me.

Lindsay Haworth

### The Real Me

To smile, to laugh, to love
Are the actions that I use
And people think I'm oh so nice
To keep them all amused.
They all think they know me
But oh how they're deceived
Because I really hate them
And my actions are only to please.
I wonder at their wisdom

That they cannot perceive
That my sweet performance
Is part of the web I weave.
My main concern's Number One
And to that end my shame will be:
If to get ahead I use people –
So what? – the rewards are for me!

Lindsay Haworth

With that name too! I felt, inwardly, do you know what you're saying?
I recalled the strange story by Emily Brontë, cauterising a bite she
received from a dog with a red-hot poker, without telling anyone.
Even Lindsay's verse-forms have a Brontëish ring, and are
delightfully and childishly primitive (she also wrote a quite terrible
Victorian love poem).

The others simply found it 'honest' – 'might as well be honest about
yourself' they said cheerfully! But I found the poem quite genuine:
about the vulnerability of one's true feelings and the need to harden
oneself at a certain cost:

The delicate things of nature
Will not survive for very long . . .
How quickly these things die . . .

They 'dance and *waver* in the breeze'. So, the young person has to
develop a kind of strength, which must be built on a stoney 'erect'
maleness which is not so vulnerable:

nothing ever hurts it
And for nothing does it care . . .

'I care for nobody, no not I, and nobody cares for me' – often the
adolescent feels he or she must cultivate this hard detachment. But
there was nothing as cynical or bitter about this girl. She was a child
emerging from *Songs of Innocence* to *Songs of Experience* – to which we
sent her (someone had already read *The Clod and the Pebble* in a
reading session and the connection established itself, I am sure). But I
thought that from my analysis of the symbols of Sylvia Plath that the
stone column in Lindsay's poem, was an aspect of the animus. I
believe the girl's need to rely on the cold animus is an aspect of our

world, that forces this on her because it does not foster her confidence in 'female element being'. I believe I sensed that many of the girls had this 'animus' problem, of having to be in some degree inauthentic, by being tough in a male way to the modern world, this involving a degree of falsification.

It should be said that many of the poems written were simply good, direct poems – about the house and the place, and about their youthful feeling and impressions. Some were simply accounts of extrovert bodily effort:

> *The Bike Ride, Wednesday*
> Riding along with the wind in our faces,
> Eating the miles
> Quickly, yet slowly
> Compared to the cars
> Whizzing past us
> Their engines straining and groaning.
>
> Beginning to rain, then raining more harshly
> blinding our eyes
> with the sharpness
> and the coldness of the huge raindrops
> each like a splinter of
> frozen glass.
>
> Contradictory weather changes once more
> The sun, although watery
> shines forth bravely
> Facing the wind and
> oppressing the raindrops,
> Suddenly as we feel the warmth on our backs.
>
> Beginning to sweat as we climb up the hill
> Then freedom once more
> when reaching the brow
> our legs can be rested
> we freewheel, quickly
> gathering speed as we fly down the hill.

Helen Riley

> *The Bike Ride, Wednesday*
> Eagerness as we set off down the road,
> Life is great!

Wind and rain blowing in our faces –
Free day.
The clank of the chain.
The grinding of gears –
Suddenly, a cry –
We stop.
People passing by, silently sniggering
Cars sending a dirty spray into our faces
Grimy, greasy oil smeared on our fingers.
It's fixed –
Muscles aching, knees creaking
As the top of the hill looms in sight –
A sense of achievement – elation?
A sign post –
One mile to go – nearly there,
Never thinking of the long climb back
Who cares? – we don't –
We're free!

                                        Christine Hannan

There were poems like water-colour sketches of the scenery:

> *Ruined Farm*
> Cold gray stone
> Covered by moss
> Broken grey slate
> Cast on the ground
> The deep deep well
> Covered by a stone
> The hand-hewn trough
> Where water still flows
> The overgrown garden
> Where a flower still grows
>
> Peaceful and gentle,
> The water laps at the lock side,
> Shredding the bladderwrack
> Borne in by the evening tide;
> And sunbeams dance on the water
> And the oyster catcher calls

To his mate
And softly the twilight falls.

                                        Lindsay Beaton


And there were poems about evocative things in the house:


    *A Picture on a Plate*
Watchfulness, wakefulness,
Will you never sleep?
Do your eyes never tire?
Those eyes –
Deep brown, kind and understanding.
I wonder,
What thoughts lurk
Behind those shadows of life –
The ages past,
The things forgotten, except by you,
If only you could but tell.
And as you look down, knowingly,
On we poor mortals,
Your pale mouth
Curves gently into a half smile
Will you never sleep?

                                        Jennifer Henderson


    *To the Gentleman on the Wall*
You stare down at me
Slightly bemused and yet with a mild understanding
If you could speak what would you say?
The tales that you could tell.

A noble lord of the 18th, no 19th century
A man who has claimed and tamed his land
Who has reached his goal and now lies on forever
In the circular window of the picture.

You may not have been tall and handsome
Perhaps your clothes were of rags
But your eyes,
Your eyes speak of truth
They live on

Ever seeing
Never dying
And you live on around them

                                    Gillian Briggs

But because of the odd 'animus' element in the poems I have discussed, I became aware that the girls revealed many forms of
frustration and alienation – alienation not in the sense they were
alienated by 'pop' propaganda, but faced with an alien world, a world
in which they did not feel they belonged. 'The world has made me old'
seems an indicative title, and remains one of some of Winnicott's
warnings of what a too-early sophistication – such as that imposed by a
dehumanized culture – may do to reduce the idealism and creativity of
the adolescent:

    *Frustration*
Why is it no one listens,
Or seems to hear
When I say something?

Is talking futile then?
Or can no-one be bothered
Any more?

Questions, questions,
Why question myself
If there aren't any answers?

No-one knows,
No-one cares any more
Life's dead!

                                    Jennifer Henderson


    *The World Has Made Me Old*
I am not sixteen
Yet the world has made me old
My brain has wrinkles
My thoughts are rheumatic

I am but sixteen
Yes I am becoming lethargic

Soon to be put out to grass
In a home, with postcards, pension and a bus pass

Diana Barnes

In these poems we hear the voice of today's anomie – even though
we allow that they may also be experiments, trials, postures
appropriate to the adolescent. Sometimes this disenchantment was
well-organized into criticism and protest, with an appropriate
idealistic dynamic:

*Different Worlds*
What do I see as I look around
This man-made 'paradise',
The architect stands at my shoulder
Pointing out the finest details
Of his self-created landscape:
Three fifty-storey blocks of flats,
An office-block, a superstore,
Pedestrian areas and roads
Over and under and through
The landscape, stretching out
Towards infinity,
New schools, glass-walled,
With all-weather playgrounds,
Prefabricated boxes which, he informs me, are

'The latest thing in houses'.
I despair. This is not my world,
We are alien beings. He the conquerer.
But there is a fifth column, invincible,
On my side.
A dandelion grows in a crack in the floor

Susan Broadhurst

*After the Bomb*
It is too quiet. The air
Lies like a sullen blanket over sound,
The sky is dark: night in day.
And the birds are still

A pile of rust – bloodred rust –
Stands to attention in the heavy air,
Grieving bones of a once proud car
And the birds are still.

A few building still stand whole.
Marble monuments to a byegone age,
Cold gravestones of the long dead.
And the birds are still.

A heavenly dome rises,
Far higher than the other ruins,
Up into the death-filled sky
And the birds are still.

A winged statue stands alone
Stone that has never lived, yet more alive
Than anything around him.
And the birds are still

One clocktower, now bell-less, stands
Where we made one last plea for common sense –
Which the others would not hear.
And the birds are still.

We did not want to make war
While others fought, we prayed. We were neutral
But they dropped their bombs on us
The birds are still now
And so is everything else.

Susan Broadhurst

The girl who wanted to murder the motor-cyclists shows in another poem that she is yearning for a transcendent sense of being and continuity that our world denies her:

*Permanence*
There is one word in our language
Which has no true existence –
Permanence,
Sweet, false permanence:
Permanence.

I thought I could dwell with the gods
On heights of Mount Olympus
From gold-oak plates to eat ambrosia,
To sip nectar from silver.

But permanence, sweet permanence,
It drifted through the sky-line
Away, away on sugar clouds
To float through seas of silence.

I want to wander in the wilds,
Wrapped in wheels of whistled winds,
Be hurled and whirled in arms of air
And held till times immortal.

But permanence, sweet permanence,
It dropped with blown-out breezes
To sink hopes to the futile fields
Dissolving in the darkness.

There is one word in our language
Which should have recognition –
Not permanence
Sweet, false permanence
But
Temporary-permanence.

                                   Elaine A. Halliwell

Susan Broadhurst's dandelion points to a tenacious attachment to hopefulness. But this group of poems enables us to relate the problem of creativity in such a context, the general problem of cultural nihilism discussed above, and what I have called the animus problem. No doubt the girls' writing here was influenced by the characteristic adolescent moodiness from *Snakes and Ladders* which I read them: can we feel enough confidence in the imagination to wrest meaning from our present existence, and to feel that we can by imagination throw meaning and value over the world? In the writing of these girls I found a similar *statis*, a frustration of potentia such as that I analyse in my book:

> *Caged*
> My brain burst with mental anguish
> And I am stuck

I want to walk to yonder crag
But I am stuck

Stuck in the hole of discontent
Where I can do everything and nothing,
For I need to walk, to think, to dream,
But I am stuck.

My spirit walks the high moor tops,
And I sit here alone
And wander with my mind,
For I am stuck.

Go away rain!
Go away now,
Free me from this watered cage
Where I am stuck.

Vivien Muir

The adolescent needs to find meanings, urgently: there are two powerful forces which threaten their creative intentionality – the arousal of black, menacing destructive dynamics within, as by a debased and sensational culture: and the blank, inhuman environment which man creates. The inner problem, the girls recognized, is a natural force (and this came out in discussions of *Full Moon and Little Frieda*). They saw it even in the river, and in the wind – and they felt it in the enmity always latent in a strange place.

### The River
The terrible giant
Crashed through trees and leafy undergrowth
To the valley below.
Down the ravine his great, heavy tread
Makes imprints in the rock,
And wears it down, down.
People, terrified, scatter
At the roar and thunder of this monster,
This alien being
That no-one really understands;
And never will.

Jennifer Henderson

G

*Wind*

**Bare-trees bare thoughts bare minds**
Wind cutting and biting cold and cruel,
Nips faces, fingers, sends hair into turmoils
Of whipping strands,
Cruel, hard wind,
Will you never cease to anger and blow

The cold, stinging raindrops on my face?
Will you never end and bring warm, warm
Summer days of leisure, play and ease?
Will you never cease to bite and fight
With unrelenting power?
Will you ever stop?

                                                              Christine Hannon


*Rain*

A constant curtain of rain
Moving from right to left,
The wind blows,
The rain takes the beating and moves quickly across my view,
The wind dies down,
The forever opening curtain is pulled again
By some weather-worn hand
Which clutches at the cord

                                                              Tracey Haworth


In one poem, the ghost of Sylvia Plath seemed to merge with memories of *Wuthering Heights,* and with the menace of painful nihilistic feelings. No doubt the students were, unconsciously, writing the kind of poems they thought we would like. Just as a Freudian analyst gets Freudian dreams and a Jungian analyst gets Jungian ones, so we were given Holbrookian and Callowian poems, no doubt.

The serious, contemplative, sometimes tragic mood, however, was theirs: and so was the essential childishness. My second stimulus was the fairytale, about a father who sells his daughter to the devil. This was not as successful as the Varèse music. But it did produce one lovely image of childhood; and a delightful, simple reminiscence of being told stories as a child.

*A Small Child Listening to a Fairytale*
　　(For Corrie and Alex)
Skin soft like a peach-coat
downy, smooth, and rose-pink
in the day:
Now, rosy-apple red
from the fiery fierce orange-yellow
in the grate.
Red lips slightly parted
unconsciously revealing
the coral mouth's-interior,
and colour of fingers
made transparent
by grasping torchlight.
Brown gentle bovine eyes
gazing unflinching, incredulous, enthralled,
Pupils enlarged in the dimming light.
Above, fair Nordic mat of hair;
thin, spiky, unruly, out with the kitchen scissors
Smelling of soap, shampoo, scarlet-striped toothpaste
and fresh laundered dressing-gown –
Living happily.

Lindsay E. Beaton

## Childhood
### by J. Henderson

One of the things I loved about my childhood was bed-time story time. In our old house we all shared a room – my two sisters and I. It was a very big room – or so it seemed, though it probably wasn't, it was just that we were very small. My bed was under the window and near the head of my bed was a huge cupboard which we kept our toys in – we used to hide in there when we were playing hide and seek. Next to that was the chimney-breast. Pam's bed was at the bottom of mine along the next wall – the head of her bed came just under the other end of the long window. At the foot of her bed was Tina's. The three beds were placed so that there was a big square area left in the middle, but we didn't have any chairs or anything – I don't think – that's blurred, and all I remember now is the vast **enormity**[1]of

---

[1] She means enormousness. Enormity implies crime.

the room and the main items in it.

Every night Mum would come and sit – I don't know where she sat, probably on one of the beds – but I no longer recollect on which she sat. Then she would tell us a story – maybe two, that depended on what time we went to bed. Of course, we got all the usual stuff – 'The Three Bears', 'Goldilocks' and so on – I remember Tina used to love 'The Three Bears' – or was it Tina? No, I don't remember. Funny, I thought I did. I used to have a favourite one, too, only now I can't remember what that was either. But the time we loved most was when Mum would tell us one of her made-up stories. Oh, how we loved them!

One of Nana's friends knitted us some little dolls – Penny-Keggies we called them and Mum made up hundreds of stories about them and the adventures they had with Tessie, Timothy, Ted and Quality Bear – mine, Pam's and Tina's teddy bears respectively – Tina's was a Koala bear but she couldn't say 'Koala'! We had nightdress cases, too – I called mine Mr. Bun after one of my favourite characters in Mum's stories – 'Timothy Red and Mr. Bun'. I don't know whether she made the stories up or not – I rather think she did. Pam was so mad with me the first day we got our nightdress cases because I said: 'Mine's called Mr. Bun.' – before she could get a word in edgeways – she wanted to call hers Mr. Bun too.

Mum made up hundreds of other stories for us – one or two ideas I vaguely seem to remember, though perhaps I'm getting mixed up with stories I read out of books. Isn't it odd how, the more and the harder one tries to remember, the less one can! We always thought it was such a shame that Mum could never remember her own stories or characters. Fortunately, though, she wrote some of them down – it's lovely just to sit now and read them and escape into memories of childhood. Our very favourite character, and the ones which I've saved to the end were the 'Moony-Boonies'. Oh, how I loved those stories! They had hundreds of adventures – they came from the moon in a nondescript space-ship. They lived with a little girl and her parents and she played with them. The one thing which sticks in my mind about them was a story about a mix-up over a tin box and a postcard. Needless to say the Moony-Boonies didn't know which was which so the little girl, Jane I think she was called, kicked the box and then told them what it was. Ever after I have memories of these little creatures delightedly kicking this poor tin box and singing each time!

'O! A tin box! O! A tin box!'

I think Mum got the idea from the old tin box which was very rusty which we found in the garden. We never did find out what happened to them in the end – whether they went back to the moon to tell everyone (I now have visions of something like the reactions of the Cadbury's smashers in their little spaceship killing themselves laughing at our antics on earth!) or what, because we moved home.

Pam and I were about nine and eleven respectively then – I was just getting ready to go up to senior school, but Tina was still only five, and she still had bed-time stories. For a while Pam and I both still crowded into her room and sat on the floor or on the bottom of the bed while Mum told her stories. But they didn't mean the same any more, they didn't have the same magic they used to – I grew up. Yet, even now, when I cast my mind back I'm still transported back with my memories; and childhood, so near and yet so far, still retains some of the magic it used to have.

Later, I read them passages from Gorki's *Childhood*, about the death of his father, and Dylan Thomas's *Fern Hill* (I acknowledge here a debt to Peter Abbs's *Autobiography in Education*). One of the most successful responses to these reveals how close to childhood the 16-year-old still is – which makes the conflict over emerging adult emotions even more acute.

### *Bear, Snowy, Teddy, Bruin, Worthington and Others*

The story this morning reminds me of Nana's house. She used to tell me stories at night. We – that is, my sister and I – had to wait at my Nana's house on Friday night until my Dad came for us after work. They used to have an oven over the top of the fire, and that's where Percy used to sleep.

Percy was an engine and had a circular track. Every Friday night he used to come out and play. I never knew why he slept in the oven but he did. My Grandad was always soft with me and he used to eat the crusts of my bread. Mum always said that crusts gave you curly hair. I never believed her and it would appear that I was right in doing so, as I am the only one in the family to have curly hair.

H

My Grandfather was the first person to buy me a TEDDY BEAR. This was fatal as it started my craze for Teddy Bears. The first bear was called 'Bear' and lasted many years, until one day we were out at Becky Falls on our holidays. Bear was lost. To pacify a distressed female girl a second bear was bought, this time called 'Snowy'. This was because he was snow white. In addition to this Snowy had a deck chair and used to sunbathe at frequent intervals throughout the day.

My mother decided that it was time Snowy passed away and one day I came home to – no Snowy! An immediate inquiry was held into the disappearance but the case remains unsolved. A new bear was bought and christened Teddy. I had my suspicions that my mother had more to do with Snowy's disappearance than she was letting on! So, when Teddy showed signs of bald patches, and Mum started making comments about 'getting rid of Teddy' an immediate Police Protection was given to Teddy, this consisted of a number of secret hiding places such as the loft, the shoe polish tin, even behind the water tank. The poor bear was subject to many indignities.

After the sudden disappearance act had failed (for when he was not behind the water tank he was firmly gripped by one paw) the devious Mum tried the new teddy bear one, and thus Bruin came to live in our house. This ploy did no good either. So in later life they tried again, this time to get rid of both Paddy and Bruin (He had by this time become rather bare himself – sorry about that one). This time a larger bear was purchased and was duly called Teddy Edward, but still the intrepid Teddy survived. But by this time the family had given up and bought Worthington (the largest bear of them all without any motives).

My collection now included

> 1 hedgehog, bright red
> 1 Womble 'Orinoco'
> 1 stuffed snake
> 4 bears
> Basher
> Fred the Gagu Basher
> 3 of my sister's Heffalumps

and    1 Mexican Thing-a-Mijig

Vivien Muir

We had an interesting discussion on this piece in which I told them about D.W. Winnicott's theories of the origin of culture in the play between mother and infant, and of the origin of the symbol in the child's first 'transitional object' – his cuddly rag or teddy-bear that symbolizes his inner possession of his mother. This symbol has a two-fold aspect – it embodies his experience of the mother, and so symbolizes separateness, too. To throw away old teddies is to make a serious breach in the child's sense of continuity in her culture: but she preserves it here by hiding her threatened transitional objects, while her family recognizes some continuity by always selecting *bears*. I said I thought it was appropriate for this account of transitional objects to appear when a group of young people were away from home for the first time, living with strangers, and concerned with creativity. Some confessed to having brought their teddy bears with them, to Lumb Bank! I didn't raise it for discussion, but secretly delighted in the charming access to childhood made so freshly in these pieces.

Marjorie Grene, criticizing the 'objectivity' of empirical approaches, declares that in order to understand things, we have to *encounter* them. The week at Lumb Bank was, certainly, an encounter. It is clear for one thing, from the girls' poems, that they were disturbed by the experience of creativity. This fact alone sets 'English' apart: it cannot be experienced without disturbance, without some kind of change in one's emotional life and one's relationship to the world.

The strangeness which the girls felt in their encounters with art is clear in the following poems, which show their awareness both of the ardours of creative work, and the tacit core of the discipline.[1]

> from *Poetry Runs Flowing*
> . . . Reading, eating, sleeping every
> every minute crammed with poetry.
> My inferior efforts annoy and baffle me
>
> Vivien Muir

> *See the Poets*
> See the poets sitting there
> And I observe
> Their faces fraught with mental strain

---

[1] A therapist friend (and poet) Will Allchin suggests, over a similar course which proved difficult, that creative work may have brought out unconscious elements which the students found too hard to deal with.

Waiting for the muse to strike them
While I in my corner sit and watch
And while away.

I wonder what they think
As poetry fills their minds:
They stare, intent upon some far-off object.
Artistic faces, firmly struck,

Trying to look . . . what?
Who knows?
They sit poetically
And I huddle in the corner,
Feet bare, and plastic-mac'd
And watch

Do they believe themselves blessed with Keats's power,
Or just try to express themselves?
Perhaps they rhyme, perhaps not.
When they leave they will stop
And put away the poetic faces they wear
In the drawer from whence it came.

I do not know.
Perhaps I also look poetic,
My face stuck on with glue
And they talk of depressing poems
And I record.

Vivien Muir

The girls seemed to enjoy the poems which Phillip Callow and I read them from our own work. I also did a good deal of work during writing sessions on my own writing: thus we tried to set an example. Graham Carey, a teacher of pottery from Bingley College of Education, came and talked with clarity and seriousness about clay and making pots, and told them that creativity was essentially a way of life. One's attitude to existence, and one's personality, inevitably made its impression in the clay, he said. The greatest delight anyone could have was in working hard, especially to establish human meaning, in symbolic forms. One can only hope that the presence of three men devoted to creative work could convey by example the serious urgency of the task of seeking meaning and values in this way.

The girls were able both to be serious, but also able to be jokey and ironic about it: of course, one could not always be 'creative', as this pleasant comic poem makes clear.

> *20 Things to do when uninspired*
> Buy a bottle of Holbrook's patent inspiration
> Buy fruit gums
> Wish the fire were warmer
> Pull your brother's socks up
> Watch people
> Twiddle your thumbs
> Make the dinner, or lunch, depending on where you come
> Pray                                                                from
> Meditate
> Shiver
> Look out of the window and admire the view
> Wash up, or down for a change
> Tickle Maura
> Draw D.H.
> Stare at D.H.
> Curse D.H.
> Feel happy because nobody else is writing much
> Thank God you dad's not a miller and you
> Haven't got silver hands;
> Think of something for twenty;
> Accept you're uninspired – and forget it.
>
> Diana Barnes

This pleasantly ironic poem, cheeky, but devoid of any hostility, brings me to the emotional strain of the course. In the end, looking over the work these students did, there is no doubt in my mind it was a success. As I left I asked some of the girls if they had enjoyed it, and they were vociferously enthusiastic (the author of *The Stone* had written home to say she *wasn't* enjoying it but she seemed happy enough as she danced about on the last day). But Graham Carey[1] made a good point; he emphasized that creative work was an on-going, long-term thing, belonging to long-term relationships between people, and between the self and the world.

---

[1] See *Proposal for a New College* by Graham Carey and Peter Abbs, Heinemann, 1977.

All the same, it must be admitted that we found the girls at times very trying. I often thought of Winnicott's essay on the need for 'confrontation' between adult and adolescent. The adolescent wants to annihilate you, says Winnicott, because, indeed, he will one day replace you. But the adult must make it clear that he is going to survive, and remain 'King of the Castle'. This then releases the young person from a false too-early maturity and responsibility, so that he or she can then be irresponsible and idealistic, set out to reform the world, stop war, and cure human hatred. This idealism is very valuable in society. But anything that forces young people into a too-early false sophistication undermines this idealistic irresponsibility. We must have a natural confrontation, says Winnicott, and 'It will not be nice' – but without the necessary, if painful, confrontation, neither adult nor adolescent is really free.

But when the confrontation came at Lumb Bank, we didn't expect it to be so painful. The girls, unfortunately, had been told that they would not be expected to work very hard. Phillip and I had other ideas: and we were on the whole, in recent years at any rate, used to working with adults rather than children. We had also, incidentally, brought up daughters. But what was our relationship to be, to these girls? We had to find out.

Everything went well, until the second day which was supposed to be a 'free' day on which the students went up on the moors, on into the River Valley to meditate, be alone, and prepare to write about themselves and the world. Unfortunately, it was wet and cold, and the girls were obliged to sit indoors, work – and chat. We alternated between fearing a lapse into the bored, desultory chit-chat of a wet day in a YHA Hostel, and something more organized, to help things along – more stimuli, more readings perhaps. At any rate, we prepared a timetable for next morning, but then, when it turned out fine, got ready to turn it back to a free morning. Everyone had agreed to meet at 9.30 am.

That morning the girls kept Phillip and me waiting for an hour and a half. They knew we were there ready and waiting. It was a real rebellion, as one could tell from their faces – that desperate, sulky and really contemptuous look adolescents direct at you, full of unconscious murder. I wasn't angry, but I was straightforward and firm. So, when they were all down, I made my confrontation. They wanted to be treated as adults, I said, but when they were involved in arrangements as adults, they went to pieces and behaved like children. I had to be careful what I said. My 'King of the Castle' act mustn't lead me to any hostile and provocative things which would spoil the atmosphere and fill everyone with what my own daughter calls 'bad vibes'. But I pointed out that they had kept two professional writers hanging about for half the morning, and everyone waiting, while we sorted out a new 'free' morning. In any case it was bad to waste their own time, and worse to waste others' time: free and responsible adults didn't do that.

But I had very painful feelings while I was talking to them in this way, because there was a sense in which they were spoiling a promising development towards self-discipline without which nothing is achieved in this work. Afterwards, however, everyone was relieved – because we had spoken out to one another as adults, asking for self-motivated co-operation.

We never cured the girls entirely of going to pieces, lapsing into hysterical giggles, spoiling the atmosphere of poetry readings by private whispers. But after we spoke as adults to adults, there was a change: a divide had been crossed, and they began to work hard and co-operatively, in a 'student' way rather than a 'pupil' way. There was a sense, of course, in which we were working within an invisible structure, which was the overall community and pattern of their college.

Many adults, including myself, are a bit afraid of adolescents – afraid of their vulnerability, their sometimes apparent (but really very superficial) hostility, their moodiness or morbid episodes. I hadn't really thought beforehand about the emotional price of being stuck with 16 female adolescents in a lonely house for a week: perhaps I hadn't dared. In the end we came to terms with one another, and liked one another. No-one was really nasty. Phillip Callow and I had many criticisms to make: the girls were poor at spoken delivery, they didn't make enough effort to speak clearly. We learned that their own choice of both their own and published poems was quite different – much was quite Victorian. But we loved their ebullience, their occasional gravity, their idealism, and even their puppyish energy. We were gratified that they worked so hard in writing. We couldn't stand their giggling, their languorous ability to pass hours without doing anything, their relapse into the anomic trance of 'pop' noise, and their inability to pull themselves together to sing or read something with an organized delivery and confident attention. There *is* a gap, and it isn't realistic to pretend that the adult can really join in their world. 'Meeting' in work like that we did may be an act of love, and so it involves hate. We hoped to have more effect by setting an example. Maybe we did: perhaps time will tell. Certainly, their created works, some quite beautiful, are in the world, where they weren't before – and this unites us. But no-one need suppose such a project was a soft option, easy, 'progressive' or 'vague'. It was very hard work, not least because so much of our environment, the ethos of the age, inhibits creativity. Even much officially approved 'art' was against us in bridging the gap. But I believe we did reach through to the true voices of those young women, and there is real engagement with meaning in their poetry.

# Chapter Ten

# The Teaching of Fiction

How do we apply philosophical anthropology to the teaching of fiction? Here I will take as a good example Dickens' *Great Expectations*. *Great Expectations*, as Mrs. Q.D. Leavis implies in the very fine essay in *Dickens the Novelist*, is one of Dickens' most successful works. It is economical, with hardly a wasted moment, and it is profound, while still being immediately accessible to even a pedestrian reader. It is in this essay, significantly, that Mrs. Leavis speaks of the difficulty of conveying the depth, sensitivity and seriousness of Dickens's art at a time when so much in our culture is facile, cynical and insensitive. But even so, when we teach *Great Expectations* we have everything on our side that it is possible to have, to help that 're-creation' of which George Sampson writes.

While it is a popular, entertaining, dramatic thriller, *Great Expectations* is also a creative work of art which deals at the profoundest level with the problem of authenticity and freedom. In this work Dickens is an 'existentialist' author. I say this not for any reason of fashion, or because Dickens needs some kind of refurbishing for the contemporary market. Dickens's preoccupation in this novel is with *potentia* (as Nietzsche called it) and how it may be fulfilled or thwarted in us.

Dickens's most positive value is love, and love is giving others their freedom, thus achieving one's own. Magwich's attempt to turn Pip into his own *potentia* fulfilled, in terms of a false cultivation imposed by wealth and spurious social graces, is not based in true love but on an idea applied from outside, and a false one at that. And so, when Magwich holds out his hands to Pip, the latter feels repelled by a bodily insult to his own authenticity. He is offended by being falsely claimed, in the light of an idea which, since it is not sprung from his Being and his true self, violates. Miss Havisham's use of the infant born of the murderess who serves Jaggers and Magwich is a violation too. She uses her power over the child Estella to use her to satisfy her own envy. This destructive hate may have arisen from thwarted love; but it is a perversion of trust and an exploitation of the child's self and being. Miss Havisham herself is an embodiment of wrecked *potentia:* but she also battens and feeds on her own impotence, and her own dynamic of cherished hate destroys her. All these violations are rejections of the natural potentialities of true self being. Pip says to her of Estella:

> 'Better,' I could not help saying, 'have left her a natural heart, even to be buried or broken.'
>
>                                        Chapter XLIX

It should be noted, despite the muted and ambivalent ending, that Dickens does not mean by this that anyone who is left 'a natural heart' must inevitably come to be broken up by life. On the contrary, he sets the disasters against the emerging awareness of true self-being in Pip – who is like most of us, from time to time, a bad chooser. We must (if we accept the existentialist position) define ourselves and find our freedom by making the right choice for ourselves: but the problem is that we become diverted from choosing truly by influences that thrust inauthenticity upon us. There are epochs in Pip's life when influences which have plans for him (malicious or benign) stand dangerously in the way of his path to fulfilment: they urge him towards a false self. These indirect forms of hate are more insidious even than death. There can be little, even in contemporary works, more painful and dreadful than Orlick's sadistic torments practised on the trapped and wounded Pip, as a picture of human interaction at its most evil. There is no doubt that Dickens was aware of what human hate can do. But the death of the spirit threatened by Miss Havisham and Magwich is even worse than physical cruelty, because (to use Lomas's words) 'the true self is so crushed or impoverished . . . it develops an alternative or false self'.[1]

And then the artistic triumph, which is also a triumph of belief in man's potentialities, is to enable Pip to 'find' Magwich and to relate to him in 'loving communion' from a self that has avoided falsification. The convict patron holding out his arms in (false) affection is repulsive: but at the end Pip is overjoyed to tell him that his child

---

[1] This may act as a 'caretaker' to the true self, 'concealing and protecting it in hope . . .' See *True and False Experience*, p.95.

Estella *has had a life* (fulfilled or no), and he feels from the movements of Magwich's hands that he is understood: the symbolism is that of a 'liebende Wirheit' achieved under the most unpropitious circumstances – and it is a kind of love. So too is Pip's development of concern for Miss Havisham, in whom he manages to bring out genuine remorse for what she has done:

> . . . to see her with her white hair and her worn face, kneeling at my feet, gave me a shock through all my frame.
> 'O!' she cried, despairingly, 'What have I done! What have I done!'

Although Miss Havisham has brought Estella up to be cold and hard, and had used her to torment hated man, there are other aspects of Estella's existence which are beyond her control. Dickens's belief in the power of love contrasts sharply with the predominant view of Sartre today and of the 'old' existentialism, that love is not possible, and that all our efforts to define ourselves and our freedom are inevitably doomed to frustration and absurdity. Throughout, Estelle is a star – and she inspires Pip with idealism and aspiration. In the end, the conclusion is tentative and untriumphant: but the real Estella is found to reflect the real Pip. Thus Mrs. Leavis is right to point out that the book is written as if told us by the mature and free Pip. He is well able both to be ironical and yet to see the transcendent reality of the human imagination, for Pip's maturation is achieved by the inspiration Estella brings into his life, even at her first appearance, and despite her cruelty and coldness.

> She answered at last, and her light came along the dark passage like a star . . .

The other important aspect of Estella's existence is that in her are the possibilities of the redemption of a heart trained in hardness and coldness.

> 'So you want me then,' said Estella, turning suddenly with a forced and serious, if not angry look, 'to deceive and entrap you?'
> 'Do you deceive and entrap him Estella?'
> 'Yes, and many others – all of them but you . . .'

This exchange comes at the very moment at which Pip's 'strong-hold' is to collapse on him, as it does in Chapter XXXIX. But in one sense it is a very positive moment: Estella's anger flares up here because he cannot see how differently she regards him from the 'others'. And whatever harm Miss Havisham has done she has also fostered this possibility of a unique loving 'meeting', by a kind of mad kindness to their boy and girl relationship. Pip suffers not only the imposition of a false identity (the 'gentleman') from a pseudo-father, Magwich: but also the petrification of his female element, Estella, by a pseudo-mother. In the background is the ghost of the Castrating (annihilating) Mother. As this happens, he denies his real love to those who are really like a mother and father to him, Biddy and Joe. His sister, who represents yet another aspect of the female element, a pseudo-male type in women, is brutally destroyed by the sadistic, libidinal Orlick, whose resemblance to Bentley Brummle makes him the aggressive father destroying the mother, in fantasy. The Orlick threat however, is only that of actual pain and death: since it concentrates Pip's mind on what is important in his life: love, gratitude and meaning – so the experience completes the 'stage of concern'.[1]

The effect upon Pip of the other inauthenticities is much more serious, as it threatens the meaning of his life altogether. It is indicative of the richness of the book that at the end – whichever end we take – we are left in the last four pages pondering the meaning of life, and what the characters' choice and acts have in fact done to their own quest for meaning and that of others. Estella in this is virtually a tragic figure – a tragedy of unfulfilment.[2] Pip may be said at least to have given us the account of his life – which, because of its existential insights, is a great work of affirmation in the face of death.

Dickens is willing in his work to confront the failure of meaning in the face of nothingness. At one point Pip declares 'I am now fit for nothing.' His potentialities have been destroyed, by the imposition upon him of a concept of what it is to be a 'gentleman' that belong to a utilitarian society. The threat directed at Magwich, who defies his exile, in which he is involved ('Don't go home'), is matched by the threat to his perception of the world, from Estella's petrified heart. At

---

[1] The parallel with *Crime and Punishment* should be evident, at the level of primitive 'unconscious' fantasy.

[2] Strangely, nearly all D.H. Lawrence's novels are tragedies of unfulfilment, too.

the beginning of Chapter XLV his scope is reduced to the dimensions of a rushlight.

> As I had asked for a nightlight, the chamberlain had brought me in, before he left the good old constitutional rush-light of those virtuous days – an object like the ghost of a walking cane, which instantly broke its back if touched, which nothing could ever be lighted at, and which was placed in solitary confinement at the bottom of a high tin tower, perforated with round holes that made a staringly wideawake pattern on the walls.
> When I had got into bed, and lay there, footsore, weary and wretched, I found that I could no more close my eyes than I could close the eyes of this foolish Argus. And thus, in the gloom and death of the night, we stared at one another.
>
> p.76

It is part of the deeply disturbing effect of *Great Expectations* that it conveys by such symbolism the attempts to impose on a human creature something that does not belong to him or her. This is, in Pip,

> the inexplicable feeling that had come over me when I last walked – not alone – in the ruined garden, and through the deserted brewery.
>
> p.299

My interpretation, taking in insights from psychoanalytical theory and existentialism, takes us more deeply into the meaning, I believe, even than Mrs. Leavis's brilliant interpretation. For Pip's problem is deeper than the question she elicits: 'Is the real life that of social reality or natural feeling?' It is rather, 'If a false social reality is thrust upon us, directly or indirectly, or if we are confused by other people's falsities, so that the natural heart is stifled, corrupted, and threatened with death (like the derelict garden and the deserted brewery) – *how do we find that which is "authentic"* for us?' Pip's own 'mature freedom' is the answer – his own creative vision, which is Dickens's, of course. But the essential anguish is, 'How do I recognize my own authenticity when I see it?' – how do I know my *potentia*, my true being in fulfilment?

The fulfilment and exertion of that creative authenticity, and in it moral choices (manifest in Pip's own placing of his people and his world as well as in every line of Dickens' prose), depend upon exploring male and female elements, and the proclivities for doing and being, of love and hate, throughout experiences of great suffering and inner debate. Dickens is not only condemning 'society' – he is also trying to define true and false experience. This makes the novel so universal. In this work there is very little sentimental falsification. Dickens' assertion of the natural heart is sound and realistic, a tremendous achievement, in upholding the primacy of imagination, feeling and vision, in his age – the age that is still ours, for the deadening falsifications in British society have been deepened both by our materialism and by our more brutal philosophical attitudes to ourselves since his day. There is a courage and trustfulness in Pip's 'better to have left her a natural heart to break, even bruised or broken' from which we can learn much: our problem is to find our true selves in the face of even greater falsification.

I have written this chapter for the teacher, and I have not spared him: it has been a difficult chapter to write. But the joy of it is that the child can read the novel and possess all these yearnings towards meaning, in the drama of its enactment, and the life of its language – without these deeper 'existential' issues even being made explicit. Even today, with reading at such a low ebb, *Great Expectations* is surely not a difficult book to teach? All the teacher has to do is help the child to enjoy the book and understand it – while the creative engagement with human existence will do its work at the deeper level of response. Such a great work of literature is an enrichment of our each living dynamics, in the quest for meaning through words, that *is* 'English'.

An English teacher who loves and respects a great creative work like *Great Expectations* will surely be dissatisfied with so much that is offered children today: the 'realist/working class' novels by Stan Barstow, Alan Sillitoe and Keith Waterhouse; the novels of 'relevance' like *Lord of the Flies* and *The Catcher in the Rye;* war stories like those of Nevil Shute, or 'science' fiction like *The Day of the Triffids.* So few of these have any genuine creative content, and are simply not works of art, but rather journalism. Some, in their existential message, are just bad. Mr Michael Saunders recently wrote a devastating critique of Jack Schaefer's *Shane* (*The Use of English*, Autumn 1977; 29/1, p.14), a novel which sells 40,000 copies a year to schools. He said, 'It is impossible to ignore the implicit and explicit savagery of the story': 'there is no interest in character, and no insight into motivation, or the subtleties of human relationships.'

If (says Saunders) it is true, as Denys Harding has said, that in a novel 'the represented participants are only part of a convention by which the author discusses, and proposes an evaluation of, possible human experience'[1] what is the effect of *Shane*? Saunders accuses the author of 'appalling taste' and suggests that teachers can only teach it by 'suspending their critical faculties' while the effect of such teaching can only be to encourage superficial reading.

Only by really possessing truly creative works of art like *Great Expectations* can teachers get a feel of fiction which genuinely satisfies the need for meaning – and become able to choose works which provide the nourishment which their charges need. If that is 'élitist', then I am élitist enough to believe we need trained dieticians in a famine.

---

[1] 'Psychological Processes in the Reading of Fiction', *British Journal of Aesthetics*, Vol.2, 1962, p.147.

# English for Meaning in Practice

---

I have tried to show that much thinking about education, even in English, tends to be sterile because in the background lurks a positivist philosophy which cannot find the tacit creative processes upon which the whole process depends. And I have tried to suggest that there is a whole new movement in philosophy which can help us to develop a more adequate approach to education – philosophical anthropology. It is supportive because it finds culture as central to man's existence. The hidden planet which we have been searching for is *meaning:* once we accept that man's primary need is for meaning, then we can find a better basis for our work.

Then I have tried to show what an existentialist approach means in practice. Today there are a number of writers striving towards an existentialist approach to education. Dr Robert Hogkin has explored the ground in his *Reconnaissance on an Educational Frontier* and *Born Curious,* though he seems to me not to have fully relinquished the chains of positivism. Philip Pacey wrote a very interesting book, *A Sense of What is Real,* out of a course at a College of Art in existentialism and creativity. Graham Carey and Peter Abbs have tried to suggest a new holistic way of training teachers in *Proposal for a New College,* while Abbs has been groping his way towards an existentialist approach to English in *English for Diversity, Root and Blossom,* and in some recent essays. In one he declares:

> We need, desperately, a concept of wholeness, of an education committed to the simultaneous development of the emotional, sensory, intellectual and imaginative faculties. Our educational system is pathologically abstract, obsessed with the transmission of facts, obsessed with examination results, obsessed with the classification of knowledge and children alike. We need, in contrast, to develop the whole person, to make him passionately

intelligent and intelligently passionate. It is vital that we impregnate scientific studies with aesthetic feeling and with moral concern, that we do not remove them from the philosophical question 'How do I know?' and the existential and moral question 'How can I be responsible for that which I know?' . . . In the arts, which are concerned above all with the development of subjectivity, the slow clarification of existence through symbolic forms, we need to develop in relationship to the concept of wholeness coherent pedagoguies and disciplines.

'An existentialist approach to education', *Times Educational Supplement*, 19 May, 1978

But how do we impregnate and develop? Fortunately, the philosophy towards which we grope simply tells us that what we do naturally, at least in English, is the best way of educating in what Abbs calls 'whole' terms.

As we pursue philosophies, alas, our words tend to get longer: and in philosophical anthropology we find ourselves involved in trying to understand difficult words from German philosophy such as *Geisteswissenschaft* and *Innerlichkeit*. It all begins to sound as daunting as the Bullock Report's discussion of 'linguistic theory with psychological links' (p.344), and 'linguistic constraints in a multi-cultured society . . . strategies and tactics used in accomplishing communication goals' (p.344). If we don't look out, we shall start using language like 'the Epigenesis of Intrinsic Motivation' or a 'symbolist interactionist approach', such as those who have had experience of certain education departments complain. The technical terms sound a thousand miles from the work we do with children and young people. How can we relate these difficult disciplines of inquiry to the everyday life of the school and college? Fortunately, philosophical anthropology recognizes the natural endowments of both teacher and child – and simply encourages them to get on with it, by Nature! That is, there is no need to suppose you can't teach until you understand the philosophy or have a theory of 'cognitive development' or whatever. We practise an art.

The phrase I would like to pick up once more from philosophy is that reference from Polanyi to how language 'points beyond the words'. When a child brings his poem to us, or when we decide to teach him Blake's *Tyger*, in what way are we concerned with 'understanding the operation of language'? Are we concerned with 'the sound system of English, with the emphasis on intonation, auditory perception and discrimination' as the Bullock Report has it (p. 345)? In the background of all such language lurks a positivist 'scientific' gesture that goes with a failure to respond to language in a poetic way, in a *whole* way. If, say, we read the opening page of *Bleak House*, we are attending to the words in a way that 'points beyond' them, towards an overall meaning. We are, so to speak, phenomenologically involved in a state of consciousness, in which we can feel the fog in our throats, and at the same time, we sense the obfuscation: we are touched, that is, by the symbolism of the fog, which stands for moral turpitude, which obscures meaning and truth – and prevents men from seeing what it is they most truly desire from life. Our response to the language illuminates problems of moral choice, by involving us, imaginatively, in 'felt life'. How else can one put it? At once we wonder what human drama is going to be played out in this obfuse setting, in Dickens's novel. It turns out to be Lady Dedlock's denial of a love that might have given her life meaning: she allows herself to be cut off from parenthood and her child in exchange for comfort, status and money. So, she becomes cut off in the end, even from the love and devotion of her husband, and dies. The fog stands for the various stages of *not-seeing* that poor Esther Summerson goes through: and for the failure of us all to see the predicament of the poor and under-privileged like Jo: and so, in a highly complex exploration, for the bleakness of our own hard hearts, because of which we do not see what really matters in our lives. These are the existential issues which the language describing the fog begins to arouse in us.[1]

The grammarian might notice that there is not one full sentence in the whole opening chapter of *Bleak House*. The linguist might find it full of surprising morphemes. But what we, as 'English' teachers, are interested in is the *moral energy* which impels Dickens to write so poetically, with such a vividness and rhythm. And we may guess that this energy is related to his universal poetic theme, which is that certain kinds of inauthenticity can destroy people's lives – can destroy the meaning in their lives. To talk like this is phenomenological, since it indicates that what Dickens is concerned with, what his poetic language is pointing to, is a phenomenon of consciousness in man, not 'social conditions' or the historical legacy behind the Clean Air Bill, or poverty, or even 'rich language'. The importance of those opening pages are in their *meaning*.

---

[1] Their symbolic roots are in the New Testament.

If our concern, then, is with 'significance', we cannot merely stick at the 'language', but must see what it points to, 'beyond'. This is true, even of the simplest child's poem. Here is one from Australia:

*The Deserted House*
The curtains are drawn,
The beds are gone.
There is not a sound.
The people have left.
The carpet is up.
The boards are bare.
There is not a sound.

Annette Chennell

This is clear and direct English – perfect for its purpose: not a word wrong. There is little for the teacher to say, except, 'Excellent!'. If we need to define the literacy at which we aim – here it is. Today, I see the Bullock Report on English is praised for its 'realism' (*The Times*, 26 January 1977): yet surely in its failure to discuss anything like the 'life' in such a poem of the naïve imagination, it is deficient in a certain kind of realism, as much as Gradgrind?

In order to become capable of fostering such clear effective English the teacher must pay attention to many tacit features. To understand the quality of this little poem we have to look beyond the words – at the intensity of *imagining*. From Winnicott's work we understand why such a good poem is a product of *trust*, in a situation in which the child feels safe to give his achievements as 'reparative' gifts of 'goodness' to an adult who will value and respect them, for example. In this, it is asking Winnicott's two questions.

How do we train English teachers to be able to respond to such qualities in a child's poem? There is one simple answer to this, implicit in such a philosophy as that of Michael Polanyi: as much *reading for enjoyment as possible*. A teacher trained to respond to (say) Dickens's description of the marshes in *Great Expectations*, or Emily Brontë's description of Wuthering Heights or to *To the Lighthouse* will be able to recognize the quality of language here. He would note how the objects *move:* the curtains come down; the vans go; the people leave; the carpet comes up. There is an uncanny movement in the little poem, and we are left with emptiness ('There is not a sound . . .'). All we can say is that we can feel that the subject of the poem is vividly imagined, and the act of imagination contributes to improved capacities to inquire into experience.

Since the introduction of the BEd, and the PGCE courses at universities, and all the rest, there has been an increasing masculin- ization of knowledge in the area of teacher training. Theses and dissertations proliferate, and there has been a concentration on 'proper academic disciplines'. But as Nicholas Grier, who experienced an education course at Cambridge, declared in a recent article in the *Daily Telegraph* (19 March, 1975)

> The long essays tend to become essays in waffle, a desperate attempt being made to fill up the required number of words with portentous educational jargon which neither student nor lecturer is likely to read again. A good arts degree teaches one how to use words precisely; an education course how to waste them.

I have looked at the recommendations of the Bullock Report – as by examining their proposed courses for students. Those who work out such schemes obviously regard themselves as 'realists', as do those who follow an academic lead into classifying children's writing, or Bernstein's sociology of language use, or linguistics, and inflict all this on students.

But they are not realists. The most realistic way of training students to teach English is to leave them ample time to read *Little Black Mingo*, *The Borrowers*, *The Jungle Book*, *Peacock Pie*, and *The Lore and Language of Schoolchildren*. They should then have seminars on the books they read: let them read *At the Back of the North Wind* and talk about the meaning of that, as when the North Wind seduces the little boy into the world of death.

And then they should read *Nicholas Nickleby*, *David Copperfield* and *Dombey and Son* – and discuss what Charles Dickens implies, about childhood, schooling, the growth of being, and love. They should know Edward Thomas's poetry, and that of Keats. They should know Mark Twain, and Jane Austen, and John Buchan. Their reading and discussion of these works should be carried out not in the context of 'how to teach' such books, but at their own level of interest. I take 'in- service' courses from time to time and I know that the really effective moments on any course occur when I am myself holding back, enjoying listening to the teacher members of the course arguing about (say) the art of *Sons and Lovers*, or disagreeing about the truth about love in a poem like *Roses on the Breakfast Table* or *Manifesto*. At such moments I know I am contributing to their professional work at a deep level by letting them do the talking. Is D.H. Lawrence right about women? Did he falsify his experience with Miriam and Clara? If teachers are in passionate discourse about such things, thumbing through the book and turning over their memories of reading it, to support their arguments – then they are re-creating their capacities as artist-teachers. So they would be if they were howling with laughter over Daisy Ashford, or *Twas Brillig and the Slithy Toves*. If I ask them to discuss the meaning of *Peacock Pie*, I am training them to teach English for Meaning.

A teacher cannot teach English well unless he or she can remember being pleased and excited by reading and writing. For this we all need continual re-creation. So the proper training for a teacher, whether in a college of education or in-service work, is the enjoyment of literature. It is the lack of such *enjoyment* that makes for so many dull English periods.

The satisfaction we get from reading good books is derived from the answers they provide to those two questions of Winnicott's. Of course, there are false answers to those questions, and the 'blood', the thriller and the pornographic book provide a kind of mental rage that offers such false answers. They provide the answers of hate, and this must ultimately lead to dissatisfaction, because hate solves nothing.[1] Such false-solution culture only deepens our starvation, and leads to endless violence, mental at first, though it is always likely to burst out into acts. Our culture today is seriously corrupt and corrupting.

A good work of art tells us what it is to be human, and, even though we do not realize it, contributes to the sense that life has a point. This can actually be quite light-hearted, as in (say) *As You Like It* or *Much Ado About Nothing*. But it can also be ultimately grave, as in *The Book of Job* or *King Lear*. The English teacher should conduct his work in the light of the recognition that he has the power and the responsibility to give his pupils nourishment in response to those two existential questions. He stands between the child's emerging self, with its own voice, its own language, and the cultural inheritance. Winnicott shows that our cultural development requires elements of union and

---

[1] See *The Masks of Hate*, by the present author, Pergamon, 1962. In a useful, if untidy, book on charlatanism and decadence in contemporary art, Mr. Giles Auty writes, 'one of the most valid objections to pornography is that its values are usually diametrically opposed to those of art'. *The Art of Self-deception*, Libertarian Books, 1977, p.69.

separateness. We need to draw on the available culture of our civilization (so that children's lives should be continually enriched by
giving them the best we can provide) while bringing out our own
emerging resources of being. So, a teacher of English must listen
intently for the child's true voice, that which speaks of what he has
within him to become. From this interchange between union and
separateness develops a sense of personal value that is the basis of all
efficiency.

As we have seen, philosophical anthropology invokes the word
*Dasein:* the need for every human being to feel that he has been
capable of *being there:* of being somewhere, and at the same moment
being conscious of his existence, and responsible for his existence, so
that a sense of existential being has been experienced that cannot be
taken away, not even by death. Without some solution to the *Dasein*
problem, men cannot live: and it is the humanities teacher's role to
concern himself with the quest for true self-being, and for meaning
and values, in this existentialist way. Out of this can emerge prowess in
the deepest sense. It is this concern with getting the best out of oneself
that is most efficient in English, even in dealing with basic literacy, as
I have shown in *English for the Rejected.* Thus English is not 'personal
growth', as in the Bullock caricature of our position. It is a subject
which can contribute to the very complex relationship between the
language in which we all exist, and the language art we can all inherit –
and the striving emergence of the young *animal symbolicum.* As for
him or her, the capacity to live a full and effective human life depends
upon the *prowess of spirit* he can develop between his own resources
and culture.

The relationship between literacy, sense of personal value, and
meaning in existence is discussed in an illuminating way in a fascinating book on teaching prisoners to write by Robert Roberts, *Imprisoned
Tongues.* This is mostly, of course, about very deprived or unstable
men. It is clear from this book that literacy goes hand in hand with the
acquisition of self-respect, while by contrast any relapse into a life of
crime often may mean the forfeiture or 'forgetting' of literacy. It also
reveals the central importance of language to the human spirit. The
stigma attached to illiteracy is evident from this book: a young
inexperienced warder, for example, once called out 'Fall out the
illiterates!, – and not a man moved! But in Roberts's classes the men
wrote moving poems:

There's a stench of fish on the wind,
And the high stone wall
Throws shadows on the waters
Of my brooding mind;
A dam that blocks the little streams
Of waking thought
And in the night invades my sleep
To censor restless dreams.

J.

Mr. Roberts' deeply human book has more in it to help with problems of literacy than the whole of the Bullock Report – not least because, again, it points beyond the words, to the problems of overcoming the effects of false choices, of false solutions, of guilt and the sense of failure. Roberts, simply by *listening* to the prisoners as tutor, saves them. His emphasis is on *encounter,* in which their teacher has established with them that he is *attending to meaning.* The meaning may even be found in their half-literate autobiographical 'placing' of original acts, such as a daring escape:

> Sir, I was once an enscape prisnor. And the way I excaped was a verry cleaver one . . . I yoused to put the musick on a readiater in the pashage to the toilet that leads from the receration Room. on the forth flor 40 foot UP. Beside this Room is the laverty and the offerser stands gard. Betwen him and the laverty is the spot where I would sit to play the pipes. when anyone would go to the WCS they would have to pass me. I would stop playing and that would be the sine for Rob to stop sawing . . .

Even in this story there is a sense of dramatic relief at the end, to be brought back to the security of justice:

> . . . I went into a pub neerby that was quiet and empty and I sat drinking giness whice somhow tastes better in the sout. Then in comes a tall man and stud by not taken anyting and then another and another and another ontill there moust of bean a dozon. Then one tap me on the sholder. I stud up. I luck at him and he lucks at me. He says noting and I say noting, but they knew they had got there man.

p.181

Robert's book makes it clear that responsiveness to the meaning of a piece of writing is an act of love, full of tacit elements of responsiveness. The more I reflect on the experience of teaching English the more I realize that one central discipline is that capacity to *listen* which Roberts displays: and this means not knowing the rules of language, but listening to meanings. This in turn means being able to *receive* symbolism. This raises again the question of how teachers should be trained. My answer would be that student teachers should spend a great deal of time discussing the symbolic content of literature and poetry, of the literature of childhood, and of children's own writing. Only a discussion of such symbolism in depth, over many hours throughout their course can equip teachers to understand the kinds of things children explore in their fantasies and creative work.

What, for instance is an appropriate response to a piece of primary school writing like this? It was read into a tape recorder by an illiterate child of eight who could not have written it down:

> Addi Sarosh
>
> Once upon a time there was an old man and an old lady and they lived together – went out to work and there was a big bad wolf and he came along and knocked at the door and said 'Old woman, open the door. I am your husband'. She said 'Show me your fingers' and she saw his fingers and said 'You are not my husband'. So the wolf went away to the butcher's and he said 'Give me some fingers and some sausages' and he said 'No, you'll have to pay for them' and he said 'Give me them or I'll kill you' so he did. And when he got the sausages he went over to a flower (?flour) stall and he said 'No, you'll have to pay for them'. He said 'I'll gobble you all up' and so he did and he got the powder and he went back to the lady's house and he said 'Little old woman, I am your husband, let me in' and then 'Show me your hands' said the mother and he showed her his paws, but they were the wolf's paws and she said 'Come in' and she opened the door and the wolf gobbled her all up, and the husband came home and he said 'Where is my wife?' and he went to the farm and the wolf had swallowed her whole and he chopped the wolf open and got the mother out. And that's the end.
>
> *Primrose Hill Primary School: from the teaching work of Miss Suki Holbrook.*

Here there are clearly archetypal elements, of the kind found in fairy tales, Hans Andersen, and the Brothers Grimm. This tale is a mixture of *Red Riding Hood* and *The Wolf and the Three Little Pigs*. It interests me because of its symbolism: would we recognize the fingers of someone we know? Why does the wolf put *flour* on the sausages to make them look like the husband's fingers? (Is it because Addi Saroch is brown, and perhaps afraid of hostility from white people?) Is there an unconscious symbolism of the sexuality of the husband-wife relationship so that the child is trying (by identifying with the wolf who is trying to usurp the husband's rôle) to offer her, undisguised, phalluses so that the old woman (mother) will accept him for a husband? Isn't the 'swallowing' a symbol of the mutual eating which a child (according to the psychoanalysts) believes adult sexuality to be? If he usurps the father's rôle in his curiosity and Oedipus impulses, perhaps (he feels) his hunger will 'eat' the mother? The end of the story, in which the real father brings the mother to life, seems a valuable recognition of the father's rights to the mother as sexual partner. So he pushes the child off to develop on his own path. Then the wolf, into whose symbolic skin the child-author had entered, must die. Something like this seems to me the meaning of this child's fairy story: a re-enactment of the Oedipus myth.

Again, I am beyond the words. Now, from my phenomenological analysis, I can return to the words, and help to edit the piece. Of course, though I ask myself those questions based on psychoanalytical theory, I never say anything of this to the child. It is a fine fairy tale, and would hold everybody enthralled. It takes its place with *The Tinderbox, Red Riding Hood* and the tales of dragons, in the mythology of gobbling up and being gobbled.

My secret understanding of its phenomenological meaning may help me, however, to help the child. For instance, it isn't clear at one point:

> 'Show me your hands' said the mother and so he showed her his paws but they were the wolf's paws and she said 'Come in . . .'

Here the unconscious elements have gotten out of hand: the child is perhaps so afraid the reader will see the (unconscious) truth, he blurts it out. What he ought to write is something like:

'Show me your hands' said the mother.

The wolf pushed a bunch of sausages covered with flour in the door. This time she thought they were her husband's hands. 'Come in . . .'

So, a teacher who can grasp the deeper meaning of the tale may be able to 'receive' it much better, and help the child edit it. A teacher may just as well respond by intuition. The only additional value of such a 'psychoanalytical' understanding is that it helps us to feel more confident in working in terms of poetic logic, dream logic – the language of the unconscious. This is not to treat English as 'therapy': it is to recognize that in English we often deal with very deep areas of experience, as all humanities subjects do, at times, and this area of creative collaboration with dream and fantasy *is* our proper area. As an imaginative energy, it is the root of being.

A teacher will not need telling all this, if he or she reads poetry. A teacher would be able to understand that strange child's story if he or she had discussed an adult poem like Bernard Spencer's *A Hand:*

> *A Hand*
> The human hand lying on my hand
> (The wrist has a gilt bangle on)
> Wore its print of personal lines
> Took breath as lungs and leaves and
> Tasted in the skin our sun.
>
> The living palm, and the near-to-bone
> Fine animal hairs where the light shone.
> The handed mole to its earth, the stoat to the dark
> And this flesh to its nature nervously planned;
> To dig love's heart till everything is shown
> To hunt, to hold the mark – this loved hand

Bernard Spencer

The child in the above story was dealing, among other things, with problems of how we recognize one another. Bernard Spencer is dealing with that uniqueness in mutual recognition which yields meaning in love. The appropriate attention of the reader is to symbolism. The woman's hand had a 'print of personal lines'. The same sun has shone on him and her, and this hand has 'tasted in the skin our sun'. The hand is alive, but, like all mortal flesh, is always 'near to the bone': the hairs against the brown flesh are animal. So he compares the hand with the little pink hands of a mole, and sees the human hand as an aspect of the dark secret life of animals, where movements are 'planned' by the nerves, and where, in the human body, there is an impulse to dig out the meaning of love. The invocation of darkness and of the flesh and nerves makes these last lines darkly erotic – 'hunt' and 'hold its mark' evoke the way in which the movements of lovers in their sexual energy are driven to their goal. In conclusion the poet comes sharply back to the present tranquil moment. All these awarenesses of body-meaning are evoked from the phrase 'this loved hand': the insights come from close attention to the language – but in a poetic way.

The poem follows a mood, and conveys it with considerable economy. By its symbolism and its metaphors ('dig love's heart'), it speaks of body-feelings and body-meanings, in their most dynamic forms, with a strong undercurrent of erotic or bodily energy (dig, hunt, hold). Again we are dealing with qualities of language the linguistic discipline cannot touch. As in Empson's *The Seven Types of Ambiguity*, in its best passages, our kind of attention to meaning points (again) 'beyond the words'. Because of its reticence and essential understatement, such a poem would be an excellent one to teach adolescents because it is 'relevant' (not in the Bullock sense) to their own puzzlement over the body, sexuality, identity and passion, but *without explicitness*. The *intention* and *tone* are part of this meaning, creating a respectful and tender attitude to love. And I am sure such a poem would prompt creative writing of a rich kind, on parallel themes, if it was read to a group of adolescents.

The value of philosophical anthropology, with its phenomeno-logical approach, for the English teacher is that it can help us understand such human themes. It helps us to recognize central human existence-problems, and so enables us to become aware of the deeper meanings of a child's poetic awareness. Such awareness gives us confidence in English as a humanities subject, and can make English very rewarding, because it becomes, in this dimension, a subject which enriches the sense of meaning in life. It is in this sense a 'religious' subject.

One of the most interesting problems in English is what I call 'matching'. From their talk and writing a teacher gets an intuitive sense of the interests of pupils – that is, their deeper concerns. How shall he provide for these? How shall he lift them, out of the mundane and ignorant, into the richer spheres of civilized interest and attitudes? This he can only solve if he is himself steeped in literature and the other arts. For instance, to take a common teaching problem, a child's poem may sink into mundanity after a promising opening.

> *The Windy Thunder Storm*
> I gaze outside at the dark grey clouds
> Soon there will be a storm,
> The rain is already spitting;
> Rumble grumble
> The whole day will be spoilt
> I turn on the TV and watch gloomily.
>
> Peter Coe

What shall the English teacher do?

The poem is disappointing, because the promise of the title is never fulfilled: the author turns from the promise of drama, and retreats to submission to the mass media. The English teacher is not necessarily enemy to the media: but he will perhaps see that much bored submissiveness must involve a forfeiture of potentialities. There is enough in the child's poem to reveal that he expected more of a meaning in the approaching storm. Here we have a clear situation where recourse to literature could help to raise the level of meaning to match the early expectations. So, the English teacher will hope to broaden his vision. He can perhaps introduce him to Emily Dickenson's storm:

> *A Thunderstorm*
> The wind began to rock the grass
> With threatening tunes and low, –
> He flung a menace at the earth,
> A menace at the sky.
>
> The leaves unhooked themselves from trees
> And started all abroad;
> The dust did scoop itself like hands
> And throw away the road.

The wagons quickened on the streets,
The thunder hurried slow;
The lightning showed a yellow beak,
And then a livid claw.

The birds put up the bars to nests,
The cattle fled to barns;
There came one drop of giant rain,
And then, as if the hands

That held the dams had parted hold,
The waters wracked the sky,
But overlooked my father's house,
Just quartering a tree.

Here the language is simple, but menacing in its strange vision which is almost surrealist: the line 'the dust did scoop itself like hands' is dream-like, and 'throw away the road' is full of that disintegrating violence that strikes us in the last line. Later, the same hands (which are the hands of God) open to 'wrack' the sky by unleashing the rain (wrecking it, and racking it – i.e. wringing it, wreaking harm).

The lightning is a kind of eagle, biting and clawing at the earth, and the images of movement in the poem convey that combination of slow ponderousness and sudden cataclysmic violence that are a thunderstorm. In the way the poem links the outer elemental rage with inner feelings: it 'builds bridges' between the objective and subjective.

I doubt very much if it is possible to lay down any kind of procedure for 'teaching' such a poem. Of course, unless attention is drawn to the effect of verbs like *rock* and *flung*, to create a feeling of threat to the very stability of the earth and sky; unless the juxtaposition is noted, of 'dust . . . scoop . . . throw' with 'one drop of giant rain', for its bizarre tactile effect – unless these are dwelt on, the teacher will not be training the necessary close attention to language. But each must devise his own method: the common policy is attention to words and their meaning, and so to what must be called the phenomenological meanings, again pointing beyond the words.

The teaching of English cannot be done without such exacting application to meaning, with a sense of living purpose.

While this may sound portentous, it is not so in practice. A great deal of good writing in English looks like this:

### My Gran

She Not very tall about 4ft 9ins to 5ft. She's got a small face,
squinting eyes, small pug nose and thin neck. She has a nosey
nature and if she goes down the pub she always telling my
grandad that men are making eyes at her, and then says he's
jealous. She's always pulling people to pieces, if she has never
moaned about you, then you must have been an angel. Her
clothes are too bad, but if she wear's a skirt 6ins above her ankle
she thinks she is showing too much leg. She's had 8 children and
thinks she knows all there is to know about bringing up children.
As well as having 8 children she got 22 grandchildren and 1 great
grandchild. Her name is the funniest of all, Blanch Izzard and
my Grandads name is Joseph Izzard (she's not bad really and is
always kind to us).

I would describe that as good, average literacy: no problems there!
But besides its good clear quality as English (albeit with a few
mistakes) it gives off a certain seriousness which speaks to me of good
English teaching, emerging from a good (trusting) relationship with
the teacher, of whom she can offer all that familial warmth, and so, in a
situation of trust, she can confront reality squarely in her writing. In
such a context the child can use words to understand and place
experiences in the ways to which Professor Britton refers. The child
can face deep existential problems in Winnicott's ways:

### My Grandad

My Grandad was eighty when he died, I saw him die. I was at
the side of his bed. He lay with a pot of tea in his hand. He
dropped the pot of tea and I thought he was asleep so I nudged
him. He did not wake up and I shouted 'Dad, dad'. He still did
not wake up. I screamed and screamed and shouted 'Mom,
Mom!' my mom came with my grandma behind her. She
pushed the door on one side and said, 'What is the matter with
you?' I showed her my grandad. The colour of his face was blue.

Girl, 11

In its simple starkness, this is like something from Gorki (cf.
*Childhood*). The event is recorded in directness and realism, and the
reader is left to ponder its meaning. An older child will be more aware
of such an event in its historical setting and in a broader human
complex – and the problems of meaning that arise:

When my father died I had many reactions, fear, anger, sadness and shock. When these passed away I was left with another feeling. I cannot describe it. If I do you will think that I am heartless but I do not know if it is true. When I thought about him in bed I wondered if he had found the key. If his life had been all that he had hoped for. I came to the conclusion that if I was him I would have been dissatisfied with my life. But when you are older what can you do to change your future? You only get one chance and that comes when you are young.

I think that there is another kind of key. A chance to expand. Perhaps if you were given an amount of money, you would have the key to travel to change your life and to fulfill it. I would like to get a chance like this one day because I am sure that when I am grown up my views will change again, will not have hazy memories, material memories and uncertain memories but from views with no uncertainty.

Very often I become scared of growing old and finding that I have failed to find the key of life. I hope that my father did not do this, but found all he wanted in his life. I hope also that I will find love, happiness and satisfaction when I find the key.

In the passages of writing I have quoted there is what can only be called a serious existential quality which, I am sure, is approved and encouraged by many of the best English teachers. It is difficult to define: and again, no theoretical preparation can help. The proper discipline for preparation to teach English is response to meaning, and the only way to judge such pieces is to have read enormously in the field of autobiography (e.g. D.H. Lawrence, Maxim Gorki, Edmund Gosse, Helen Thomas: See Peter Abbs, *Autobiography in Education*). Subtle problems are involved, to do with sincerity and authenticity – critical terms which could perhaps only be given substance in a series of seminars among teachers – where one could work by reading phrases aloud, and exchange comparisons, of rhythm, image, tone, symbol, intention and manner, between children's work and published literature.

Literary critical problems are involved, too. Today, an 'open', honest approach to human experience is cherished – and with this openness, a certain seriousness and directness of language. If this kind of English is practised, it does foster development: children become more trusting and honest, as anyone can tell who spends time in a

good, human school. I am equally sure that when it comes to writing
personal letters or using words orally in the most significant moments
of relationships, or telling others of one's love or anger, pupils find
that 'English' of this kind makes an important contribution to 'life',
because the satisfactions of dealing with real problems of existence
does stimulate the use of language as an instrument of understanding
in Polanyi's sense. As an example of the kind of 'voice' I would wish to
encourage I cannot think of a better example than the voice of 'E.T.'
describing the end of her affair with D.H. Lawrence:

> In the front garden the clumps of narcissi stood in shadowed
> stillness. I began to expect Lawrence soon after midday, but the
> afternoon passed, and when at last he wheeled his bicycle
> through the big yard-gate he was not the Lawrence of the night
> before.
>
> 'You said you were coming early,' I reproached him. He made
> no answer and avoided my glance. When tea was over he
> suggested that we should read some French and we went into the
> stackyard and sat on a log beside the hay-stack. Our dog Trip, a
> big white bull-terrier, came up to us with doggish delight and lay
> at our feet. To my surprise Lawrence drove him away:
>
> 'Go away, Trip,' he said. 'We don't want you, you're not nice.'
>
> We read a little, but soon Lawrence closed the book and began
> to speak in a strained voice.
>
> 'This . . . this friendship between us . . . is it keeping even . . . is
> it getting out of balance, do you think?'
>
> My mind barely grasped his words. It was his voice that
> warned me.
>
> 'I think it is keeping in balance,' I replied, bewildered. 'I don't
> know what you mean.'
>
> 'I was afraid,' he went on, as if the words had to be forced out,
> 'that the balance might be going down on one side. You might, I
> thought, I don't know, you might be getting to care too much for
> me.'
>
> I felt my heart turn cold, and replied: 'I don't think so. I
> haven't thought about it.'
>
> He was silent.
>
> 'But why are you saying this?' I asked in deep dismay.
>
> 'Well, they were talking last night, mother and E. E. asked
> mother if we were courting.' He spoke with difficulty. 'They say

we either ought to be engaged or else not go about together. It's the penalty of being nineteen and twenty instead of fifteen and sixteen,' he concluded bitterly.

I began to understand.

'Ah – I always thought your mother didn't like me,' I said quietly.

*A Memoir*, 'E.T.'

It is illuminating to compare this with the parallel passages from *Sons and Lovers:* which is the true account? Could there be one? Here is the basis for an illuminating discussion about the nature of art in relation to 'life', among English teachers.

I refer to these passages to support my argument that what we are seeking in English is not merely a technical skill – a 'language for life' in that sense – but a particular kind of orientation towards the world through words, which devotes itself to the discovery of the truth and meaning of experience. When we ask for directness and sincerity in English, we mean this kind of clarity and frankness, indivisibly there in the plain good words. The English language is a superb instrument of this pursuit of truth in the human world because of its range and quality, with their roots in its complex, multi-racial history.[1] Our language extends from the simplest of expressions of body-meaning in the sigh, sob or *crie de joie,* through rhythmic and metaphorical richness in poetry, to the highest abstractions of scientific work. In the act of struggling with words and with meanings the individual is not only 'representing experience to himself' or 'processing experience' – or even 'creating new forms of behaviour', to use Bullock's terms. He is trying to find the meaning of his life and to solve the *Dasein* problem. E.T. (Jessie Chambers), Helen Corke and Lawrence obviously could not go on living until they tried, in words, to make sense of the experience of early courtship.

Of course, in a great deal of children's writing, the encounter with the *Dasein* problem is still a game: a good deal of their writing is *serious play.* But play, as Winnicott and Buytendijk show, has a serious purpose. Such word-play is a valuable kind of exercise, as here in recognition of mortality:

---

[1] See Owen Barfield, *History in English Words.*

*Death*

The light of life is failing
The doom of death is near
The end is slowly coming
In your eyes I see the fear.
Your eyes are glazing over
There's no colour in your cheek,
You're dying my friend, you're dying
You're humble small and weak,
The angel of death is coming
I hear her mournful moan
Death is black and black is death
For now you stand alone.
Oh Death is cold as ice my friend
Yet hotter than the sun.
For now you don't stand alone my friend
For death and I are one
For death and I are one, my friend
Yes, death and I are one.

I see you tremble in your bed
Your heart is cold as ice
Your heart is cold, your hands are cold
And death you do entice
But death is not so easy
Like a child he loves to play.
Perhaps he'll hold you in his grasp
Or let you live another day.
I see the sweat upon your brow
Now your heart is hot as fire
You beg for life, you pray for life
Oh life's your one desire.

Oh death is cold as ice my friend
Yet hotter than the sun
For now you don't stand alone my friend
For death and I are one.
Can you see the fires of hell my friend
The fires so hot and red?
All sinners come to these fires
As soon as they are dead.

Don't lay there and shake with fear my friend.
Your time is almost done.
The angel of death is here my friend.
Now it is time to come.

Oh death is cold as ice my friend
Yet hotter than the sun
For now you don't stand alone my friend
For death and I are one
For death and I are one my friend.
Yes, death and I are one.

Ranjit Wandi
From a collection of pupils' work, source unknown

But the well-read English teacher could find a relationship between this and the gravely playful poem by Emily Brontë, *Cold in the Earth*, or the folksong *The Unquiet Grave*, or the strange poem about Youliana above (p.149) which has that 'folk' quality of anonymous suffering.

We are today sternly reminded of the 'practical' requirements we must serve in English. But it is as well to insist that unless the underlying problems of our fear of death, and our need to create some kind of sense of meaning in life against it are solved – *practical powers may be locked up, or wasted.* The arguments of Rollo May's *Love and Will*, and Maslow's symposium *New Knowledge of Human Values*, suggest that widespread powers among human beings are wasted because of a failure of intentionality, a loss of confidence in the future, and in the creative possibilities of self-realization. As Heidegger argued, our society distracts us, with gadgets and comfort, from a necessary engagement with the meaning of life, and this leaves us unsatisfied.

Developments towards literacy cannot be seen merely in practical terms. The capacity to use words goes with the capacity to find oneself as a human being able to relate to others and the world, in the quest for a meaningful life, devoted to life-tasks. To find our best potentialities, to 'hear the call' in life, we need vision – these are imaginative acts. Hence the importance of literature, and the elements of play in culture explored by D.W. Winnicott, in working on existential questions. So, in this area of mortality and the *Dasein*, teaching such a poem as the following is relevant, at a depth which cannot be made explicit easily:

*Delay*
If you were coming in the fall,
I'd brush the summer by
With half a smile and half a spurn,
As housewives do a fly.

If I could see you in a year
I'd wind the months in balls,
And put them each in separate drawers,
Until their time befalls.

If only centuries delayed,
I'd count them on my hand,
Subtracting till my fingers dropped
Into Van Diemen's land.

If certain, when this life was out,
That yours and mine should be,
I'd toss it yonder like a rind,
And taste eternity.

But now, all ignorant of the length
Of time's uncertain wing,
It goads me, like the goblin bee,
That will not state its sting.

                                                    Emily Dickinson

This is a good existentialist poem, about choice and action in time: its effect is to urge us that, since we do not know how long anything, especially any relationship, will last, and cannot be sure of eternity, we must allow ourselves to be goaded by the 'unstated' sting of death, to use every moment at our disposal. We must not allow our lives to be a 'thoughtless accident', as Nietzsche put it, but use every moment responsibly, in the pursuit of meaning: to exercise our existential choice, in defining ourselves.

The English teacher influenced by the practical and pseudo-scientific implications of the Bullock Report might think such a strangely metaphysical poem 'remote' or 'irrelevant'. It could even seem 'morbid', in the light of today's materialist optimism. But this only reveals the Gradgrindian inefficiency of the utilitarian view. Children respond eagerly to the mysterious and challenging, and gladly seize any opportunity to explore metaphysical questions. It is just the failure to pay attention to such deep thoughts about life and death through symbolism that is making for paralysis and impotence in our society, not least verbal impotence.[1] On the other hand, secure inner resources stimulated by such art enable an individual to become more effective in his dealings with the world, by examining the primary function of symbolism. Better language use comes thus *incidentally* from the existential excitement.

When we are discussing English in general terms, of course, there is always a tendency to be portentous. Then we always have to bring ourselves down to earth, and say – all right, but how do I do all this in Monday's poetry lesson? Perhaps, then, we shall teach a poem like this by Bernard Spencer, or use it as a stimulus for creative work, or drama?

> *On the 'Sievering' tram*
> Square figures climb off and on;
> mufflers, Astrakhan hats.
> A wintry night for a ride to a clinic
> to visit a new-born boy and his mother;
> and the bell hurrah-ing.
>
> Too many life-bullied faces
> packed on the Sievering tram.
> Yet a woman smiles at a baby near her
> and beckons and beckons, as we run lurching,
> and sigh and restart.
>
> The baby views the woman steadily;
> (and the floor is all mucked with snow.)
> What do I bring to the boy and his mother
> lying in the clinic? Daffodils,
> bewilderment and love.
>
> Ready money, a clock and a signature,
> A Neon-light Pegasus glows in the sky
> (Somebody's Oil) as we swing corners

---

[1] The church's abandoning of the Authorised Version of the Bible and of the traditional Liturgy is a blow of colossal proportions to the nation's capacities, through language, to pursue the meaning of life. See the group of articles in *New Universities Quarterly*, Vol.33, No.3 and also Ian Robinson in *The Survival of English*.

past bakers' and laundries and snow,
                    with the traffic
–gongs ringing like glory.

                                        Bernard Spencer


Here, the intention to visit a new-born child sharpens the poet's awareness, and raises every moment that question, 'What is the point of life?' The faces at first look 'Life-bullied': but then a woman smiles at a baby near her and beckons – invites someone to respond to her. The baby itself stares with its inquiring gaze at the snow muck – trying to piece it all together. The protagonist is bringing daffodils, which have some symbolism he doesn't declare. All round him there is a bewildering flux of life, out of which we can make no coherent pattern (except the poem) to relate to his triumphant mood. The gongs of the tram and the bell (*hurrah-ing*) seem, however, to be echoing the joy in his heart. Though there is no order or coherence to the odd things he notices, one theme emerges – he is glad to be alive, and the things are united by his expectancy and joy. It conveys a bodily, sensuous excitement that is 'beyond the words' and has to do with the sense of being a human being bewildered by the surrounding world, when elated.

In response to such a poem, with its deep human awareness of the flux of life all round one, a child may write a 'realistic' poem like the following. The poem is not merely a practical description of a super-market. It offers the *experience* of the supermarket, as a dehumanizing one – and so upholds human value against the depersonalizations of commerce, on behalf of the experiencing of consciousness.


### The Supermarket

I managed to squeeze through the door
And greet the hot, bustling crowd which awaited me.
It's as though I were squeezed into a small sardine tin.
I reached for a tin of peas
And found the whole lot rushing at my feet –
The pressure, the heat, the tension.
I moved on, trying not to crash against the wall,
Everyone seems in a hurry

As though the world were to end in five minutes.
I finally managed to get my few bits and pieces together,
And now the wait,
The wait that really depresses,
That really tenses my nerves.
I stand lonely, uneasy –
The line moves,
I relax my muscles and fight to keep my place
As a fat lady snatches at a packet of Cadbury's Smash,
And another lady lashes out furiously at a small child

Who pesters her for an ice-lolly.
Once again the lines moves
And I move too.
A wasp stings an assistant –
This holds up the line even more.


I wait, now annoyed and still depressed,
I wait for ten minutes.
The assistant finally comes back,
Her arm clumsily bandaged.
I await my turn . . .
At last it comes.
I put my bits on the counter –
She tried to reckon up my things,
She reached for a bottle of orange squash
But knocked it on the floor
Causing an even longer delay.
At last my chance came
To greet the fresh air once again.
I rush to the door,
A refreshing breeze greets me –
Everything so different
So calm, so free.

Ramona Harris

From *Stepney Words:* from the English teaching of Chris Searle

This poem conveys very well the intensity of tension that may be afflicting a young person, even in everyday circumstances. Exploring such feelings and expressing them helps him towards any sense of meaning he can achieve, asking questions about how one can remain human in such an environment. It is a phenomenological record of consciousness, and because of its truth upholds that consciousness as of primary importance. 'English' is at least one subject capable of healing some of the dissociation which our world causes in such circumstances - not least by helping children to understand their world. As a humanities subject it enables them to see what is wrong with the environment, when it threatens to reduce human beings. So, more meaningful.

I have quoted elsewhere the statement by a character of de la Mare's – 'the meaning has gone out of what we call reality'. The task of English is no less than to help put meaning back. It may sound a Herculean task. But how else are we going to train human beings to create a better world to live in, except in education and except in the humanities? It is here, and in art and music, that we must restore vision: and, one hopes, contribute to changing the world and making it a better place to live in.

In our present economic and social crisis, there is in fact a greater need to foster such inner resources and potentialities than ever before: we only have to consider here the predicament of the unemployed: enforced idleness is promised to many for a very long time, if not for ever. Yet, to some, 'imagination' seems the last thing to save us, even when millions are faced with this kind of leisure with its threats of boredom and meaninglessness. When schools are hard-pressed to buy books, who is going to buy *poetry* – expecting *that* to save us? But maybe poetry, or, at least, the kind of inner strength of the kind poetry gives, may be just the thing to save the unemployed from meaninglessness? Can anything as remote from practical life as poetry save us, whatever Matthew Arnold said? Can it be true today that 'the future of poetry is immense'? The answer is *yes*, because in a world stripped of meaning, it is just the exercise of fancy, dream and imagination that we need to throw meaning over it, and to find a way to restore a sense of *future* to the world. To some, today, it seems that we have reached a point of clinging to the concrete present which is almost psychopathological in its failure to hope for and find promise in the future. So even a fairy-tale poem may be more relevant to children at school than a documentary photograph of a slum:

*Gone*

Where's the Queen of Sheba?
Where King Solomon?
Gone with Blue Boy who looks after the sheep:
Gone and gone and gone.

Lovely is the sunshine;
Lovely is the wheat;
Lovely the wind from out of the clouds
Having its way with it.

Rise up, old Green-Stalks!
Delve deep, Old Corn!
But where's the Queen of Sheba?
Where King Solomon?

Fantastic as it is, it raises the question of our rôle in time: 'What is the point of life?' This is where we must begin – both in our own lives, trying to regain our creativity, and in teaching. The poem is a symbolic utterance, about death and continuity. Where is King Solomon? He exists only 'in the criss-cross of utterance between us': as a symbolic myth figure, he embodies wisdom, and so his life seems to triumph over dust. All our myths refer both to dead heroes and heroines: but in their existence they left meanings which assert the *Dasein* against nothingness. Someday every one of us will be 'gone and gone and gone'. The wind strokes and seduces the wheat – 'caught in that sensual music', life passes by, and we may neglect those achievements which could solve our problems of existence. Between the rising shoots of new life and the deep creative effort of maturity we may find something that triumphs over death and time: some meanings that nothingness cannot eradicate. Some of these meanings will be in words. English is the means to promote this triumph of the *Dasein*. English in this sense is a *tragic* subject. It is not a 'religion': but it is a discipline in which we use language, to grope beyond language, as the possible meaning that life may have. Even our practical literacy depends upon this 'spiritual' dynamic, while teaching English in this spirit (I say once more, and finally) is an art, which itself requires a training of the imagination, not of linguistic theory or dry rules and abstract injunctions. The English teacher or student teacher engrossed in *Middlemarch* or *Huckleberry Finn* or Donne's *Songs and Sonnets*, is preparing himself in the best possible way for his arduous task, and all he has to do is to read what he can from his inheritance to his pupils, matching as best he can their own speaking voice, each expressing a unique existential need.

# BIBLIOGRAPHY

ABBS, P. (1976). *Root and Blossom*. London: Heinemann.

BEVERIDGE, W.I.S. (1950). *The Art of Scientific Investigation*. London: Heinemann.

BUBER, M. (1964). 'Distance and relation.' In: FRIEDMAN, M. (Ed) *The Knowledge of Man*. London: Allen and Unwin.

BURTT, E.A. (1967). *In Search of Philosophical Understanding*. London: Allen and Unwin.

CASSIRER, E. (1944). *An Essay on Man*. New Haven: Yale University.

CHALONER, L. (1964). *Feeling and Perception in Young Children*. London: Tavistock.

CHOMSKY, N. (1972). *Language and Mind*. New York: Harcourt Brace Jovanovitch. (For discussion of his other books see ROBINSON, I. (1975). *The New Grammarian's Funeral*. Cambridge: Cambridge University Press.)

DEPARTMENT OF EDUCATION AND SCIENCE (1975). *A Language for Life* (Bullock Report). London: HMSO.

DRURY, M. O'C. (1973). *The Danger of Words*. London: Routledge & Kegan Paul.

FRANKL, V. (1958). *The Doctor and the Soul*. London: Souvenir Press.

FRANKL, V. (1970). *Psychotherapy and Existentialism*. London: Souvenir Press.

FRIEDMAN, M. (Ed) (1964). *The Knowledge of Man*. London: Allen and Unwin (Contains Buber's essay 'Distance and relation').

FRIEDMAN, M. (Ed) (1967). *The Philosophy of Martin Buber*. Cambridge: Cambridge University Press.

GEDIN, P. (1977). *Literature in the Market Place*. London: Faber and Faber.

GRENE, M. (1966). *The Knower and the Known*. London: Faber and Faber.

GRENE, M. (1968). *Approaches to a Philosophical Biology*. London: Basic Books. (Discusses F.J.J. Buytendijk, Helmuth Plessner and Adolf Portman.)

GRENE, M. (1968). *Dreadful Freedom: an Introduction to Existentialism*. Chicago: University of Chicago.

GRENE, M. (1976). *Philosophy in and out of Europe*. California: University of California.

GUNTRIP, H. (1961). *Personality, Structure and Human Interaction*. London: Hogarth Press.

GUNTRIP, H. (1968). *Schizoid Phenomena, Object Relations and the Self*. London: Hogarth Press.

HODGKIN, R.A. (1976). *Born Curious*. Chichester: John Wiley.

HOURD, M. and COOPER, G.E. (1959). *Coming Into Their Own*. London: Heinemann.

HUSSERL, E. (1970). *The Crisis of European Sciences*. Evanston: Northwestern University Press.

ISAACS, S. (1929). *The Nursery Years*. London: Routledge & Kegan Paul.

ISAACS, S. (1932). *The Children We Teach*. London: University of London.

JUNG, C. and von FRANZ, M.-L. (1964). *Man and His Symbols*. London: Aldus.

KLEIN, M. (1960). *Our Adult World and Its Roots in Infancy*. London: Tavistock.

KOESTLER, A. and SMITHIES, R. (1969). *Against Reductionism – The Alpbach Seminar*. London: Hutchinson.

LAING, R.D. (1960). *The Divided Self*. London: Tavistock.

LANGER, S. (1942). *Philosophy in a New Key*. Cambridge, Mass: Harvard University Press.

LEAVIS, F.R. (1975). *The Living Principle*. London: Chatto and Windus.

LOMAS, P. (Ed) (1961). *The Predicament of the Family*. London: Hogarth Press.

LOMAS, P. (1973). *True and False Experience*. Harmondsworth: Allen Lane.

MARCEL, G. (1948). *The Philosophy of Existence*. London: Harvill Press.

MARSHALL, S. (1963). *An Experiment in Education*. Cambridge: Cambridge University Press.

MASLOW, A. (Ed) (1959). *New Knowledge in Human Values*. New York: Van Nostrand Reinhold.

MASLOW, A. (1969). *Towards a Psychology of Being*. New York: Van Nostrand Reinhold.

MAY, R. (Ed) (1958). *Existence: a New Dimension in Psychiatry*. London: Basic Books.

MAY, R. (1969). *Love and Will*. London: Souvenir Press.

MAY, R. (1972). *Power and Innocence*. London: Souvenir Press.

MILNER, M. (1950). *On Not Being Able to Paint*. London: Heinemann.

MILNER, M. (1969). *In the Hands of the Living God*. London: Hogarth Press.

MERLEAU-PONTY, M. (1962). *The Phenomenology of Perception*. London: Routledge & Kegan Paul.

PACEY, P. (1977). *A Sense of What is Real*. London: Brentham Press.

POLANYI, M. (1958). *Personal Knowledge*. London: Routledge & Kegan Paul.

POLANYI, M. (1958). *The Tacit Dimension*. London: Routledge & Kegan Paul.

POLANYI, M. (1969). *Knowing and Being*. London: Routledge & Kegan Paul.

POLANYI, M. and PROSH, H. (1975). *Meaning*. Chicago: University of Chicago.

POOLE, R. (1972). *Towards Deep Subjectivity*. Harmondsworth: Allen Lane.

RENOIR, J. (1962). *My Father*. London: Collins.

ROBINSON, I. (1973). *The Survival of English*. Cambridge: Cambridge University Press.

ROBINSON, I. (1975). *The New Grammarian's Funeral*. Cambridge: Cambridge University Press.

RYLE, G. (1949). *The Concept of Mind*. London: Hutchinson.

SAMPSON, G. (1934). *English for the English*. Cambridge: Cambridge University Press.

**SPENCER, B. (1965), *Collected Poems*, London; Alan Ross.**

SPIEGELBERG, H. (1965). *The Phenomenological Movement*. Atlantic Highlands, N.J.: Humanities Press.

SPIEGELBERG, H. (1972). *Phenomenology in Psychology and Psychiatry*. Evanston: Northwestern University Press.

STERN, K. (1966). *The Flight from Woman.* London: Allen and Unwin.
STRAUS, E. (1963). *The Primary World of Senses.* New York: Free Press.
SURGEON GENERAL OF THE USA (1976). *Report on Screen Violence.*
Washington DC: US Government Printing Office.
TOMLIN, E.W.F. (1948). *Living and Knowing.* London: Faber and Faber.
WHITEHEAD, F. (1968). *The Disappearing Dais.* London: Chatto and
Windus.
WHYTE, L.L. (1951). *Aspects of Form.* London: Lund Humphries.
WINNICOTT, D.W. (1958). *Collected Papers.* London: Tavistock.
WINNICOTT, D.W. (1971). *Playing and Reality.* London: Tavistock.
WINNICOTT, D.W. (1971). *Therapeutic Consultations in Child Psychiatry.*
London: Hogarth Press.
WINNICOTT, D.W. (1977). *The Piggle.* London: Tavistock.

Essays on politics, meaning and culture by the author have been
published in the following symposia edited by Ross Fitzgerald PhD in
Australia: 'Politics and the Need for Meaning', in *Human Needs and
Politics,* Pergamon Australia, 1977; 'What it Means to be Human' in
*What it Means to be Human,* Pergamon Australia, 1978; and 'Sources
of Hope' in *Sources of Hope,* Pergamon Australia, 1979. These books
may be obtained from Pergamon Press, Headington Hill Hall, Oxford.

The author's *Selected Poems* are to be published by Anvil Press in 1980.

# BOOKS ABOUT EXISTENTIALISM

Those seeking an introduction to existentialism may like to read the following (most are also included in the general bibliography too). As Colin Wilson explains in his *Introduction to the New Existentialism* (Hutchinson, 1966), one can speak of two kinds of existentialist philosophy. There is the 'old' existentialism which fails to find any reality except the nothingness beyond, offers only limited choice to shrink back, if we can, into numb, unthinking, decent living; or to embody the futility and chaos by indulging in decadent unnaturalness. Sartre's freedom (says Philip Pacey) is freedom for nothing. We must choose, in order to define ourselves: but all choice is ultimately futile. Love inevitably turns to sadism, masochism or indifference. But there is also the 'new' existentialism, which asserts that it is possible to find the other and to establish meaning through love; and to solve the *Dasein* problem, as by achievements which cannot be reduced to nothing, by death or nothingness. This school is much influenced by existentialist psychotherapy: obviously, it is impossible to work with a patient in need, and tell him that every effort he makes to define himself and to find his humanness is doomed to futility! Here Rollo May, Viktor Frankl, Abraham Maslow and Ludwig Binswanger are important figures, while in Britain Peter Lomas follows on from the work of D.W. Winnicott, who really gave an existentialist twist to Freudian psychoanalysis by bringing culture, symbolism and meaning to the centre of the human picture.

PACEY, P. (1977). *A Sense of What is Real.* London: Brentham Press. A book written out of a course given at a College of Art on existentialism and creativity.

ROUBICZEK, P. (1964). *Existentialism: For and Against.* Cambridge: Cambridge University Press.

A useful philosophical introduction, mostly about the 'old' existentialism.

MASLOW, A. (1973). *The Further Reaches of Human Nature.* Harmondsworth: Penguin.

ROSZAK, T. (1973). *Where the Wasteland Ends.* London: Faber and Faber.

WILSON, C. (1966). *Introduction to the New Existentialism.* London: Hutchinson.

STERN, K. (1966). *The Flight from Woman.* London: Allen and Unwin.

ABBS, P. (1976). *Root and Blossom.* London: Heinemann.

ABBS, P. and CAREY, G. (1977). *Proposal for a New College.* London: Heinemann. An attempt to turn an existentialist approach to education into practical suggestions.

FRANKL, V. (1962). *The Search for Meaning* (originally *From Death Camp to Existentialism*). Boston: Beacon Press.

FRANKL, V. (1970). *The Doctor and the Soul*. London: Souvenir Press.

FRANKL, V. (1970). *Psychotherapy and Existentialism*. London: Souvenir Press.

GRENE, M. (1948). *An Introduction to Existentialism*. Chicago: Chicago University Press.

LEDERMANN, E.K. (1972). *Essential Neurosis*. London: Butterworth.

MARCEL, G. (1948). *The Philosophy of Existence*. London: Harvill Press.

MAY, R., ANGEL, E. and ELLENBERGER, H.F. (Eds) (1968). *Existence – a New Dimension in Psychiatry*. London: Basic Books.
The first historical chapters are of great importance for an understanding of the emergence of the 'new' existentialism.

LOMAS, P. (1973). *True and False Experience*. London: Tavistock.

POOLE, R. (1972). *Towards Deep Subjectivity*. Harmondsworth: Allen Lane.

TOMLIN, E.W.F. (1960). *Great Philosophers of the West*. London: Arrow.

TOMLIN, E.W.F. (1960). *Great Philosophers of the East*. London: Arrow.

HOLBROOK, D. (1977). *Education, Nihilism and Survival*. London: Darton, Longman and Todd.

MASLOW, A. (Ed) (1959). *New Knowledge in Human Values*. New York: Van Nostrand Reinhold.

MASLOW, A. (1968). *Towards a Psychology of Being*. New York: Van Nostrand Reinhold.

GRENE, M. (1976). *Philosophy in and out of Europe*. California: University of California Press.

HODGKIN, R.A. (1970). *Reconnaissance on an Educational Frontier*. London: Oxford University Press.

CURTIS, B. and MAYS, W. (Eds) (1978). *Phenomenology and Education, Self-consciousness and its Development*. London: Methuen.